CONDUCTING THE REFERENCE INTERVIEW

A How-To-Do-It Manual for Librarians

Catherine Sheldrick Ross
Kirsti Nilsen
Patricia Dewdney

HOW-TO-DO-IT MANUALS FOR LIBRARIANS

NUMBER 117

NEAL-SCHUMAN PUBLISHERS, INC.
New York, London

Published by Neal-Schuman Publishers, Inc.
100 Varick Street
New York, NY 10013

Printed and bound in the United States of America.

Library of Congress Cataloging-in-Publication Data is available.

ISBN 1-55570-432-8

CONTENTS

PREFACE

The seed for *Conducting the Reference Interview: A How-To-Do-It Manual for Librarians* was a workshop that Patricia Dewdney and Catherine Ross developed in the mid-1980s to teach the skills required for effective reference interviews. Over the past fifteen years, this workshop has been presented to thousands of information professionals in Canada and the United States. Participants have come from public, academic, and special libraries as well as community information centers, legal advice centers, and software support providers. We called this workshop "How to Find Out What People Really Want to Know," although privately we thought of it as "Why Didn't You Say So in the First Place?" Anyone who has ever worked in any kind of information will instantly recognize the problem: "Everything you have on travel" turns out to be a request for "information about inexpensive motels in Jamaica" and "information on allergies" turns out to be "side effects for a particular antihistamine." The "the financial page for February 24" does not need to be retrieved so long as you can find the price of gold on that day.

During these years, all three authors were also teaching the basic reference course in the Masters of Library and Information Science at The University of Western Ontario. This teaching environment provided the opportunity to involve students in conducting the Library Visit study, more than a decade's research on the users' experience of asking questions in libraries. We use this assignment because we want beginning librarians to have a vivid sense of the experience of being a user. The Library Visit project convinced us, if we needed convincing, of the crucial importance of taking a user-centered, rather than a system-centered approach to thinking about reference service. In *Conducting the Reference Interview*, we consolidate findings of the Library Visit study that have previously been reported in scholarly articles scattered across different journals. The Library Visit study produced over 250 accounts in which real library users recorded what happened, step by step, when they went to a library and asked a question that mattered to them personally.

To complement this material based on users' perceptions, we have also drawn extensively on the verbatim transcripts of 332 reference interviews that Patricia Dewdney tape-recorded in public libraries. We also have access to the data from the Mental Models study, in which Patricia Dewdney and Gillian Michell observed reference transactions in three different public library settings and afterwards interviewed the librarians and 33 users about their perceptions of the transaction. With these rich sources we are able to illustrate discussions of particular aspects of the reference interview—e.g., the physical environment of the library, communication accidents, ill-formed queries, appropriate use of specific skills such as open questions, what happens when appropriate skills are not used, etc.—with specific examples drawn from real reference transactions and real statements from users. Although the challenge of finding out what the user really wants to know is the same in public libraries, academic, government, and special libraries, we have tended to illustrate our discussion with straightforward examples drawn from public libraries, so that a specialized subject background is not needed to understand the context of the user's question.

We believe in the integration of theory and praxis and are convinced that a really useful book on reference must be informed by relevant theory and research while making a point of being very practical as well. Hence there is a double genesis of this book in the workshop and in a research agenda engaging a number of researchers at The University of Western Ontario with the topic of reference (e.g., Dewdney, Harris, McKechnie, Michell, Nilsen, Ross). The reference workshop, though rooted in a sense-making theory of information and based on current research in reference, was essentially practical in emphasis. Through a combination of methods including small lectures, modeling, group exercises, role plays, and discussion, the workshop explored communication problems occurring between library users and library staff and presented some skills for coping with these problems. Workshop participants over the years shared with us their experiences of reference interviews gone right and wrong and we fed this material back into the workshops. Some of these earlier findings were included in Ross and Dewdney's *Communicating Professionally* (2nd ed., Neal-Schuman, 1998). Unlike that book, which covers the broad range of speaking and writing skills applied to many library-professional contexts, this manual is focused on the reference transaction exclusively.

Conducting the Reference Interview: A How-To-Do-It Manual for Librarians is a response to the many librarians, educators, and students who have asked us, "Where can we read about skills for the reference interview" or "I have to develop a training package for my staff/ my course, and I need any help I can get." This book is *not* about reference sources or about where to look for information, although we think that knowing the sources is crucially important. It is about finding out enough about the user's information needs that the librarian understands quite specifically what to look for. The process of finding out what the user really wants is the bedrock of successful reference, upon which everything else depends. The most comprehensive understanding of the sources is wasted if the information intermediary is looking for the wrong thing. The need to understand what the user really wants to know remains the same, whether the reference transaction is face-to-face, over the telephone, or computer-mediated through asynchronous e-mail or real-time chat.

ORGANIZATION

In Chapter 1, "Conducting an Effective Reference Interview," we describe the theoretical foundations for this book and review perspectives on the need for conducting a reference interview. We argue that taking questions at "face value" does not work because the initial question rarely reflects three essential aspects of the user's information need as defined in Brenda Dervin's sensemaking theory—the situation (how the need arose), the gap (what is missing in the user's understanding), and the uses to which the user hopes to put the information. Chapter 1 also introduces mental models theory (with previously unpublished examples) to explain why users do not always present their questions clearly and completely. If librarians want to provide helpful answers beyond "the 55 percent rule," they must hone their communication skills to perform "the art of translation."

In the next three chapters we use Allen Ivey's microtraining approach to identify those communication skills most helpful in the reference interview. We illustrate these with examples, both positive and negative, from our own research and training programs. Chapter 2, "Using the First 30 Seconds to Set the Stage for the Reference Interview," covers the basic skills needed for the crucial first few seconds of contact—non-verbal, listening, and verbal skills that establish a positive communication climate. (Some of the material, including the definitions and examples of specific skills required, is repeated here as it was presented in *Communicating Professionally*, in some cases with only minor changes since the definitions of the skills have not changed. We repeated this material rather than simply referring the reader to the earlier book because we wanted to provide readers with a single stand-alone source on the reference interview.)

Chapter 3, "Finding Out What They Really Want to Know," begins with some common problems observed in reference interviews, such as negative closure and unmonitored referrals, then sets out the major skills for the reference interview—asking open and sense-making questions, avoiding premature diagnosis, paraphrasing, summarizing, and achieving closure. Chapter 4, "Moving Beyond Negative Closure," includes skills useful for later stages of the interview—inclusion, one-to-one bibliographic instruction, and essential follow-up techniques. We also give tried-and-true tips for practicing and integrating skills into everyday behavior.

Chapters 5 and 6 cover a variety of special contexts where librarians must adapt these skills for particular purposes and user groups. Chapter 5, "Exploring Special Contexts for the Reference Interview," includes telephone reference service, voicemail, and handling imposed queries (where one user presents a question on behalf of another). Sections are devoted to working with children and young adults and people who have disabilities or special language-related needs. This chapter also brings together for the first time the many communication problems arising from medical and legal reference questions. Chapter 5 finishes with a substantial section on the readers' advisory interview. In Chapter 6, "Performing the Reference Interview in an Electronic Environment," we deal with the principles of communicating effectively in the electronically-mediated reference interview, specifically e-mail reference, real-time reference, and instant messaging.

Finally, in Chapter 7, "Establishing Policy and Training for the Reference Interview," we consider the broader institutional context—library policies and training programs designed to support librarians improve information service through more effective reference interviews. At the end of each chapter, we provide comprehensive annotated references that can also be used as suggestions for further reading so that helpful sources appear at point-of-use for the reader, rather than in one bibliography.

APPLICATIONS

We have written this book to provide a single accessible source that draws together the scattered findings of research and praxis and translates them into practical guidelines and exercises that can be used for training and for individual learning. Over the past 15 years, research studies conducted in LIS graduate programs have filled in a lot of gaps in our understanding of the reference interview—what works and what doesn't, what can go wrong despite the best intentions of the librarian, and what explains puzzling user behavior (why *do* users ask for "everything on refrigeration" when they want to know how to repair a refrigerator?). Our goal here is to integrate the most valuable work done by ourselves and others on the reference transaction. Materials presented here have been adapted and developed from numerous studies of human communication, especially sense-making and microtraining. *Sense-making* is an approach developed by Dr. Brenda Dervin, now at Ohio State University, that focuses our attention on how people use information to make sense of their lives. Instead of assuming that information is a commodity that is valuable in itself, sense-making directs us to ask, "How will this information help this particular individual deal with a particular situation in the context of his or her own life?" *Microtraining* was developed by Allen E. Ivey as an effective way to teach interview skills to counselors and is based on the idea that complex communication behaviors can be broken down into constituent parts that can be taught, one at a time. We have modified these innovative models to focus on the strategies and skills most useful for the reference interview.

The pages that follow combine our most useful training materials for the reference interview together with a map to the most helpful research—all set within a framework for thinking about information service. Like the workshop, this book is based on the idea that people learn best when they are actively engaged. Therefore each chapter combines explanatory text together with modeling, many examples drawn from actual reference interviews, exercises that provide opportunities for practice, and annotated references that provide recommendations for further reading. We have designed *Conducting the Reference Interview: A How-To-Do-It Manual for Librarians* to be useful both to individual learners and to trainers/supervisors who want support materials for staff training on the reference interview.

ACKNOWLEDGMENTS

This book could not have been written without the help and co-operation of the librarians who participated in Pat Dewdney's field study of the reference interview and who participated in the Mental Models study. We especially want to thank the more than 200 graduate students from the University of Western Ontario who participated in the Library Visit study over the period of a decade and wrote the library visit accounts from which we have freely quoted in this book. Particular acknowledgment is due to two leaders and researchers whose work has been so influential on our own thinking: Allen Ivey and Brenda Dervin from the fields of counselling and communication respectively. Within the library field, we are greatly indebted to Mary Kay Chelton, Joan Durrance, Gillian Michell, Marie Radford, and Bernie Sloan. Special thanks to Lynne McKechnie, who wrote the section in this book on the reference interview with children and young adults. The excellent staff at Neal-Schuman prompted us to write this book and supported us throughout its development. And finally we want to thank Gail Schlacter and the RASD selection committees who encouraged this research by awarding the Reference Services Press Award to four of our *RQ* and *RUSQ* articles that reported our work on the reference interview: "Flying a Light Aircraft," "Oranges and Peaches," "Negative Closure," and "So Has the Internet Changed Anything in Reference?" We thank them all—and others too numerous to list here.

1 CONDUCTING AN EFFECTIVE REFERENCE INTERVIEW

In this chapter . . .

1.1 WHAT IS A (REFERENCE) INTERVIEW?

An interview is a special kind of conversation directed intentionally to some purpose. There are, of course, many different types of interviews, and these vary widely along many dimensions (e.g., the power relations established between the participants, the degree of trust involved, the duration of the interview, the length of responses, the degree of structure in the questions, the purpose of the interview). Consider the difference between two kinds of interviews. On the one hand, there is the police interrogation in which the interviewer is totally in charge and sets the agenda for the questioning, trust is low, questions are structured and often closed ("Did you leave your house on the evening of the 20th?"), answers are often unforthcoming ("No."), and the purposes of police interrogator and suspect are usually diametrically opposed. On the other hand, there is the oral history interview or research interview in which both parties are equal partners, trust is relatively high, questions are often open-ended and geared to the interests and priorities of the interviewee, answers are often very lengthy, interviews may last an hour or more, and the purpose of the interview is mutually shared.

Clearly one of the most important factors in any interview is the extent to which the interviewer and interviewee share a common purpose. At one end of the scale, both parties share a common purpose and know that they do. At the other end, each party has a separate and opposed purpose. Sometimes an interviewer makes an erroneous assumption about the interviewee's purpose, as in the case of a young library user who asks for "a book about a classic novel," hoping to find a brief plot summary for a book report due today. He wants the minimum possible to get through the assignment and is not really interested in reading the book. The librarian, on the other hand, thinks that everyone should take advantage of educational opportunities to read classic works such as *War and Peace*. Such interactions are likely to go badly unless the interviewer takes the view that the goal of the reference interview is to find out what the user wants to do and then provide materials that will help him reach that goal (however different the librarian's own goal would be in the same situation).

Despite obvious differences among different types of interviewing, all interviews share some common features. A growing body of literature has been developed to explain what some of these important features are. Although interviews seem to resemble ordinary conversations, they actually differ from ordinary conversation in important ways. It is the job of the interviewer, not the interviewee, to keep in mind these differences between a well-conducted interview and a friendly conversation:

- Participants in conversations are expected to follow the rule of turn-taking, allowing each person a relatively equal share of talking and listening. In interviews, on the other hand, it is not only acceptable but highly desirable for the interviewer to do a lot more listening, while encouraging the interviewee to talk. See listening, section 2.4.5.
- Unlike typical conversations, interviews involve the asking and answering of questions; one person normally asks the questions and the other answers. See open and closed questions, section 3.2.1, and sense-making questions, section 3.2.3.
- Unlike typical conversations, interviews are directed toward a purpose. Any topic not relevant to the purpose of the interview can appropriately be excluded by a comment that brings discussion back to the purpose of the interview (e.g., "That's interesting about your vacation, but to get back to your question, what aspect of submarines interests you?"). See closure, section 3.2.5.
- Redundancy and repetition are drawbacks in conversa-

tion but desirable in interviews; interviewers often ask the same question in different words in order to get a fuller picture. Interviewees often don't spill the beans right away, because they are following the rules for conversationalists (don't be boringly repetitive or talk at length about yourself) rather than the rules for interviewees (provide as full an account as is useful about the topic of the interview). Effective interviewers use encouragers and probes to reassure the interviewee that they are not bored and to get the interviewee to expand on a statement ("What else can you tell me about your research project on bagpipes?" "Uh-huh, anything else?" "That's interesting. Anything else?" "Could you give me an example of that?") See minimal encouragers, section 2.4.4.

- Unlike a participant in a typical conversation, a good interviewer uses a number of strategies to make sure that the interviewee has been fully understood and that the message has been accurately received. These strategies include paraphrasing and summarizing what has been heard (e.g., "OK, so it sounds as if X is the case/you feel Y/you want Z to happen. Did I get that right?") and note-taking, and sometimes recording and transcribing, when the interview is long and complex. See reflecting of content, section 3.2.4.
- Unlike ordinary conversation, an interview has a structure that must reflect its purpose. The stages of an interview usually are

    1. establishing rapport,
    2. general information gathering or getting the big picture,
    3. specific information gathering,
    4. intervention such as giving information, advice, or instructions,
    5. ending, including feedback or summary.

These stages may be iterative, occurring in loops throughout the interview, as for example when the interviewer needs to reestablish rapport or do some more general information gathering before the interview ends.

But what about the reference interview? The term *reference interview* suggests to most librarians a short face-to-face interview conducted for the purpose of finding out what the user really wants to know so that the staff member can match the user's question to the library's store of information. It is generally agreed that users' initial questions are often unclear or incomplete. The purpose of the interview is to elicit from the user sufficient information about the real need to enable the librarian to understand it enough to begin searching. The user's initial question often needs to be clarified, narrowed down, made more detailed, and contextualized. Questioning during the reference interview may elicit information about what the user wants to know; how the user plans to use the information; what level of detail, technical specialization, or reading ability would be useful; what format of information is preferred; and any other restrictions, such as how much work the user is willing to do to get the answer, whether there are time limits or deadlines, and whether only the most recent information will do.

The typical reference interview is shorter than most types of interviews that are described in the literature, such as counseling interviews, ethnographic interviews, oral history interviews, or journalistic interviews. Normally, reference interviews last three minutes or less, but a reference interview with a client who has complex research needs or with a genealogist may last for twenty minutes or longer. Variations on the basic form often occur. There's the readers' advisory interview (section 5.7), in which the adviser has a directed conversation with the user about her reading tastes, experiences with previous favorite books, and current preferences before making recommendations. There is the interview in which the librarian cannot communicate directly with the user who wants the information but must work through a delegate who is asking the question on behalf of someone else—the interview resulting from what Melissa Gross (1995) has called "the imposed query" (section 5.3.1). As a special case of the imposed query, there is the interview with a child who is trying to get enough material to complete a school assignment about which she might have no personal interest whatsoever (section 5.4.3), and there's the interview that is mediated electronically either by telephone (section 5.2) or, increasingly, by e-mail (Chapter 6). Sometimes the latter involves the user in filling out an electronic form in order to provide specified details concerning the information need.

All of these interviews in their various guises can be defined simply as a purposive conversation between the librarian and the user in which the librarian asks one or more questions in order (1) to get a clearer and more complete picture of what the user wants to know, and (2) to link the user to the system. In addition to these purposes of query negotiation, the reference interview may include related functions: giving information, advice, or instruction; getting feedback; and following up to assess the user's satisfaction with the help provided.

DID YOU KNOW?

According to Solomon (1997), research on the physician/patient interview has found that doctors ask all the questions and patients provide the answers. When patients do ask questions, the question often is not heard.

Although all reference interviews are unique, they have common structural features and go through similar stages: establishing contact with the user, finding out the user's need, and confirming that the answer provided is actually what was needed. There is a standard set of skills that staff members can learn, practice, and use to increase the likelihood that the interview will be productive. The interview can go wrong in predictable ways, and there are standard ways of recovering from "communication accidents." Whatever the purpose of the interview, the interviewer should have a clear idea, before the interview starts, of why she is conducting the interview and what she hopes to have accomplished by the end.

1.2 SERVICE ORIENTATION OF LIBRARIES

Is a reference interview really needed? Reference as a core function in libraries has been around for scarcely more than a century, and for the first half of that period, all attention was directed to learning about sources, not to communicating with users. Patrick Wilson, in his article "The Face Value Rule in Reference Work" (1986) points out that the literature seems to be divided on this issue. Some authorities say that a reference interview is almost always needed; others say that a reference interview is needed only under certain circumstances and definitely not for directional queries or for ready reference questions. Wilson quotes one commentator who seems to be putting himself forward as a spokesperson for bluff common sense speaking out against ivory-tower concepts taught in library school: "the reference interview can't—and shouldn't—be applied as readily in public libraries as we were taught. Time and common sense won't permit it" (McCoy, 1985).

There are two arguments—we call them myths—that have been advanced against putting much effort into worrying about reference interviewing skills. Both arguments, in our view, are wrong because the result of acting upon them is that users don't get the service they need. This book is based on the principle that libraries must take a service orientation. We are convinced that the institutions that will survive the 21st century and beyond are those that serve their clients and give them the help they need. If libraries don't provide helpful information services, users will turn to other service providers who are more service oriented. As the ALA "Guidelines for Information Services" state, "Provision of information in the manner most useful to its clients is the ultimate test of all a library does."

Myth 1: Because users are often pretty clear about their information needs, the reference interview is unnecessary.

According to this view, the user's question is straightforward, and the tricky part for the intermediary is knowing the range of tools that contain the answers. There are still a few writers, such as Dennis Grogan, who maintain that "most of the library users who put questions to the librarian know exactly what they need and ask for it clearly" (1991: 63). Robert Hauptman (1987) has called the reference interview a "myth," claiming that in a study he conducted, only six cases out of 1,074 demanded an extensive interview. We aren't advocating "extensive" interviewing in any case. Several properly focused questions are usually enough, but there's a big difference between the claim that *extensive* interviewing is not needed and that *no* interviewing is needed. The view that finding out the user's information need is unproblematic has changed as research increasingly has drawn attention to the complex nature of human interaction. Although it is true that some users are able to ask an initial question that explains exactly what they are looking for, we know that about 40 percent of users do not, especially those who are unfamiliar with how libraries work. For these novice users in particular, the reference interview is a crucial tool, but for *all* users it enhances the likelihood of receiving a helpful answer. In short, it is important to give every user the chance to elaborate on the query; if it turns out to have been unnecessary, then no harm done.

Myth 2: The onus is on the user to know what he or she wants and express the need clearly. Librarians should take the user's question at "face value."

One response to the fact that users' initial statements of their information need can be incomplete or misleading is Patrick Wilson's "face value" rule: "Assume that information requested is information wanted; interview only to clarify the initial formulation of the request" (1986: 469). When the user asks, "Where is your history section?" the face value rule would direct the librarian to take the user to the history shelves and say, "The history books are on these shelves." If the user asks for the wrong thing (what he actually wanted to know was how tall the Eiffel Tower is), that's his problem. The face value rule puts the onus on users to become more informed about libraries and the

---

ANALYZE THIS REFERENCE TRANSACTION

Case 1: System routines vs. user needs

Librarian:	Can I help you?
User:	Do you have the third section of the Million Dollar Directory?
Librarian:	No, we don't. We didn't subscribe to it.
User:	Pardon?
Librarian:	We didn't subscribe to Volume 3.
User:	You don't get it?
Librarian:	No. The reason is that the companies included tend to be mostly smaller companies and not in our area. So we haven't found we needed it. Did you find a reference to it? (closed question)
User:	I thought it was here—the brown one.
Librarian:	The brown one. (acknowledgment) No, that's a periodical directory. [She explains.] If you need Volume 3 of the Million Dollar Directory, the University has a copy in the business library. (referral)
User:	I can get it if I want it. OK. Thank you.

Dewdney, Million Dollar

Comment: Does this user really need Volume 3 of the Million Dollar Directory? Maybe not. We'll never know. This 75-second transaction focused almost exclusively on the library's subscription policy. No headway whatsoever was made into finding out what information the user hoped to locate in the Million Dollar Directory because the librarian chose not to conduct a reference interview. Admittedly, there are some circumstances in which a user absolutely needs to see a specific reference tool and not a substitute—to write a review on it, for example, for a library school assignment. But in the majority of cases, the requested reference tool is just a way station on the path of finding a specific piece of information. In this case the question was taken at face value and the user was directed off to another library at some distance. But without conducting a reference interview, the librarian has no way of knowing whether there are other tools within her own library that could have answered the user's question. It's quite possible that the user's question could have been answered by another directory that the library did possess, or perhaps by another type of reference tool altogether.

DID YOU KNOW?

Herb White (1992) says that librarians need to emphasize their strengths. As computers increasingly take over clerical tasks that computers are good at, librarians should focus attention on aspects of service that computers can't do well: human communication. Let computers get involved in document identification, document delivery, overdue notices, interloans, and cataloging, White argues, and let librarians take a proactive role in information intermediation.

organization of information so that they can ask for exactly what they want. This rule makes the reference interview unnecessary in many cases, but a lot of users won't get what they need. Patrick Wilson acknowledges that the face value rule "is plausible if the conception of library service that it reflects is acceptable": "The Face Value Rule seems to be a perfectly proper rule to follow if one conceives of the reference librarian as an intermediary, prepared to respond to requests for information, not professionally responsible (though sometimes personally interested) for the consequences of the use of the information" (1986: 474–75). A big drawback to accepting this conception of service and following the face value rule is that libraries with this limited orientation to service are less likely to be perceived as helpful institutions that are worth funding and preserving.

William Katz puts his considerable authority behind the view that "the original question . . . is rarely the real question" and "the purpose of the reference interview . . . is to clarify the question" (1997). However, according to research carried out since the late 1970s, in half of transactions in libraries, the reference staff follows the face value rule and bypasses the reference interview. When researchers such as Mary Jo Lynch (1978) and Patricia Dewdney (1986) audiotaped actual reference transactions and began to look closely at exactly what the users and the staff members said and did, three things became very clear: (1) users don't express their information needs clearly and completely in the initial question; (2) in half of the cases, staff members accept the initial question at face value and don't conduct a reference interview; and (3) when the initial question is taken at face value, users often wind up not getting the help they want. In this book, we will be arguing vigorously against the face value rule and advocating instead that a reference interview (the asking of one or more questions intended to discover the user's information needs) must be conducted in *every* transaction. Users should be offered the invitation to expand or clarify. To the objection that librarians are too busy, we argue that some additional seconds spent in finding out the user's real information need saves time in the long run. Less time is spent by library staff looking for the wrong thing; less time is spent within the library system processing book transfers and interlibrary loans for the wrong materials; and less time is spent by e-reference staff in typing out answers that direct users to the wrong electronic sources.

An important part of providing good service is the willingness to try to understand the user's perspective. A research study by Patricia Dewdney and Gillian Michell called "Mental Models of Information Systems: A Study of 'Ill-Formed' Queries Presented

DID YOU KNOW?

In an unobtrusive study of reference service in Suffolk County public libraries on Long Island, Thomas Childers (1980) used "escalator" questions so that librarians would have to use probes to discover the specific question. No matter how general the initial question was, in 67 percent of cases, library staff members asked no questions to clarify what information was required, with the result that they got to the last step only 20 percent of the time and hardly ever provided an accurate answer. By contrast, the third who did use probes to arrive at the specific question provided an accurate answer 62 percent of the time.

in Public Libraries" (1996) demonstrates how the users' initial questions are influenced by their "mental model" of how libraries work. Dewdney and Michell observed and recorded reference transactions in public libraries, conducted in-depth personal interviews with 33 adult public library users who had asked for help from a librarian, and later interviewed these same librarians. Among other questions, both the user and the librarian were asked how easy or hard they thought the question would be at the outset and how easy or hard it actually turned out to be. Here are some of their findings:

1. **Users depend on librarians to help them find the information they need.** Even frequent library users do not have a very accurate or complete understanding of how library resources are organized and how to use them. Despite a general willingness to help themselves, they rely heavily on professional librarians to help them cope with this complexity, which is increasing with new information technology.
2. **Complex information needs are presented in small libraries as well as large ones.** Even in small branch libraries, people ask difficult reference questions that require staff assistance. It is important for staff to be able to make effective referrals and be knowledgeable about resources in other locations.
3. **Users' questions appear to be easily answered, but often they are difficult.** Apparently simple requests (e.g., "Can I look at the city directory?") often mask complex information needs that require a range of resources and often a referral. Neither librarians nor users could initially predict how difficult a question might be to answer. Users in general thought their questions were easier than they turned out to be. Furthermore, users who thought questions had been easy to answer gave the presence of the librarian as the explanation: users thought their questions were easy for the librarians because of the librarians' skills, knowledge, helpfulness, understanding, technological abilities, and so on.
4. **Nearly half of these questions could not have been answered without the librarian's help.** About 40 percent of these questions probably would not have been answered completely without the help of a professional librarian. One reason is that users often have unreasonable expectations of electronic information systems: for example, that entering a company name into the public access catalog will result in information about that company. Even when users are

---

EXERCISE

IS AN INTERVIEW NEEDED?

Examine this interview, which lasted 17 seconds, as tape-recorded in Dewdney's field study. The librarian followed the face value rule, asking a question only to clarify the initial formulation of the request:

Librarian: Hi. Can I help?

User: Where can I find the city directory?

Librarian: For [local city name]? (closed question)

User: Yes.

Librarian: Right here. You can take it to a table and just bring it back when you're finished.

Dewdney, City Directory

For group discussion, consider the following: Do you think any further interviewing was needed here? Under what circumstances would further questioning be unnecessary? Under what circumstances might it be needed? How can the librarian distinguish in advance between these two sets of circumstances? What else could the librarian have said during this interview to enhance the likelihood that the user would not leave the library without finding what she was looking for?

Compare the 17-second interview quoted above with this one, conducted by the same librarian in the same library a short time later:

Librarian: Can I help?

User: I have a list of publications [reads from paper]. I don't know if those are magazines or journals or . . .

Librarian: They're all magazines [looking at paper. Reads names of magazines and gives directions on where to find them.] But before you look at magazines themselves, you'd want to know where—. Which particular articles you are looking for? (open question)

User: Do you have an index?

Librarian: Yeah. Are you looking at a particular topic? (closed question that functions as an open question)

User: Yes. I'm looking at wage restraint in the federal government.

Librarian: OK. You might want to use the business index. [Explains index, shows index.] Have you used an index before?

User: No.

Librarian: [Explains and instructs. Together they find several headings related to wage restraint. Librarian gives directions on how to find the specific articles on wage restraint in the magazines themselves.]

User: OK. Thank you.

Dewdney, Wage Restraint

EXERCISE

JUST SAY NO

Karen Hyman's "Rule of 1965" is that anything the library did prior to 1965 is basic and everything else is extra, to be offered grudgingly—for decades. Check how well your library is following the Rule of 1965 by giving it one point for every Yes answer to the following:

1. You offer services that you don't publicize because too many people might want them.
2. The telephone reference staff won't fax answers to users, even though the technology is now cheap and available, because "that's not how it's ever been done in this department."
3. Your telephone voicemail says that you are too busy to answer and that the caller should phone back or come into the library in person.
4. On the Web page describing the electronic reference service, the very first thing users see is a disclaimer or a statement about the kinds of users or questions that are ineligible for service. Give an extra point if the e-reference Web page advises users to come to the library in person for really good service.
5. The library restricts and rations Internet access through complicated sign-up procedures. Reference librarians don't treat free Web resources as a library tool to be used with the user, but instead recommend that users "check out the XYZ Web site when you get home."
6. Your policy disallows the use of the Internet for personal communication (e-mail, chat).
7. The link to your electronic reference service is at least three clicks away from your main page.
8. The library's e-reference service tells users that they should use the service only for "ready reference questions." Give an extra point if no examples or explanation are provided to help the user understand what libraries mean by a ready reference question.

If the score is 0 or 1, the library deserves congratulations. If the score is 2 to 4, more could be done to put a positive face on the library service. If the score is 5 or more, the library is in trouble and needs to review its policy on service and its communications with its users (if it still has any users).

(Adapted from Hyman, 1999. Used with permission.)

knowledgeable about the library system, unexpected barriers may intervene, such as material that is missing or misshelved. If the user's own strategy does not work, the user might not be able to get an answer unless the librarian is available to suggest alternative strategies.

5. **Users depend heavily on librarians not only to find the information they need but also to find out how to use the system.** Users spoke of "learning one new thing each time I come to the library," usually through instruction by the librarian.

The data repeatedly showed that *the librarian is the key to the information seeking process* for users. The solution to current stresses on library systems is not to reduce the human element but to make it stronger, more efficient, and more effective. The most important resource of a public or academic library may be the staff who link people with collections, virtual or otherwise. Their findings have implications for the concept of the do-it-yourself virtual library. One wonders first how many questions go unanswered when users do not come to library staff for help, and secondly how many more will go unanswered if remote access becomes the norm. In an era of electronic resources, the role of libraries as intermediaries between users and information has not diminished—it may actually be even more crucial.

1.3 BEYOND 55 PERCENT

Unobtrusive studies have shown that when users ask reference questions in academic and public libraries, they get accurate answers from 50 to 60 percent of the time. So frequently has this result been found that it has been enshrined in the literature as the "55 percent rule," first articulated by Peter Hernon and Charles McClure (1986, 1987) in their analysis of unobtrusive studies of reference service. Unobtrusive observation was given impetus in Social Science research with the work of E. J. Webb *et al.* on unobtrusive measures in the 1960s. The advantage of unobtrusive measures is that they are unreactive. That is, subjects who are observed unobtrusively are less likely than subjects who know they are being observed to change their behavior as a result of being studied. Unobtrusive observation and testing got its start in the library field after Terence Crowley and Thomas Childers published their two studies of reference service in 1971.

In these two pioneering research reports and the many that replicated their methods, the researcher typically developed a list of questions with a known right answer, and a research assistant or proxy asked the question in a library and tabulated the percentage of correct answers provided. In these studies, accuracy of the answer is the single measure used to evaluate information service effectiveness. Accuracy of the answer recommends itself as a measure to researchers because it is one of those reliable variables (like "precision" and "recall") that are not dependent on subjective judgments.

Yet no one would deny that an answer might be accurate and still fail on some other criterion of adequacy. It might, for example, be incomprehensible to the user, it might be provided too late to be useful, or it might be unacceptable because it was provided by a surly librarian. Moreover, accuracy is a useful criterion only for questions to which there really is a single right or wrong answer—factual questions such as the height of the Washington Monument or the address of the Australian High Commissioner in Zimbabwe. But most reference questions have a range of acceptable answers. Users' questions typically take the form of "I want information on X." Hence they might say, "I'm looking for information on prostate cancer" or "Do you have anything on carbon dating?" or "Where can I get information on the care of grapevines?" So even if we could agree that correctness of answer is the best measure for factual questions, we might wonder about the validity of this measure for overall reference service.

Joan Durrance asks the rhetorical question "Does the 55 percent rule tell the whole story?" and her answer is no. She proposed and tested a new indicator: the user's willingness to return to the same staff member at a later time. In her study of 266 reference interviews in academic, special, and public libraries, Durrance found that a user's willingness (or unwillingness) to return was significantly related to eleven interpersonal and search skill variables. She found that users were "far more forgiving when library staff members had weak interviewing skills or gave inaccurate answers than they were if the staff member made them feel uncomfortable, showed no interest, or appeared to be judgmental about the question" (1989: 35). In fact, in some cases in which the answer was rated as largely inaccurate, more than one-quarter of Durrance's users said they would return to that same librarian. Her study raised some interesting questions: Are users more impressed by the demeanor of the librarian than by the quality of the information provided? What factor or combination of factors influences the user's willingness to return?

In her book *The Reference Encounter* (1999), Marie Radford makes a valuable contribution to our knowledge of what factors enter into the users' perceptions of reference success. Drawing on communication theory, she makes a key distinction between the content-oriented dimension and the relational dimension of interpersonal communication. Unobtrusive tests of accuracy measure only the content-oriented dimension. The relational dimension of the reference transaction includes the feelings of the participants and their attitudes toward one another and toward the reference encounter itself. Radford gathered the data for her study by observing reference transactions in three different academic library settings and then interviewing both parties to the transaction. In total she observed 27 reference encounters and tape-recorded and transcribed in-depth interviews with nine academic reference librarians and 29 users. Her real interest was in perceptions of the reference transaction, and specifically whether the user's perception differed from that of the librarian involved in the same transaction. You won't be surprised to learn that there were substantial differences.

According to Radford's book, users almost always attributed the success or failure of a reference transaction to relational factors—they said the librarian was "nice and helpful and pleasant" or "went out of her way" or, contrariwise, was "not very patient" or was "really sour" (1999: 76, 80). In contrast, librarians, especially when discussing successful transactions, were apt to talk about issues of content, such as the amount or quality of information available on particular topics. However, when discussing transactions considered unsuccessful, librarians focused on the relational factors of feelings or attitudes. Interestingly, librarians explained unsuccessful transactions in terms of the users' poor attitudes either toward the librarian or toward the task. Users were described as having "a closed mind," being "angry, he was angry when he started," and "interrupting" (1996: 76–77).

There is a growing body of research that acknowledges the narrowness of accuracy of question-answering as a sole indicator of reference success. Typically, these studies emphasize the importance of other factors, including the relational dimension, and use other indicators, such as the user's willingness to return to the same librarian with another question. However, like the unobtrusive studies that use accuracy as the measure of success, these studies have also found a 50 to 60 percent success rate. In the Library Visit Study, which used willingness to return as a measure of reference success, Dewdney and Ross (1994) found that only about 60 percent of users of public and academic libraries expressed a willingness to return. The troublesome fact remains—whether we examine public, academic, or special libraries and whether we measure reference success by accuracy of the answer or by willingness of the user to return—that the success rate for information service hovers in the 50 to 60 percent range, in the absence of a concerted effort to improve success. Fortunately, training programs such as the Maryland Training Program described by Lillie Dyson (1992) and the STAR program described by Laura Isenstein (1992) do work to improve reference success. We can and must get beyond a 55 percent success rate.

The good news is that it seems that progress is being made, at least in the libraries observed in the Library Visit study. When we compared the reference transactions in phase one (1991-1993) and phase two (1998-2000) of the Library Visit study, we found that overall success rates improved from 60 percent in the earlier period to 69 percent, measured by willingness of the user to return to the same librarian. This improvement is entirely explained by improvement in the users' satisfaction with public library service.

Percent saying Yes, they would return:

Phase 1: 1991-1993, 100 library visits
In both public and academic libraries:	60%
In 71 public library visits:	53.5%
In 29 academic library visits:	76%

Phase 2: 1998-2000, 161 library visits
In both public and academic libraries:	69%
In 111 public library visits:	66%
In 50 academic library visits:	74%

SIX COMMON CAUSES OF COMMUNICATION ACCIDENTS

The reference interview tends to go wrong in predictable ways that can be avoided or at least remedied through the use of basic microskills described in Chapters 2, 3, and 4. Avoiding these predictable communication accidents can go a long way toward increasing reference success well beyond 55 percent. Here are six common problems, together with suggestions for how to avoid them.

DID YOU KNOW?

Accuracy is highly prized by librarians, but it is not the only, or even the most important, element that users look for. Users want information packaged in a certain format; they want it within a specified period of time; they want a certain amount of it; and above all they want it not to take more than a certain amount of effort to get it. Depending on what they are trying to do, users may be quite justified in feeling that a ballpark answer is helpful—they don't always need it to be more exact. Part of conducting the reference interview successfully is to find out how finely grained the helpful answer needs to be.

EXERCISE

THE 55 PERCENT PROBLEM

Read "Unobtrusive Reference Testing: The 55 Percent Rule" by Peter Hernon and Charles R. McClure. This article reviews many research studies that indicate that only about 55 percent of the answers provided by reference librarians are accurate. For group discussion: To what extent do you think the accuracy rate could be increased by a more effective reference interview? Since the Hernon and McClure article was published in 1986, there have been many changes in libraries. Do you think that the Internet has made a difference to reference success rate? In what way?

1. **Not acknowledging the user.** Establish immediate contact with the user by acknowledging her presence through eye contact (section 2.4.2) and gestures and by restating the initial question (2.4.3).

2. **Not listening.** The inexperienced interviewer talks more than the experienced interviewer, who does more listening. Librarians who are talking or thinking ahead about search strategy might be trying to help, but they aren't listening (section 2.4.5) and they will probably miss important clues. Practice active listening. Pause (2.4.2) or use an encourager (2.4.4) instead of responding at length to everything the user says. To show that you are listening, use appropriate body language and show that you have understood what was said by using the skills of reflecting content or summarizing (3.2.4).

3. **Playing twenty questions.** An open question (section 3.2.1) or sense-making question (3.2.3) such as "What would you like to know about X?" will get you further in less time than playing twenty questions and asking, "Is it this? Is it that?"

4. **Interrupting at inappropriate times.** If you are talking or cutting off a user who is telling you something that's relevant to the query, you're not listening (section 2.4.5). Use pauses or encouragers to signal to the user that it's her turn to talk. When you need to redirect the conversation back to the purpose of the interview, wait until the user finishes and then use closure (3.2.5).

5. **Making assumptions.** Some assumptions (e.g., that the user would like some kind of help) are necessary. But assumptions based on the user's appearance or on your own perception of the problem are usually inaccurate and may offend if you make them explicit. Avoid premature diagnosis (section 3.2.2). Instead, ask sense-making questions (3.2.3), such as, "Could you tell me a little bit about how you plan to use this information?"

6. **Not following up.** Recover from other communication accidents by following up (section 4.1.3). Ask a closed or open follow-up question such as, "Did that help you?" or "What other help would you like?" Even when you're busy, invite the user to ask for further help or give instructions ("If you don't find it, ask the person at the Information Desk.") (Reported in Ross and Dewdney, 1998)

1.4 WHY DIDN'T YOU SAY SO IN THE FIRST PLACE?

If users were all experts in ways in which information is gathered, organized, and retrieved, they would think about information differently, more like the way librarians do. They would also ask for information differently. Because they are *not* all experts, they often phrase their information needs in terms that reference librarians find indirect, incomplete, or misleading. The mirror image of this is that your extensive knowledge of the library system makes you unable to think about information the way that users do. Therefore it is important to examine how users actually do ask questions. The reference librarian's job is to be the intermediary, linking users to the system, and this function involves understanding how users think about information and how they ask questions.

Consider the following reference requests, which are the initial questions of users who came to various public libraries for reference help. The questions look diverse, but they all have something in common:

> I'm looking for information on ethnic arts and crafts, especially Mexico.
> What I'm looking for is information on stockbrokers—articles that have been written about stockbrokers.
> Where could I find information on a particular company—what they make?
> Do you have an industrial park listing?
> Is there a listing of companies and addresses?
> Can you tell me where I'd find a directory of museums?
> A friend of mine says that the government has a book out that lists all the different departments, their addresses, and all that.
> Can you tell me where the newspapers are?
> Do you have any idea when the next *Vancouver Sun* will be coming out?

These questions were captured on tape as part of a field study conducted by Patricia Dewdney (1986) in which she recorded and transcribed reference transactions in public libraries. She recorded these transactions for a doctoral dissertation undertaken in the Library and Information Science program at the University of Western Ontario. We know more than is usually known about

---

ANALYZE THIS REFERENCE TRANSACTION

Case 2: Job search

User: I'm looking for information on ethnic arts and crafts, especially Mexico.

Librarian: Mm-hmm. There's quite a lot in the section on arts and crafts—745.5. (acknowledgment) Then you would have to find crafts of Mexico. You probably just have to browse through the shelves and see what comes out of crafts of various countries. That's the sort of thing you want, is it? (closed question for confirmation)

User: Yes.

Librarian: [Checks catalog.] OK, there's crafts of Japan, crafts of Mexico, crafts of New England, crafts of Papua, New Guinea. They should all be in the same area, but you may have to go further afield for some of them. I'll write these numbers down for you. Crafts of the Indians—you'd like that too?

User: Mmm.

Librarian: Right. That one is crafts of the world, so it should have different crafts in it. And then check these other ones. [Gives directions.]

Dewdney, Crafts

Comment:

This transaction is a good example of the so-called simple question that some people claim needs no reference interview. In fact, no reference interview took place here. The librarian accepted the initial question at face value and did not try to find out anything further about the user's information need.

When the user was interviewed after this reference transaction as part of the research project, she explained that she was applying for a job for which she would need to plan children's programs. She wanted to get some ideas for crafts that were "out of the ordinary" to impress a potential employer. What she really wanted, however, was to be put in touch with "someone who has done this before" so that she could talk to someone involved with arts and crafts programs for children. The user was only "somewhat satisfied" with the service she got and probably would not go back to the same librarian with a similar question. When the user tracked down the call numbers, many of the books were not on her topic. She said she felt that she had been left to sink or swim on her own and had hoped to get more actual help.

For discussion:

How typical do you think this transaction is? What aspects are typical/not typical?

Do you think it would have made any difference to the information that the user received if she had started out the interview by saying, "I'm preparing for a job interview." What difference, if any?

Was the user right to feel she had been given very little help? How do you account for the user's assessment of the service provided?

EXERCISE

REMOVING COMMUNICATION BARRIERS

Consider the communication barriers suggested in the list provided in WHY CAN'T THEY JUST ASK US FOR WHAT THEY WANT? Which of these factors do you think might be barriers for the users of your library? For each factor that you think might be problematic, what solution(s) can you think of to address the problem? How many are solutions that would need system-wide administrative support? How many are within the control of the individual librarian?

WHY CAN'T THEY JUST ASK US FOR WHAT THEY WANT?

The library literature is full of guesses and attributions, as librarians try to come up with explanations for why users don't think about information the way they themselves do. Here are some of these explanations:

- Users don't understand that it is the job of the reference librarian to help get them the right answer.
- Users think that a library is like a supermarket, where they are expected to be self-reliant and find everything themselves and the most they can expect is to be pointed at the right aisle. Therefore they don't want to "bother" the librarian.
- Users think libraries are simple. Hence they could do everything for themselves, if only they had a tiny bit of direction or instruction.
- Users are inexperienced in asking for help because they do not really expect to get help. They haven't much confidence in the librarian's ability to find the information or even that there is any helpful information to be found on their topic or problem.
- Users don't think librarians have the subject expertise to be able to understand their specialized topic.
- Users sometimes avoid self-disclosure, especially with legal, medical, or financial questions. Some want to protect their privacy because the particular topic is sensitive, while others are reserved and generally avoid talking about themselves to strangers, whether the topic is sensitive or not.
- Users are just beginning on a problem and don't really know what they want.
- Users know what they want but they can't articulate it in system terms. They don't know what information the librarian needs to know in order to find the information they need. Users will not volunteer information that they do not perceive as relevant, and they don't always understand the relevance because they don't know how the system works.
- Users ask for broader subjects than necessary because they know that libraries are organized by broad subjects.
- Users don't know the enormous extent of information available. When they ask for "everything on transportation," they are not envisioning thousands of items.
- Users don't know how information is organized and packaged and lack the specialized vocabulary to distinguish accurately among different reference tools. They might think that all top-

---

WHY CAN'T THEY JUST ASK US FOR WHAT THEY WANT? (Continued)

ics come in book-size packages and so they ask for a book on topic X when actually the answer that they need is to be found in government statistics or in a directory or on a Web page.
- Users think they are being helpful by suggesting a source.
- Users are unaware of the ambiguity of subject requests (e.g., "information on fish" = catching fish? cooking fish? caring for pet fish? starting up a salmon-farming business? the diseases of fish? the symbolism of fish in Christian iconography?).
- The initial questions that users ask are just a way of starting the conversation.

(Adapted and summarized from Mount, 1966; Nahl, 1997; and Dewdney and Michell, 1996).

---

the context of these questions because follow-up interviews were conducted in which the users were asked, among other things, how they had hoped the information requested would help them. The element linking these questions is that all were asked by people who needed help to prepare themselves for finding a job. The user asking the question about ethnic arts and crafts turned out to be getting ready for a job interview involving programming for children. The question about stockbrokers was really a request for something describing what stockbrokers actually do in their day-to-day work; the user wanted to decide whether stockbroking was the sort of job he would enjoy. The questions about the listing of companies or industrial parks, the museum directory, and the listing of government departments were all asked because job-hunters needed names and addresses of potential employers to whom they could send résumés. The users asking for newspapers wanted to find advertisements for job openings.

This juxtaposition of reference requests provides a striking illustration of the way that users typically formulate their questions. None of these users said, "I'm job-hunting and I want . . . ." Rather, the three users with questions about ethnic crafts, stockbrokers, and a specific company had a particular answer in mind, but each phrased the question as a request for general information on a broad topic. The other users asked questions one step more remote from their original questions. Starting with their job-hunting problem, they translated their specific need into a gen-

---

WHAT PEOPLE REALLY WANT TO KNOW

Initial question	Negotiated question
1. Do you have anything on housing?	What are the rights of a tenant in a rental situation?
2. Do you have a copy of the Ocala, Florida, newspaper?	Does Ocala, Florida, have a car rental agency that I can contact?
3. Where are your books on alcohol?	I would like the times and places for meetings of local AA groups.
4. Where are your books on Canada?	I need a picture of an attacking grizzly bear for a book I am illustrating.
5. Does anyone on your staff speak German?	Will the library buy my collection of German books?
6. How extensive is your library?	I need a book on wedding etiquette that tells me what to do as best man at a wedding.
7. I would like a book on carving a duck. (assumed to mean carving a cooked duck)	I want books on woodcarving with instruction on how to carve a duck decoy.
8. Do you have Animal Graveyard?	Do you have Stephen King's Pet Sematary?
9. Where is your ancient history section?	I need to read about the causes of World War I for a school assignment.

---

eral topic and then *prescribed* the reference source that they thought most appropriate for their topic: an industrial park listing, a directory of museums, a book listing government departments, newspapers in general, a particular city newspaper. Unfortunately, the farther the presenting question gets from the actual information the user needs to know, the greater the chance of mistranslation, misunderstanding, and mistaken requests for inappropriate reference sources.

On the basis of these initial questions alone, it is unlikely that the librarian would understand what the user really wanted to know. Well, so what? Why be concerned, as long as the librarian provides the list or directory or newspaper that the user has asked for? Would knowing about the job-hunting context of the question change the kind of answer that the librarian would provide? Well, yes. Surely with at least some of these questions, it would make a difference to know the particular context of the question. (But see section 3.2.3 on why librarians should not ask why directly.)

The rest of this section explores, from a variety of perspectives, the contrasts between the ways in which users and librarians think about information.

1.4.1 THE ILL-FORMED QUERY

Librarians are familiar with the phenomenon of the "ill-formed" query—a term from linguistics given to a question that doesn't work because it leads to erroneous inferences. In fact, one experienced librarian in the Mental Models study said she had come to expect to encounter incomplete or misleading initial questions: "He was quite specific in what he wanted. He knew exactly what he wanted and that's what he asked for. And it threw me. Because you're not used to people asking for what they want." Over the years, Dewdney and Ross have asked workshop participants for examples from their own experience of cases in which the real question had turned out to be different from the question as initially presented. Participants rarely have any difficulty in thinking of a recent situation. "Yes it happens all the time," they say, nodding. From the workshops and other sources, we have collected examples of ill-formed queries and now have a database of 945 examples of question pairs. The box WHAT PEOPLE REALLY WANT TO KNOW gives some typical examples of question pairs: the initial question and the negotiated or "real" question.

The problem—and the reason the reference interview is needed—is that people don't always express their information needs clearly and completely. As we have seen, the user's initial question is often not the real question. We call these problematic initial questions "ill-formed queries," which we define as initial questions that do not provide a statement of the information need that is sufficiently clear or complete for the librarian to be able to give effective help. The questions may be perfectly well-formed semantically and syntactically, but in context they are somehow incomplete and even misleading. The key point is that the queries are "ill-formed" with respect to the information system; that is, they do not match the structure or "expectations" of the system.

While every question is different, an analysis of a large collection of ill-formed queries reveals some repeated patterns. Here are some typical problems:

1. **Users ask for something very broad and general** when they actually want a very specific piece of information within the broad category they have asked for. Example 1 (anything on housing) falls into this class. Other examples that recur frequently are initial questions that take the following form: "Where do you keep your medical books?"

A QUICK TIP

QUESTIONS ABOUT THE SYSTEM

Often questions about how to use an index or catalog or some other library system mask an information need. If a user says, "I'm having trouble with this index catalog" or "Are the books arranged in any particular order?" it is often helpful to ask, "What are you trying to do?" or "What are you trying to find out?" Here's a case in which the librarian didn't follow this advice:

User: Have you got a book that writes down the Dewey Decimal System? Like in the 700s. I want to copy the divisions for the 700s.

Librarian: Do you? Sure. [Gives him the Dewey schedule.] There you go. Start there.

Dewdney, Dewey

After the user spent a long time with the book, he came back and asked, "There's nothing in your filing system that gives series? Like a neighbor brought to my door a music book. This book had piano pieces with very simple arrangements by this man Tyndall. I thought the library might have some more of his arrangements."

"Where is your law section?" "What have you got on transportation?" The question "Where is your law section?" can mask many different information needs requiring different sources (e.g., I want to get out of a lease; I want to do background reading before seeing a lawyer about divorce; I want to verify a legal opinion on a problem with a neighbor; I'm doing a project on copyright legislation for my college course). If the initial question is treated as a directional question, it is unlikely that the user will find the specific piece of information that is wanted. The user who asked about the location of medical books was worried about her daughter and wanted to find out more about anorexia, its diagnosis, treatment, and long-term effects.

2. **Users ask for something specific but there is a mismatch** between the specific thing they ask for and what they actually need to answer their question. Often the mismatch happens because users ask for a specific source, thinking that the answer is either there or in that general vicinity, as in examples 2 and 3. Because most users aren't experts on sources, they are often wrong in their diagnosis of the best source. For example, a user who asked, "Where do you keep your encyclopedias?" actually wanted job listings in Australia. The users who asked for books on alcohol and books on Canada in examples 3 and 4 have diagnosed wrongly what the best source would be (the mismatch problem) and then added a second problem by asking for something very broad and general. A variant on the problem of asking for something specific that involves a mismatch happens when the user becomes confused about library terms. Requests for bibliographies are often made in error when biographies are wanted, and vice versa.

3. **Users aren't exactly sure how the library system works** and ask a question based on a misunderstanding or to clarify a confusion. Examples 5 and 6 fall into this class. Sometimes a question about the library system ("I'm having trouble with this index" or "Excuse me, are the books arranged in any particular order?") is the user's way of saying he has run into a barrier and needs help—not necessarily bibliographic instruction on how to use an index or understand classification schemes, but assistance with finding a helpful answer.

4. **Keywords in the user's question are ambiguous.** There are two basic kinds of ambiguity here: ambiguity caused by either the user's pronunciation or the staff member's faulty hearing, and ambiguity caused by homophones, words that sound the same but have different meanings, as in example

A QUICK TIP

TRANSLATE THOSE LOCATION QUESTIONS INTO PROBLEM-CENTERED QUESTIONS

Dewdney and Michell ("Oranges and Peaches," 1996) point out that users typically present their information needs as questions about locations and subjects as in "Do you have books/information/a section on X?" rather than as problem-centered statements. So users ask, "Where are your books on houseplants?" and not, "I have whiteflies on my aspidistra." Unlike problem-centered statements, questions about locations and subjects provide no context and increase the chances that a request for X will be heard as a request for Y (e.g., "house-plants" heard as "house plans"). Dewdney and Michell recommend that you don't immediately rush to provide directions for where information on Y is shelved, but instead that you ask a question about Y: "What would you like to know about house plans?" The user's answer almost always elicits the context from which you can distinguish between X and Y, between houseplants and house plans, for example.

7. A typical example of the pronunciation problem is the Scottish user whose request for military badges sent the librarian off on a fruitless hunt for military budgies. Other examples of acoustic failures include the question about venom that turned out to be about the Vietnam War. Ditto Tolkien books/talking books; bird control/birth control; hairpieces/herpes; hairdressers in Saudi Arabia/addresses in Saudi Arabia; house plans/houseplants; bamboo hearts/baboon hearts; silver service/civil service test; and the sick in California/the Sikhs in California. A typical example of ambiguity caused by homophones is the request for "something on whales," which may easily be heard as a request for "something on Wales" or, depending on the dialect, "something on wills." China, Greece, Turkey, and Chile are also good candidates for confusion. Workshop participants have provided us with many examples of ambiguous keywords, some of them humorous: eunuchs/UNIX; tofu/TOEFL; super vision/supervision; reproductive technology (interpreted as artificial insemination)/reproductive technology (photocopiers); makeup (cosmetics)/psychological makeup; and of course, the old standby, which we have heard so often that we suspect it's an urban legend: youth in Asia/euthanasia. One of the best examples of a user's mishearing is the "Oranges and Peaches" case that provided the title for the Dewdney and Michell article on the ill-formed query (1996). A user asks for a copy of *Oranges and Peaches*, but it turns out that he has misheard the teacher's instruction to find Darwin's *Origin of Species*.

A further complication that can occur with either of these two kinds of ambiguity is that the staff member may interpret the ambiguous words in the context of a particular mental set, predisposition, or expectation. For example, one librarian was busy weeding the sports books when he misheard a request for books on Socrates as "soccer tees" and began scanning the soccer books. Another librarian was engaged in bibliographic checking when she misheard a request for books on sea lamprey as a request for books on C. Lamprey, presumed to be an important person.

5. **The user's question involves a reconstruction,** as the user tries to remember specific terms or details and sometimes gets it wrong. The user reconstructs the meaning but not the form of a forgotten item. Sometimes the reconstruction involves substitutions of synonyms or near synonyms, as in example 8. Hence a user may say, "Where is your gynecology section?" when she wants to research her fam-

DID YOU KNOW?

ily tree. The user may ask for information on Clinton's closet when he wants Clinton's cabinet, or ask for the book *Sex Before Dinner* when he wants *The Naked Lunch*. Or the user asks for a book recommended by a friend in England, *Shame on the Princess*, when she wants *Tales of a Shaman's Apprentice*. Other examples are sugar mommy/ sugar daddy; IUD/*OED*; Rockin' Jim/*Rock and Gem*; the President of Utopia/the President of Ethiopia; the Kingdom of Phyla/an overview of biological classification; Malcolm the Tenth/Malcolm X; chow mein/Charlemagne. This type of problem is more apt to happen with what Melissa Gross has called the "imposed query" (see section 5.3.1), in which the question is generated by someone else, such as a teacher, and the user has not completely understood the assignment.

6. **The user's question contains an error or misconception,** not about the library system itself but about the outside world. In example 9, the student may regard anything before 1950 as ancient history, but this view, though understandable, is idiosyncratic and not consistent with accepted conventions of periodization. In this category of ill-formed question, the error is embedded in the question as a taken-for-granted fact and is not easy to spot without asking a question such as "What are you looking for when you say 'ancient history'?"

1.4.2 MENTAL MODELS

We can explain the prevalence of ill-formed queries in terms of the users' mental models of how libraries work. The act of asking a librarian for help is a microcosm of information-seeking behavior governed by the participants' mental models of the system. A useful theory of mental models has been associated with Donald Norman and Philip N. Johnson-Laird in the field of artificial intelligence and cognitive science. Norman and Johnson-Laird describe a mental model as a working model that individuals construct in their minds to facilitate interaction with the environment, other individuals, or technology. Such a mental model contrasts with the "real" model or "conceptual model" of the same object, which is, according to Norman, an appropriate representation of the target system "in the sense of being accurate, consistent and complete" (1983:7).

An individual's mental model of any system is, by definition, inaccurate and incomplete in relation to the conceptual model. The degree of discrepancy between an individual's mental model of the system and the conceptual model is important. When users' mental models of the library system are at odds with the "real"

DID YOU KNOW?

Dewdney and Michell (Mental Models, 1996) decided to find out what the chances are of providing a helpful answer when the librarian takes the initial question at face value. Their field study was based on observing 33 reference transactions and afterward interviewing both the user and the librarian. For each case they asked, "What are the chances of the librarian's being able to understand the real information need from the initial question alone?" and rated the chances from 1 (not at all) to 5 (excellent—little or no question negotiation required). The following is a summary of the findings for the 33 cases.

Somewhat good,
   very good, or
     excellent: 60.6%
   (ratings of 3, 4 or 5)
Not at all
   possible or not
   very good: 39.4%
   (ratings of 1 or 2)

That is, in 40 percent of the cases, the librarian has practically no chance of discovering the real information need without conducting a reference interview or unless the user decides to volunteer more information. Words from these ill-formed initial questions could not be entered as keywords into an information retrieval system with any hope of finding something useful.

or conceptual models of the library system, they are more likely to generate ill-formed questions. Librarians, on the other hand, have mental models of libraries that are much closer to the conceptual model. The crucial questions are: Does the users' understanding of the library system (including the collection and its organization, the physical layout, the role of the librarian in the system, and the types of service that a user can expect) differ in any important way from the librarian's understanding of that system? If there is an important difference, does either the librarian or the user discover it, and how does that discovery affect the outcome of the transaction? What can the librarian do to increase the likelihood of discovering such differences?

The mismatch between the user's mental model and the librarian's mental model can be used to explain communication accidents and misunderstandings that arise in the reference interview, with implications as described below.

SOME IMPLICATIONS OF MENTAL MODELS RESEARCH FOR REFERENCE STAFF

1. Remember that users tend to phrase their initial questions in a way that they believe meets the requirements of the system. However, users' models of the system tend to be oversimplified, incomplete, and sometimes wrong, even in the case of frequent public library users. The problem of the inadequacy of the users' mental models becomes greater as computerized library systems become more complex in the options that they offer.

2. Be aware of the likelihood of the discrepancy between the user's mental model of the library system and your own and take steps to check for discrepancies. The less experienced the user is with the system, the more likely he or she is to have an inaccurate mental model. Use the questioning skills described in Chapter 2 to find out what the user's mental model is. For example, when a user says, "Can you help me find some good historical books to read?" a good readers' adviser checks by saying, "Can you tell me about a historical book that you have read recently and enjoyed?" or "What sort of historical books are you in the mood for?" The user might want Jean Plaidy or some other historical romance, not Winston Churchill on the second World War. Fortunately, there are particular communication skills that librarians can learn, or refresh, that reduce the chances that the librarian never finds out what the user wanted.

3. Mental models change through an incremental learning process. Each time users come to the library, they learn a bit

EXERCISE

MENTAL MODELS

Reread the case provided in MENTAL MODELS OF THE LIBRARY SYSTEM. We have tried to suggest the beliefs that may have been part of Mary's model of libraries when she asked, "Where's the science section?" in order to get rabbit pictures. What beliefs about libraries do you think were held by Arjun, Julia, and James that led each of them to ask their different initial questions?

DID YOU KNOW?

In her study of academic library users, Virginia Massey-Burzio (1998) discovered that users, even those who were at advanced levels in their fields, had an inaccurate understanding of the library system and its complexity. Here are some misconceptions that she uncovered: They don't understand the difference between a keyword and an assigned subject term. They try to look up the title of a journal article in the on-line catalog. They can't find fiction books in a Library of Congress–arranged collection because they expect to find them all alphabetically arranged in one sequence, not divided by country. They don't understand that the reason they are not finding anything is that the database or index that they are looking in does not cover their subject area. They feel overwhelmed by all the different databases and so they stick to the one or two that they know, irrespective of subject coverage.

MENTAL MODELS OF THE LIBRARY SYSTEM

Four different users are all looking for colored photographs of rabbits because they want to draw their own pictures. Mary says, "Where's the science section?" Arjun says, "Do you have Encarta?" Julia says, "I want information on rabbits." And James says, "I want to see the head librarian."

All four of these users have a goal, which is to find a color photo of a rabbit from which to draw their own pictures. All four have a plan to achieve that goal. Underlying the plan is a model that includes various beliefs about the world in general and about library systems in particular. Each person has developed his or her model on the basis of past experience, prior learning, and other factors. Mary's model of libraries may include some beliefs that can be stated as propositions:

1. Photos of rabbits are often found in books.
2. Books can be found in large numbers in libraries.
3. Books in libraries are organized by general subjects.
4. The general subject for rabbits is animals, but perhaps this is unduly narrow, so the subject is probably biology or even science. Based on past experience with libraries and their signage, science seems like a good bet.
5. If I can be pointed toward the science section, there will be a book there that contains a photo of a rabbit. I'll be able to make my own copy.
6. I should be able to find what I need on my own with a minimum of help. Libraries are self-help places, just like supermarkets.

These assumptions are not completely wrong. However, the librarian knows, because of her more accurate model of libraries, that the more efficient procedure is not to start with a broad subject area because (and these are the librarian's underlying beliefs):

1. Users don't always ask for what they want.
2. Not everything to do with science will be classified as science.
3. Science is a huge section. It is inefficient to search for "science books."
4. If I give directions to the science section, the user will probably not find what she needs.
5. My job is to help users find what they need. Once I find out what the user's goal is, I can substitute a more effective and efficient plan.
6. The appropriate step is to ask the user what she wants.
7. Photographs of rabbits can be found easily in a specialized picture file or children's book of animals.

When the librarian acts on these beliefs by conducting a reference interview and providing the desired rabbit picture, she can modify the user's beliefs or model of the library in a way that will help the user better negotiate her way through the library the next time she has a question.

A QUICK TIP

A GRAIN OF SALT

When users ask for books, they are not necessarily intending to put a restriction on the format of the acceptable answer. An experienced librarian in the Mental Models study reported that a user's question "Where are the books on coins?" was very typical. "The one before that asked, 'Where are the books on needlepoint?' It happens a lot. They say, 'Where are your books on back pain?' It's the way users phrase the question when they want information. They say, 'Where are the books on . . . ?' Their assumption is that the information is in a book and that the books are all together in one place." In such cases, the user's mental model of the library may be inexact and the librarian knows of additional or better sources.

more about what the librarian is doing and how to do it for themselves. This suggests that the user's model of the library is fluid, changing, and in fact may change quickly, even over the course of one interaction with the librarian. The librarian can help the user develop a more accurate mental model of the library system by explaining, not necessarily in great detail, what she is doing; this skill, called inclusion, is discussed in section 4.3.1. It is especially effective when you are working with users who value their own incremental learning.

In many cases, the most useful thing you can do to help users develop a more accurate mental model is to help them become more aware of the system's capacity. For example, users who think that all information comes in book-size packages could be helped to understand that the library has a large range of sources available in different formats, or that the sources on their topic may be scattered in different parts of the library, or that there are other formats available, including Web-based resources. Once users understand a bit more about the complexity of resources available, they are in a better position to choose whether to proceed on their own with some instruction or whether to ask you to draw on your knowledge of the system to help solve the problem.

4. You should not, however, insist on giving unwanted instruction; you must assess (and not by guessing) what the user's level of knowledge or ability is and whether or not the user wants to learn more on that particular day. In their Mental Models study, Dewdney and Michell occasionally observed librarians instructing users in the use of the library catalog, when some users told them later they already knew how to use it and others said they were not at all interested in learning how to use it. Users don't necessarily need to be given a detailed picture of how libraries work. Your job as intermediary is to link the user to the system in whatever way the user finds most helpful. One of the interesting questions for our field (especially in bibliographic instruction) is the point beyond which it is counterproductive for individuals to have a more complete understanding of the model. Some users want bibliographic instruction; others, such as students, are expected to want it; and still others just want the answer. For this last group, their rudimentary mental model of how the library works is sufficient for their purposes, even if librarians are reluctant to believe that some people are content to be uninformed about

indexing systems. When users get helpful answers to their questions, their mental model of the library is at least likely to include certain understandings: the library is the right place to come for help with information questions; librarians are likely to be willing and able to help.

DID YOU KNOW?

If you think that information is a commodity—and a precious commodity at that—then you will believe that the more information that the user is given the better. The reasoning here is that a big stockpile of information is always a good thing because information is a resource that is valuable in itself. However, most people would much rather have a small amount of information exactly tailored to their needs. Library users, especially novices, feel overwhelmed when offered dozens of book titles, hundreds of articles, or thousands of Web pages. In fact, people commonly refer to "information overload," or "infoglut" and talk about feeling "swamped," "inundated," "overwhelmed," or drowning in information. Sara Fine has coined what she calls "the Saturation Principle" to cover this situation: "If the user is already saturated with information, additional information will not help in making a decision or aid in solving a problem" (1995: 17–20).

1.5 THE HELPFUL ANSWER: TWO WAYS OF THINKING ABOUT INFORMATION

Everyone who works in libraries operates from a set of assumptions about what information is. Often these assumptions are unacknowledged and unexamined, but they have a powerful influence on what kind of service is provided to users. In this next section we make the case for critically examining the way we think about information and for making explicit the metaphors we use to talk about information and its provision.

1.5.1 INFORMATION AS A COMMODITY

In the profession of librarianship, several factors combine to make us think of information as a commodity. Most pervasive of all is the language we share, which provides us with a way of talking and thinking about information that is essentially metaphoric: we "store" information; we "retrieve" it; we "transfer" it, we feel "buried" in too much of it, and so on. These metaphors for information are part of a larger pattern that Michael Reddy (1993) has called the "conduit metaphor" for language. He has argued that the way we talk about language is structured by the following metaphors: Ideas are *objects*. Linguistic expressions are *containers*. Communication is a process of putting idea-objects into linguistic containers and sending them along a *conduit* to a listener, who takes the idea-objects out of their word containers.

Normally, of course, we are not aware of the metaphors we use. But once we start paying attention to them we can see how strongly what we think of as ordinary reality is structured by metaphor. George Lakoff and Mark Johnson (1980) have analyzed the entailments of the conduit metaphor as follows: If we think of ideas as objects, then we think of meanings as existing independently of people and contexts. Moreover, if words are thought of as containers for meanings, then we think of words and sentences as having meanings in themselves, independent of any context or speaker.

Likewise, if we think of information as a commodity, it too can be thought of as existing apart from people or contexts—an object to be transferred, retrieved, exchanged, stored, and stockpiled. This way of conceptualizing information makes it seem "natural" to think that a question can be posed and can be answered correctly with no reference to its context in the life of the asker. That is, no matter who asks the question and in no matter what context, the answer to the question "How did Senator Williams of New Jersey vote on the Panama Canal treaties?" remains the same: He voted Yes on both treaties.

There is another reason librarians tend to think of information as a commodity with no context: the way reference is often taught in library schools and the way it is evaluated in the literature. Library program instructors (we ourselves do this in our own introductory courses in reference) typically teach basic reference by giving students a list of questions to answer: How many goats are there in Bangladesh? What was the first short story that Alice Munro published and where was it published? What is a Fowler's octagon? What is the highest annual milk production for a dairy cow? What does a manticore look like? Where does the expression "the whole nine yards" come from? The working assumption here is that there is one correct answer and the library student should be able to find the answer and verify it in a second source. In addition, as we have seen in section 1.3, reference service has often been evaluated by studies that use proxies posing as real users. These proxies ask scripted questions and unobtrusively measure the accuracy of answers to queries like "Where is the nearest airport to Warren, Pennsylvania?" Here again, it is understood that there *is* a correct answer (in fact, the way to develop such questions is to work backward from a known answer to a question that will elicit this answer). The students in the reference course or the librarians undergoing unobtrusive observation are being tested on whether or not they have succeeded in discovering this one predetermined correct answer. In these contrived cases, the questions truly do fit the paradigm of information as commodity. They are decontextualized and exist independently from any user; probably no real user has ever asked them.

1.5.2 QUESTIONS IN CONTEXTS

Now we come to a different situation, that of a real user asking a genuine question in a library setting. Whereas contrived questions have no context and no history, real questions are embedded in the context of users' day-to-day lives. Users ask questions out of

DID YOU KNOW?

In a study of reference service at the Johns Hopkins University library, Virginia Massey-Burzio discovered that paraprofessionals at the information desk referred only 6 percent of questions to the librarians. "Because Information Desk staff were trying to deal with questions beyond their abilities, patrons viewed them as ignorant and unhelpful" (1998: 212).

the contexts of their immediate concerns. They don't take the trouble to go to the library to ask a question for the fun of it; they ask the question as a means to an end important to them. They are trying to *do* something: apply for a job, make a decision, complete a school project, finish a grant proposal, remodel their kitchen, make a complaint, join a support group, understand an illness they have been told they have, give a speech at a wedding, contact a professional colleague, complete a literature search, draw a rabbit. They ask questions to fill in gaps in their understanding so that they can get on with these concerns. Therefore, a necessary part of understanding the question is knowing the situation out of which the question arose. The question is meaningful in its context, and its context is part of its meaning. We understand the question when we recover its framework.

The user may ask, "Do you know when the next *Vancouver Sun* is coming out?" and the librarian may choose to treat it as a decontextualized question requiring the answer, "The *Vancouver Sun* is still on strike and no one knows when it will be out." But a more appropriate way of thinking about information and information-seeking in this case would be to think of the question as having a context in the life of the person who asked it (see section 1.4 on the job-hunting context). A more helpful answer to this question, when it is asked because the user is job hunting, may be, "The *Vancouver Sun* is on strike just now, but we do have other sources for western news. What specifically were you looking for?" More generally, a helpful answer for job hunters is one that helps them, in their own terms, to get on with the business of job hunting. Users are helped to the extent that the answers they get in libraries help them to do something that they want to do. Hence it is conceptually useful to distinguish between the "*correct*" answer for the disembedded, contextless question and the *helpful* answer for a particular person in a particular situation. The librarian who answers a question without knowing anything about the context in which the question became a question could provide an answer that is correct but not helpful.

Now we come to the hard part. To be able to provide this helpful answer, the librarian needs to know the context. But as we have seen, users normally don't present the initial question by volunteering the context. Users also have learned to think of information as a commodity that must be asked for in libraries in decontextualized terms. Rather than saying, "Next week I'm going on a trip to Perth, Australia, and I want to know what the temperature is likely to be, so I can pack appropriate clothes," a user may ask, "Where is your travel section?" Users often try to translate their questions into what they think are library categories or classifications.

As the Mental Models research indicates, the problem here is that users are unlikely to understand the full complexity of how information is organized in libraries. A user who wanted names and prices of ski resorts in Colorado said, "I'm interested in your ski section." We can assume that he had a rather nebulous view of what the "ski section" might include. He had probably not considered the differences among such aspects of skiing as ski resorts, learning how to ski, buying ski equipment, biographies of famous skiers, sports injuries connected with skiing, and so on, or among such formats as vertical file materials, books, periodical articles, Web sites, etc. Librarians know all this, but can't use their professional expertise unless they have more to go on than just "ski section." The purpose of the reference interview is to find out, quickly and tactfully, the context for the user's question, including the user's goal.

EXERCISE

PROVIDING THE HELPFUL ANSWER

In the Mental Models study, a user and an experienced librarian were each asked to talk about their experience with a reference transaction. The user said that she needed information on the city of Cambridge (UK) because she was getting ready to do a presentation for her book club: "I'm doing a book that takes place in Cambridge and I want to compare the reality with the fiction. It's my turn to do a report." The user had done a keyword catalog search on the word Cambridge but had become discouraged when she got hundreds of irrelevant matches, including everything published by Cambridge University Press. The user's initial question was: "I would like to find material on Cambridge." The librarian said that his first thought was "Cambridge what? University? Travel? It could be a whole range of things." He said that if he had been downstairs in the education area where the college calendars are kept, he could easily have assumed she wanted Cambridge University.

Evaluate each of the following possible responses that the librarian could have made to the user's initial request: "I would like to find material on Cambridge." Rank the responses in order of helpfulness from most to least, with helpfulness defined as providing users with the information they need in order to advance their own goals. What are your reasons for your ranking? (You might want to skip ahead to sections 3.2.1 and 3.2.3 on questioning techniques for useful background for this exercise.)

1. Have you checked the catalog?
2. The calendars for Cambridge are downstairs. You should ask the librarian at the downstairs desk for the Cambridge material.
3. What kind of information on Cambridge would help you most?
4. Do you want travel information?
5. Do you mean Cambridge, Massachusetts?

1.6 REFERENCE AS AN ART OF TRANSLATION

A great deal has been written on the necessity for translating a reference question into a representation of the user's information need that the system will accept. By *system*, we mean the interacting components of an organization for providing information service, including not only the collection and its finding aids but also the library policy and the roles of the staff. An obvious example of translating the user's natural language request into the specialized language of the system is the need to transform keywords in the information need statement into subject headings or controlled vocabulary. However, we should be aware that translation is happening all along the line.

As we have seen, users often try to do the translation themselves. They want a picture of a rabbit, so they try to translate that need into system terms, asking for "the science section." Because users are translating into an unfamiliar language—the language of the information system—it's not surprising that sometimes their translations are not helpful to the librarian. The proper person to do the translation into system terms is the librarian, not the user, just as the proper person to diagnose a drug prescription is the doctor and not the patient. When a patient comes into the doctor's office and says, "I need a prescription for prednisone," the doctor doesn't reach immediately for the prescription pad. He or she first asks some questions in order to understand the nature of the original problem and its symptoms. Similarly, the purpose of the reference interview is to get back, as far as possible, to the original information need. Until you do this, you don't really know what kind of question you are dealing with. One experienced librarian in the Mental Models study reported, "The woman came in and said she wanted books about the *Titanic*. It turned out she had a great aunt who had survived the *Titanic* sinking and she wanted the passenger list to find this lady's name. So it was a genealogy question masquerading as information about the *Titanic*." The job of the savvy librarian is to strip off the masquerade.

For this reason, standard ways of categorizing reference transactions can be misleading. A common approach is to provide a classification scheme for different kinds of reference questions and suggest escalating levels of interviewing to deal with each. Hence directional questions require pointing; ready reference questions require a quick confirmation; complex questions require an extensive interview; intensive research questions may require appointments. Here's what Sutton and Holt suggest:

> In any library setting, various types of reference questions are asked. Some are straightforward and require only brief confirmation leading to short, factual answers; others require a fairly comprehensive search of literature on a complex or obscure subject. The latter type of inquiry often requires an extensive interview process in which the subject is increasingly better defined. (1995: 36)

A variant of this approach is the adoption by some libraries of a "two-tiered" reference service, in which nonprofessional or paraprofessional staff members handle the front lines and answer routine questions. Only the difficult reference questions get referred to librarians, who stay behind the scenes. The fallacy here is the assumption that difficult questions are easily recognized as such and that users' information needs can be sorted into straightforward or complex on the basis of the initial question. The reality is that you can't classify the reference question until *after* you have conducted a reference interview to discover what the real query is. There is a real danger that what these categories really capture is a decision on the part of the librarian about how much service to give to the user: treat it as a simple directional question, point, and hope that the user can do everything independently. Treat it as a complex question, find out what the person really wants to know, and then provide help in finding specific sources.

DID YOU KNOW?

Karen Hyman recommends that you "[t]reat every customer like a person." She says, "When we categorize people— problem patron, angry mother, deadbeat borrower, greedy computer user—we feel free to ignore their feelings and messages and transform ourselves into hall monitors or victims" (1999: 58).

1.7 THERE ARE NO BAD-GUY USERS

Communications scholar Brenda Dervin has coined the term *bad-guy user* to describe the person who won't use the system in system terms—the one who refuses to read signs and follow instructions or the one who asks for "books on transportation" when it should be obvious that there are thousands of such books. In *The Reference Encounter*, Marie Radford reports that when academic librarians were asked about barriers to good reference outcomes, they tended to think mostly of problems caused by bad-guy users:

DID YOU KNOW?

In a posting to LIBREF on August 28, 1997, Dr. Diane Nahl reported that in her research with undergraduates, she has asked them to report what was said during their reference interview with a librarian, along with what they were thinking during the interview: "It was shocking and sad to discover that they were fearful that they were doing something wrong, stupid, or inappropriate throughout the entire exchange, in spite of the librarian's being usually helpful. [They castigated themselves] for being stupid, for having to ask, for not knowing, for bothering a professional, for boring a professional" (1997, used with permission).

DID YOU KNOW?

A study of 59 information exchanges between a librarian and hospital staff revealed that almost 30 percent of them contained specialized technical language or acronyms relating to the library system. The study concluded that the librarians' ability to use unfamiliar insider language served the purpose of establishing the librarians' own status as specialists and their right to be considered part of the medical team. (S.M. Schultz, "Medical Jargon: Ethnography of Language in a Hospital Library." Medical Reference Service Quarterly 15(3), 1996: 41-7)

DID YOU KNOW?

In Marie Radford's study (1999), one librarian said that the librarian's difficulty in understanding what users really wanted was the result of the users' lack of skill at "self-disclosure" or their unwillingness to trust the librarian. No mention was made of interviewing skills.

The poor library user . . . is one that has not done the proper preparatory work, has not . . . read the assignment prior to the reference interview . . . .

They don't understand indexes at all.

They don't know what they want, so no matter how much of a reference interview I did, I could never find it out.

They really expect to be handed everything, and that's become far more prevalent in the last couple of years.

[Poor users are] the ones who wait until two days before the assignment is due before they start thinking about it.

The information that he was requesting was available in these particular sources, but he refused to even consider [using them].

[T]hey're not interested in the options, they're not really interested in learning how to use the library, they just want the quickest way in and the quickest way out . . . . If they had come in earlier and were more willing to put more into it, maybe they would be better off.

I don't know why they sometimes ask for something and then, you know, they practically throw it away as soon as you give it to them. (1999: 60–62, 113, 122)

All of us, from time to time, are bad-guy users in other people's systems, particularly when that system is unfamiliar. It's easy to label as bad guys library users who are ill-prepared, lazy, and procrastinating. However, to understand why users behave this way, it helps to think about ourselves trying to negotiate other people's unfamiliar systems. For example, we appear at the airline ticket counter with our ticket to Australia but somehow didn't realize a visa is also needed and so the ticket agent has to get us one at the last minute. We call up the telephone company to report a problem and erroneously call the problematic service "call waiting" when it is really "call answer." We phone a government agency to ask about nursing homes but it turns out we should have asked for retirement homes (or vice versa). When we order a "regular coffee," we are given coffee with cream and sugar added, but we really meant we wanted regular as opposed to decaffeinated coffee. We ask the driver, "Is this the bus to Albuquerque?" when the sign clearly says "Albuquerque." In short, people get things wrong because they don't know the specialized vocabulary of an unfamiliar system and are unable to make distinctions that are self-evident to system insiders. This is why library users may ask for a bibliography when they want a biography, or an encyclopedia when they need a directory. Library staff must conduct a reference interview, not simply blame the users.

A QUICK TIP

REASSURE THE USER

Users may worry that their questions might not seem important enough or that they might be made to feel foolish or a nuisance. In the Library Visit study, users often said things like, "I worried about having the librarian scoff at my question." One user who was delighted with the reassuring treatment he received said, "I believe that one of the worst mistakes a librarian can make is to make a user feel they are wasting the librarian's time and that their question is not important. It is an intimidating feeling to approach a reference desk, and a good librarian can turn this experience into an enjoyable and fulfilling one." When this reassurance is given, it changes the users' mental model of the library from a self-service operation to a place where they can expect expert help.

We have found that in some cases, users themselves take the blame for a less than successful encounter, in effect sharing the librarian's sense of them as bad guys. For example, one user in the Library Visit study excused a staff member's manner by saying, "I have worked in retail and know it's not always easy to be pleasant when people ask dumb questions." Others apologized for asking a hard question or blamed themselves for not formulating the initial question clearly enough: "I may have asked my initial question too fast or with an overly British accent." "I was embarrassed that I had been so inept at formulating my question," said a user who asked about the location of the children's science section when his real need was for a diagram of the earth tilted on its axis to explain to his seven-year-old son the cycle of the seasons.

In short, when staff members think of the users of library services as bad guys, this sometimes unconsciously held attitude can impair service and harm public relations. In the Library Visit study, one user reported unhappily, "I distinctly overheard her remark that the reason there was so much need for shelving was because patrons always take out more books than they need and, what's worse, they don't even read them."

1.8 ANNOTATED REFERENCES

1.8.1 PRINCIPLES OF INTERVIEWING

Benjamin, Alfred. 1981. *The Helping Interview*. 3d ed. Boston: Houghton Mifflin. Written by a famous practicing counselor, this book contains many concrete examples to illustrate principles of how to conduct the helping interview.

Conroy, Barbara, and Barbara Schindler-Jones. 1986. *Improving Communication in the Library*. Phoenix, Ariz.: Oryx Press.

Ivey, Allen E., and Mary Bradford Ivey. 1999. *Intentional Interviewing and Counseling: Facilitating Client Development in a Multicultural Society*. 4th ed. Pacific Grove, Calif.: Brooks/Cole Publishing Company. Chapter 12, "Skill Integrations: Putting It All Together" provides an overview of the counseling interview, with a sample transcript illustrating individual microskills.

Shipley, Kenneth G., and Julie McNulty Wood. 1996. *The Elements of Interviewing*. San Diego and London: Singular Publishing Group. A useful introduction to basic interviewing skills in various contexts.

Spradley, James P. 1979. *The Ethnographic Interview*. New York: Holt, Rinehart and Winston. Written for the student of ethnography, this book clarifies the difference between a conversation and an interview. It distinguishes between an interviewer style whereby the interviewer learns the language of the interviewee vs. the style where the interviewee has to learn interviewer language.

Stewart, Charles J. 1999. *Interviewing: Principles and Practices*. 9th ed. Dubuque, Iowa: Kendall/Hunt. This little book is a classic guide to various kinds of interviewing. Based on extensive research, it is both practical and easy to read. Each chapter includes training exercises.

1.8.2 BIBLIOGRAPHIC GUIDES TO THE REFERENCE INTERVIEW

Dr. Matthew Saxton of the University of Washington and Dr. John Richardson of UCLA have developed a selected bibliography of 1,000 citations on reference to supplement their book *Understanding Reference Transactions* (New York: Academic Press, forthcoming). The list is alphabetically arranged by the name of the first author and contains many items of interest on the reference interview.

Elaine Zaremba Jennerich and Edward J. Jennerich have included a 300-item bibliography on the reference interview in their book *The Reference Interview as a Creative Art*, 2d ed. Englewood, Colo.: Libraries Unlimited, 1997.

Bernie Sloan has been updating a bibliography on Digital Reference Services and making it available on the Web. A 200-entry bibliography updated to November 7, 2000, can be found at www.lis.uiuc.edu/~b-sloan/digiref.html. A 100-item supplement became available on July 19, 2001, at www.lis.uiuc.edu/~b-sloan/bibsupp. More than half of the items in the supplement are Web-accessible.

Whitlatch, Jo Bell. 2000. *Evaluating Reference Services: A Practical Guide*. Chicago and London: American Library Association.

1.8.3 WHEN IS A REFERENCE INTERVIEW NECESSARY?

American Library Association, RUSA Access to Information Committee. 2000. "Guidelines for Information Services [online]." Rev. ed. Available: www.ala.org/rusa/stnd_consumer.html [17 February 2002]. Revised from guidelines prepared by the Standards and Guidelines Committee, Reference and User Services Association, 1990, under the title "Information Services for Information Consumers: Guidelines for Providers."

Dewdney, Patricia H. 1986. "The Effects of Training Reference Librarians in Interview Skills: A Field Experiment." London, Canada: The University of Western Ontario. Unpublished doctoral dissertation.

Hauptman, Robert. 1987. "The Myth of the Reference Interview." In *Reference Services Today: From Interview to Burnout*, edited by Bill Katz and Ruth Fraley. Binghamton, N.Y.: Haworth Press. First published in *The Reference Librarian* 16 (1986): 47-52.

Katz, William A. 1997. *Introduction to Reference Work*. Vol. 2, *Reference Services and Reference Processes*. 7th ed. New York: McGraw Hill.

Lynch, Mary Jo. 1978. "Reference Interviews in Public Libraries." *Library Quarterly* 48, no. 2 (April): 119–42. A report of a pioneering and still valuable study of 751 reference transactions that occurred in four New Jersey public libraries and produced 366 reference interviews.

Wilson, Patrick. 1986. "The Face Value Rule in Reference Work." *RQ* 25, no. 4 (summer): 468–75.

1.8.4. MEASURES OF INFORMATION SERVICE EFFECTIVENESS

American Library Association, Reference and Adult Services Division (RASD), Evaluation of Reference and Adult Services Committee. 1995. *The Reference Assessment Manual.* Ann Arbor, Mich.: The Pierian Press. Contains summaries of instruments and includes a detailed 140-page annotated bibliography that covers a variety of aspects of evaluating reference, broadly defined.

Burton, Paul F. 1990. "Accuracy of Information Provision: The Need for Client-Centered Service." *Journal of Academic Librarianship* 22 (October): 201–15.

Childers, Thomas. 1980. "The Test of Reference." *Library Journal* 105 (April 15): 212–17. The first to test reference accuracy by the use of "escalator" questions that required probing by the reference staff.

———. 1987. "The Quality of Reference: Still Moot After 20 Years." *Journal of Academic Librarianship* 13 (May): 73–74.

Crews, Kenneth D. 1988. "The Accuracy of Reference Service: Variables for Research and Implementation." *Library and Information Science Research* 10, no. 3 (July): 331–55. A meta-study that provides a useful table summarizing 39 unobtrusive studies of reference accuracy in terms of percentage of correct answers reported, type of library, type of contact that proxy questioners made with the library being observed, etc.

Crowley, Terence, and Thomas Childers. 1971. *Information Service in Public Libraries: Two Studies.* Metuchen, N.J.: Scarecrow Press. These two pioneering studies, "The Effectiveness of Information Service in Medium Size Public Libraries" by Crowley and "Telephone Information Service in Public Libraries" by Childers, introduced the technique of unobtrusive observation into library research on reference evaluation.

Dewdney, Patricia, and Catherine Sheldrick Ross. 1994. "Flying a Light Aircraft: Reference Service Evaluation from a User's Viewpoint." *RQ* 34, no. 2 (winter): 217–30. The first report on the Library Visit study, this article summarized the experiences of 77 library users who asked a question that mattered to them personally. Users' detailed accounts of their library visits yielded contrasting lists of "most helpful" and "least helpful" features of the service received.

Douglas, Ian. 1988. "Reducing Failures in Reference Service." *RQ* 28, no. 1 (fall): 94–101. Argues that the uniformity of the 50 to 60 percent success rate is "as much an artifact of the methodology [of getting research confederates to ask a set of previously devised test questions in libraries as of] the quality of reference services offered by libraries."

Durrance, Joan C. 1989. "Reference Success: Does the 55 Percent Rule Tell the Whole Story?" *Library Journal* 114 (April 15): 31–36. Questions the use of accuracy of the answer as the appropriate measure and suggests instead the more user-centered measure of "willingness to return" to the same staff member in the future.

———. 1995. "Factors that Influence Reference Success: What Makes Questioners Willing to Return?" *The Reference Librarian* 49/50: 243–65.

Dyson, Lillie Seward. 1992. "Improving Reference Services: A Maryland Training Program Brings Positive Results." *Public Libraries* 31 (September/October): 284–89.

Hernon, Peter, and Charles R. McClure. 1986. "Unobtrusive Reference Testing: The 55 Percent Rule." *Library Journal* 111, no. 7 (April 15): 37-41. A frequently cited study that coined the term *the 55 percent rule* for the repeated research finding that library users get the right answer slightly more than half the time. Reports results of unobtrusive testing in 26 U.S. libraries, specifically accuracy of answers, duration of the interview and search process, and use of referral.

———. 1987. *Unobtrusive Testing and Library Reference Services*. Norwood, N.J.: Ablex. Describes the role of unobtrusive testing in evaluating reference service, research design, and methodology, as well as analysis of some actual study results.

Isenstein, Laura. 1992. "Get Your Reference Staff on the STAR Track." *Library Journal* 117 (April 15): 34–37.

Katz, Bill, and Ruth A. Fraley, eds. 1984. *Evaluation of Reference Services*. New York: Haworth Press. A theme issue that includes articles on various types of evaluation methods, including unobtrusive testing, interviews with users, and output measures.

Larson, Carole A., and Laura K. Dickson. 1994. "Developing Behavioral Reference Desk Performance Standards," *RQ* 33, no. 3 (spring): 349–57. Reports the process used by the University of Nebraska Library system to develop a customized set of behaviorally based reference standards.

Massey-Burzio, Virginia. 1998. "From the Other Side of the Reference Desk: A Focus Group Study." *The Journal of Academic Librarianship* 24, no. 3 (May): 208–15.

Radford, Marie L. 1999. *The Reference Encounter: Interpersonal Communication in the Academic Library*. Chicago: Association of College and Research Libraries. Chapter 1, "Literature on the Reference Interaction," reviews evaluative studies that report on percentages of correct answers, providing citations for a number of typical studies of this kind as well as criticism of research on the 55 percent phenomenon.

Tyckoson, David. 1992. "Wrong Questions, Wrong Answers: Behavioral vs. Factual Evaluation of Reference Service." *The Reference Librarian* 38: 151–73. Argues that the unobtrusive testing of accuracy of answer received is too narrow because it neglects the process involved. Tyckoson recommends instead the obtrusive evaluation of reference by a supervisor who uses a behavioral checklist containing 25 indicators clustered into four groupings: availability, communication skills, search strategy skills, and individual attention given to patrons.

Westbrook, Lynn. 1989. *Qualitative Evaluation Methods for Reference Services: An Introductory Manual*. Washington, D.C.: Office of Management Services, Association of Research Libraries. An introduction for librarians to qualitative methods for evaluating reference service: observation, interviews, surveys, and content analysis.

White, Marilyn Domas. 1989. "Different Approaches to the Reference Interview." *The Reference Librarian* 25/26: 631–39.

1.8.5 THE ILL-FORMED QUERY AND USERS' MENTAL MODELS

Dewdney, Patricia, and Gillian Michell. 1996. "Oranges and Peaches: Understanding Communication Accidents in the Reference Interview." *RQ* 35, no. 4 (summer): 520–36. Classifies ill-formed queries into four main categories and recommends specific interview techniques to avert communication accidents.

———. 1996. "Mental Models of Information Systems: Results of a Field Study of Ill-formed Queries in the Public Library Reference Interview." Paper presented at the American Library Association summer conference, in New York.

Eichman, Thomas Lee. 1978. "The Complex Nature of Opening Reference Questions." *RQ* 17, no. 3 (spring): 212–22. Explains how the user's initial question functions more as a greeting than as a fully elaborated question.

Massey-Burzio, Virginia. 1998. "From the Other Side of the Reference Desk: A Focus Group Study." *The Journal of Academic Librarianship* 24, no. 3 (May): 208–15. A focus group study of users of Johns Hopkins University library focused on users' experiences in order to find out what kind of reference service would most help users.

Michell, Gillian, and Patricia Dewdney. 1998. "Mental Models Theory: Applications for Library and Information Science." *Journal of Education for Library and Information Science* 39, no. 4 (fall): 275–81.

Ross, Catherine Sheldrick. 1986. "How to Find Out What People Really Want to Know." *The Reference Librarian* 16 (winter): 19–30. Discusses reasons why initial questions are often not complete and describes skills that librarians can use, including open questions and sense-making (neutral) questions.

Wang, Peiling, William B. Hawk, and Carol Tenopir. 2000. "Users' Interaction with World Wide Web Resources: An Exploratory Study Using a Holistic Approach." *Information Processing and Management* 36, no. 2 (March): 229–51. In a study of 24 student-searchers' attempts to answer two test questions using Internet sources, researchers concluded that users are likely to develop incomplete and fragmentary mental models of Web resources.

1.8.6 USEFUL CONCEPTUAL FRAMEWORKS FOR THINKING ABOUT INFORMATION, MENTAL MODELS, ETC.

Johnson-Laird, Philip Nicholas. 1983. *Mental Models: Towards a Cognitive Science of Language, Inference and Consciousness*. Cambridge, Mass.: Harvard University Press.

Lakoff, George, and Mark Johnson. 1980. "Conceptual Metaphor in Everyday Language." In *Metaphors We Live By*. Chicago: University of Chicago Press.

Norman, Donald A. 1983. "Some Observations on Mental Models." In *Mental Models*, edited by Dedre Gentner and Albert L. Stevens. Hillsdale, N.J.: Lawrence Erlbaum Associates.

Reddy, Michael J. 1993. "The Conduit Metaphor." In *Metaphor and Thought*, edited by Andrew Ortony. New York: Cambridge University Press.

Reilly, Ronan G., ed. 1987. *Communication Failure in Dialogue and Discourse: Detection and Repair Processes*. Amsterdam: Elsevier Science. Pages 99–

120 provide a useful overview of research on communication accidents in ordinary conversation, as studied by researchers from various disciplines, including linguistics, education, cognitive science, and artificial intelligence.

Solomon, Paul. 1997. "Conversation in Information-Seeking Contexts: A Test of an Analytical Framework." *Library and Information Science Research* 19, no. 3 (fall): 217–48. Provides an analytic framework that looks at linguistic features of interactions such as turn taking, turn allocation, gaps, openings, closings, frames, repairs, etc., to examine how information-seeking conversations differ from ordinary conversation and conversations in other restricted domains such as physician-patient or teacher-student.

1.8.7 MISCELLANEOUS

Bidwell, Pam. 1997. "Re: Humor: Oranges and Peaches." In *Academic Computing and Technology Listserv* [online]. Available: http://libref-1@listserv.kent.edu [9 August 1997].

Cramer, Dina C. 1998. "How to Speak Patron." *Public Libraries* 37, no. 6 (November/December): 349.

Fine, Sara. 1995. "Reference and Resources: The Human Side." *The Journal of Academic Librarianship* 21 (January): 17–20.

Grogan, Dennis. 1991. *Practical Reference Work*. London: Library Association.

Gross, Melissa. 1995. "The Imposed Query." *RQ* 35, no. 2 (winter): 236–43. Deals with the theoretical and practical aspects of "secondhand" reference questions, whereby the inquirer is asking on behalf of someone else.

Hyman, Karen. 1999. "Customer Service and the 'Rule of 1965.'" *American Libraries* 30, no. 9 (October): 55–58.

McCoy, Michael. 1985. "Why Didn't They Teach Us That? The Credibility Gap in Library Education." *Reference Librarian* 12: 174.

Mount, Ellis. 1966. "Communication Barriers and the Reference Question." *Special Libraries* 57 (October): 575-78.

Nahl, Diane. 1997. "Re: Why don't they ask for what they want?" In *Academic Computing and Technology Listserv* [online]. Available: *http://libref-1@listserv.kent.edu* [28 August 1997].

Shultz, S. M. 1996. "Medical Jargon: Ethnography of Language in a Hospital Library." *Medical Reference Service Quarterly* 15, no. 3, 41–47.

Sutton, Ellen D., and Leslie Edmonds Holt. 1995. "The Reference Interview." In *Reference and Information Services*: *An Introduction*, 2d ed., edited by Richard E. Bopp and Linda Smith. Englewood, Colo.: Libraries Unlimited. (36).

White, H. S. 1992. "The Reference Librarian as Information Intermediary." *The Reference Librarian* 37: 23–35.

2 USING THE FIRST 30 SECONDS TO SET THE STAGE FOR THE REFERENCE INTERVIEW

In this chapter . . .

2.1 BEING APPROACHABLE

The reference interview begins when the user approaches a staff member and asks a question. Because users with information needs are often hesitant to ask for help, a lot of potential reference interviews never happen. Being approachable is the first step in giving good customer service. You have to be physically available and you must appear willing to help. At the most basic level, you have to be located where users can see you, not behind a high desk or in an out-of-the way location. And you have to look as though you genuinely want to serve users. Looking approachable involves using nonverbal skills such as a welcoming posture, smiling, and eye contact, wearing an identification tag, and being constantly on the alert for users who need help. Even if you have other work to do, scan the area every few minutes so that you don't miss people who look as if they could use some help.

Taking a proactive stance in offering help is important because many users who need help hesitate to ask. Virginia Massey-Burzio (1998) conducted focus groups with users at the Johns Hopkins

University library to find out their experiences using the library and its services. At all levels, from undergraduates to graduate students to faculty, focus group participants said they felt uncomfortable asking questions. Here are some comments:

> I'm not a question asker. Maybe I'm just an idiot wasting time wandering around the library, but I'd rather do that. (undergraduate)
> If I know what I'm doing [in my field], I should be able to find stuff. (graduate student)
> There's a fear that someone is going to say—not that it ever happened—"Why didn't you come to our open house? We discussed that at length." (faculty)

How can you tell if a library user needs help? In the Mental Models study, experienced librarians identified five signs that they used to identify those users who want help but don't ask:

> They're standing at the catalog, maybe standing back from it, and not writing anything down.
> They walk aimlessly among the computer terminals looking lost or confused.
> They look frustrated or even disgusted as they go through an index or other reference tool.
> They walk slowly past the reference desk and glance repeatedly in your direction.
> As they are looking at materials, they often stop and make eye contact with you, even though they don't come and ask.

The ALA "Guidelines for Behavioral Performance of Reference and Information Services Professionals" (1996) suggest that the librarian who wishes to communicate approachability adopt the following seven behaviors. The approachable librarian:

- is poised and ready to engage approaching patrons and is not engrossed in reading, filing, chatting with colleagues, or other activities;
- establishes initial eye contact with the patron;
- acknowledges the presence of the patron by smiling and/ or with open body language;
- acknowledges the patron through the use of a friendly greeting to initiate conversation and/or by standing up, moving forward, or moving closer to the patron;
- acknowledges others waiting for service;
- remains visible to patrons as much as possible;

EXERCISE

WHY DON'T THEY ASK QUESTIONS?

An early study found that more than one-quarter of users in the catalog, index, and stacks area had a question that they would like to ask, but would not ask a librarian. They told the research interviewer that they would ask a friend or another student or even the interviewer, just not the librarian whose job it is to answer such questions. And why not? The most common reason was that they were unhappy with previous service (42 percent), while 29 percent feared their question was too simple for a librarian and another 29 percent said they didn't want to bother the librarian (Swope and Katzer, 1972).

For this exercise, pick a particular library, possibly the library where you work. Put on your user hat. Imagine that you are a user with a question, but you are unfamiliar with this library. What elements in the library environment would encourage you to approach reference staff with your question? What might discourage you from asking your question?

ANALYZE THIS REFERENCE TRANSACTION

Case 3: "This person is really helping me"

In the Mental Models study, both the user and the librarian were interviewed to discover the perceptions both parties had regarding a reference transaction. Users were asked how often they visit or phone a public library, how familiar they are with this particular branch, and something about their purpose for coming to the library on this visit. Then they were asked to recollect, step by step, what they said and did during the reference transaction, what the librarian said and did, and what they were thinking at each of these steps.

In this next case, the user was from out of town and had never been to this particular library before. He had come along with a friend. While he was in the library, he thought he might as well look up information on fish—specifically, whether or not his big Oscar would eat baby ones, if he were to buy some at the pet store. He was trying unsuccessfully to find information on the computer when the librarian asked if she could help:

User: She told us that the computer I was using was for this and that [he was using a computer dedicated to CD-ROMs], but that this other computer [with access to the online catalog] was the one I needed. So we walked over there and got that computer and then she showed me exactly where the books were. Next she took me over to the books, and she just asked me questions about what I would like to know about. Then she went to get my book for me.

Interviewer: What were you thinking?

User: That this person's really helping me. It's their job— they're librarians. [laughs] I was really being looked after. Like in my library at home, they just sit at the desk. Me, I'm not much of a book person and I have trouble reading too, and I can't find my way through the library. But this librarian actually took time and helped me look for what I needed. The book she gave me had a picture of an Oscar on the cover.

Interviewer: Thinking back to when you first spoke to the librarian, how easy did you think it would be to get an answer to your question?

User: I didn't think it would be that easy to find. If I had to do it myself, I would have been looking right now. But she made it real easy. She just typed in the thing on the computer and she knew exactly where to go and what to do. I think it was worth coming here. She actually took time to help me and figure out what I was doing.

When the librarian was interviewed, she said that the user seemed surprised when she took him to another computer: "People assume that all the computers are the same," she said, but in fact the computer that the user chose was set up for searching Books in Print on CD-ROM:

Librarian: Because of where he started, at the CD-ROM computer, I don't hesitate to approach people there. I don't assume that they know what they're doing when they sit down there, because they don't. People may spend ten or fifteen minutes there and find books on fish in Books in Print, but it will still be the wrong place to be. And the next thing you know, you're at the point where you have to interloan some book from another library. Users just see a computer [and assume they are interchangeable]. And we're probably lax that we don't label the computers so that users can tell which ones provide access to the catalog.

Comment: Unlike the librarians in the user's home library who "just sit at the desk," this librarian is a rover whose working principle is to offer help to anyone looking puzzled. Computers all look the same, and novice users in particular are likely to end up searching in the wrong place: they look for local library holdings in Books in Print or they look for a journal article in the library catalog.

In this case, the librarian provided such an apparently effortless mediation between the needs of the user and the complexity of the system that the user was unaware of all the steps involved. The user said that the librarian "knew exactly where to go and what to do," but the successful outcome of this transaction depended on a lot of background knowledge as well as activity that was invisible to the user, including the reference interview. The user said, "She just asked me questions about what I would like to know about," but the librarian said she had to do a lot to narrow the topic. "When he said fish, I asked him if he wanted aquarium fish or fishing for fish or fish cookbooks. Then I had to establish if it was saltwater or freshwater fish.

For discussion:
Brainstorm all the ways in which this librarian's intervention could have made a difference. Consider immediate effects and more distant effects, such as the user's mental model of the library, his likelihood of using libraries in the future, etc.

- roves through the reference area offering assistance whenever possible.

Some libraries have successfully experimented with a "roving librarian" whose job is to move around and approach users to see if they need help. Not every library can afford to have a position dedicated to a "rover," and sometimes it's too busy for librarians to leave the reference desk, but everyone can occasionally rove. Roving is particularly important in "the electronic arcade," the area where public access electronic systems are installed. In *Teaching the New Library*, LaGuardia says that "one of the main attributes of a good rover is excellent interpersonal skills: you have to walk the line between offending or frightening some patrons, while gently sending others off on their own to fly after the first couple of hand-holding sessions. You need to be able to sense who invites approach and who will skitter away or refuse offers of assistance. If in doubt, approach" (1996: 110). When offering help, a low-key, nonintrusive approach works best: not "You look like you need some help" or "That's not the right way to search," but rather something like "Excuse me, but are you finding what you're looking for?" (Thanks for this tip to Gary Klein, Willamette University, Salem, Oregon.)

DID YOU KNOW?

A questionnaire administered at the University of Chicago Regenstein Library tried to find out why catalog users don't approach the reference staff for help when they need it. The barriers turned out to be a lack of accurate information concerning the location, function, and identification of reference librarians. Recommendations included making an effort to orient the user, particularly the first-year user, to the reference desk (Westbrook, 1984).

2.2 THE LIBRARY AS A PHYSICAL SPACE

The physical setting of the library has a large impact on what happens in the reference transaction, as we discovered in the Library Visit study. We asked beginning students in the early weeks of a basic reference course to go to a library of their choice and ask a question that mattered to them personally. They then wrote up an account of the library visit that included (1) what happened step by step until the end of the transaction and (2) what they found helpful and unhelpful about the experience. They were also asked to rate the success of the transaction in terms of the helpfulness of the answer and their willingness to return to the same librarian with a similar question.

More than half the users in the Library Visit study began their account with some comment about the library as a physical space. They praised well-marked reference areas and "large, well-placed easily identifiable signs," while singling out for criticism the lack of convenient parking, confusing floor plans, the lack of clear signage for reference desks and subject areas, and the lack of means of identifying the professional librarians. The reference desk itself could become a barrier to users, who sometimes perceived library staff as hunkering down with their terminals behind the garrison of the desk. One user said, "The high counters reminded me of a taxation office." When staff members were occupied with other work, they sometimes seemed "too busy to be approached."

Because the environments we work in can become invisible to us, we need to cultivate what anthropologists call "anthropological strangeness" to get past our habituated ways of seeing. We need to make a deliberate attempt to look at the library's physical environment through the users' eyes. Having done that, we can take steps to remedy the problems identified. Sometimes the solutions can be quite simple. As one approving user commented, "Approximately three seconds after I entered the library, I noticed a sign that said, QUESTIONS? ASK ME. I was very surprised and glad. . . . I also thought that this sign was more effective and generally understandable than a sign indicating REFERENCE."

Here's what library users in the Library Visit study said about the physical setting as a barrier. The most important factors turned out to be signage; the layout of the library, including the positioning of desks; and the cues (or lack thereof) that allow users to identify reference staff.

> The first thing I noticed was the absence of any specific orientation aid for patrons seeking help.
>
> Since there were no signs, it took me a couple of minutes to ferret out that the reference desk was behind a wall, making the desk invisible to anyone looking for information.
>
> None of the staff wore name tags or any other identification clarifying their professional function.
>
> The librarians were working behind their big desks and I didn't want to disturb them.
>
> The placement of the computer screen is such that the client cannot see what is going on and it obscures the reference librarian. I had the feeling that in this particular situation the catalog was being used as a shield.
>
> I noticed in this reference area that the librarians were shut in. They couldn't get out. I suppose there were doors, but my impression was that they stayed in that little pen all day. My idea of a librarian is that they go to the shelves with you—not always, but that they would browse around and look for you and interact with books too. But they just sat there with this machine [the computer]. That was their job.

A common problem for library users was not knowing where to go to ask questions. It is not uncommon to find that users go to the first likely-looking desk they see, which may be the circulation counter or the desk of the security guard. This is what happened in the following case, in which a student user was interviewed about her reference experience by another classmate:

User:	As I went into the public library, right in front of me was a desk, so I approached that and asked my question. She directed me to the reference desk.
Interviewer:	Did you know if she was a reference librarian?
User:	No, I didn't know who they were. I just saw this woman as I walked in. I realized afterwards that it was the circulation desk.
Interviewer:	And then what did you do?
User:	I went up to the reference desk. The woman said, "Yes?" Didn't smile.
Interviewer:	Did you ask her if she was a reference librarian?
User:	No. She was sitting behind the reference desk, but my impression was that she was a library assistant. One of the things I've always felt is that it's very hard to find out who's the librarian. I think they should wear name tags.

A QUICK TIP

RECOGNIZING THE EXPERTS

Joan Durrance (1989) has pointed out that libraries are different from all other professional settings in making it difficult for users to identify professional staff. Users have a better chance of recognizing the experts when the library uses well-designed signage and when staff members are identified by badges.

In addition to the physical layout of the library and the desk, users rely on other physical cues, among them the appearance of the staff. One reason to adopt a professional appearance is that it helps library users identify you as an employee. From an unobtrusive study conducted in various types of libraries, Durrance concluded that:

Appearance of the staff member (including age and dress) plays an important role in helping observers make decisions, especially when the environment fails to send a clear message; 56% used environmental clues to decide if they had been working with a librarian. Well-dressed, older individuals were assumed to be librarians while casually dressed younger people were thought to be students.

EXERCISE

APPROACHABILITY

If you don't normally wear an identification tag, make one and wear it for an hour while you stand near your public access catalog. Do you find that more people tend to ask you questions? If people still do not ask you for help, try asking them if they found what they wanted. The results may be surprising.

In this study, one of Durrance's participant observers approached a young man seated behind the reference desk; he said that he was not the librarian, but a friend of the librarian. When "the librarian emerged from the stacks, the observer concluded from her age, her casual clothing, and her bright pink hair that she was not a librarian either" (1989: 9, 33).

These examples raise the much debated issue of whether or not library staff who serve the public should wear identification tags. Some research indicates that library users feel that they have been better served if they know the name of the staff member who is helping them, in much the same way as they like to know the name of the doctor who treats them in an emergency ward. For those employees who are concerned about privacy and security, the purpose is served by tags that indicate their function or position. Some libraries give employees the option of using an "alias" on tags. The key consideration in the name-tag debate, and indeed in the entire issue of appearance, is really accessibility: Can people identify you as someone who is able to help them, and do they feel comfortable in approaching you?

2.3 ESTABLISHING CONTACT

As we have seen in section 1.4, reference interviews often start out in one of two ways: the user asks a very general question ("What information do you have on health?") or the user asks a very specific question ("I'd like to see the University of Wisconsin's academic calendar"). When these questions are answered literally ("Thousands of books, articles, clippings, and Web pages" or "Here's the academic calendar for the University of Wisconsin"), the answers might not help the user. Suppose, for example, the users in these examples wanted to locate research that compares St.-John's-wort and Prozac as treatments for depression or needed the first name of a scientist thought to be on the faculty at Wisconsin.

But why would a person wanting articles on specific drugs ask for general information on health? Why don't people say what they want in the first place? On off-days, a librarian may be tempted to think that users do this to be difficult. It might help, however, to think of the user's initial question not as a fully articulated query, but as a way of making contact and of opening the channel of communication. Remember that the user may have gone to the wrong place and already asked someone else—the clerk at the circulation desk or the person at the security desk—before bringing the question to you.

Linguists have an explanation for what sometimes seems to be the perverse way in which people phrase their initial requests for help. This explanation is based on the fact that language can have a number of different functions, among them exchanging information and establishing contact. During a reference encounter, two strangers meet in a public place. As Thomas Eichman (1978) has pointed out, the librarian expects from the user an exchange of information in the form of a clear statement of the information need. The user, on the other hand, feels the need to establish contact. He has unspoken questions in mind that need answering before he will be willing to invest time telling the whole problem: Am I in the right place? Are you available and listening to me? Are you the person who's going to help me? Can you help me with a problem that falls into this general area?

You need to respond in a way that answers these unspoken questions. PACT is an acronym for remembering what the user wants to know first.

P	Place is right
A	Available and listening
C	Contact made
T	Topic (in general) understood

Communicate these responses (yes, you've come to the right place; I'm the person to help you, etc.) through nonverbal skills such as eye contact, smiling, and standing up (see section 2.4.2) and through verbal skills such as acknowledgment (2.4.3) and encouragers (2.4.4). When the user asks for health information, look up, perhaps stand up, smile, and acknowledge the user immediately (e.g., "Health information, uh-huh."). By using PACT, you establish the contact that will encourage the user to tell you more. It also is very useful in cross-cultural transactions or in cases in which the user's primary language is not English.

2.4 SKILLS FOR THE FIRST 30 SECONDS

In this section we focus on a cluster of skills, known as attending skills, that you can use to establish contact and set the stage for the rest of the interview. In the first 30 seconds, you won't have a chance to say much, but you still are conveying strong messages of one kind or another to the user. When you use attending skills,

A QUICK TIP

HELLO, CAN YOU HELP ME?

Think of the user's initial question not as a fully formed request but as a kind of greeting. In this greeting, the user is asking for some reassurance that you are listening and are the right person to help. Thomas Eichman (1978) uses John Searle's speech act theory to make the case that the initial question has the illocutionary force of performing a greeting. To the librarian, the initial question may seem to have the linguistic function primarily of exchanging information, while to the user the initial question often has the linguistic function of establishing contact and saying, "I wonder if you might help me."

DID YOU KNOW?

Over and over again, the users in the Library Visit study expressed concern that their questions might not seem important enough or that they might be made to feel foolish or a nuisance. For them, a crucial first step in the reference transaction was the librarian's confirmation that the question was valid and they had come to the right place. For example, a user who ended up getting exactly the information he wanted about trees in an arboretum said, "I had been worried that this might not be an appropriate question for the library." And these users weren't novices; they were graduate students. Inexperienced users are even more in need of the reassurance you provide by using PACT.

many of which are nonverbal, you show an interest in others by paying attention to the other person. The use of attending skills in interviewing has been explained best by Allen E. Ivey, who has developed a framework called microtraining for teaching interview skills to counselors. In her doctoral dissertation, "Microcounseling in Library Education" (1974), Elaine Jennerich was the first to recognize the value of Ivey's microtraining approach in relation to the reference interview.

2.4.1 THE MICROTRAINING APPROACH

In the early 1960s at Stanford University, Ivey developed the microskills approach as a way of teaching new counselors to use the basic communications skills necessary in any interview. He identified the smallest components of effective interviews as "microskills," beginning with the basic listening sequence that includes attending behavior such as eye contact, body language, and verbal tracking skills like acknowledgment. These formed the basis of his hierarchy of microskills, which continues through asking questions and culminates in skill integration. Attending skills are the foundation of Ivey's microskills hierarchy because they establish a good communication climate for further conversation. Attending behavior, including acknowledgment (or restatement) and minimal encouragers, is the most basic skill that we must learn before moving on to other skills such as questioning or summarizing.

Briefly, microtraining is based on the idea that complex communication behavior can be broken down into its constituent parts or small (micro) skills, and that these skills can be taught, one at a time, in a systematic way that involves the following steps:

1. Defining the skill and identifying its function
2. Observing the skill modeled
3. Reading about the skill and the concepts behind it
4. Practicing the skill in a context that provides feedback (e.g., audiotaping or videotaping; getting a peer coach to provide observations on your use of the skills)
5. Using the skill in a real-world context and observing what happens
6. Teaching the skill to others

A key principle of microtraining is that you learn the skills one at a time and practice each one. For each skill, you first learn to identify or recognize the skill by observing others' behavior or by picking out the skill in a transcript, videotape, or some other exercise. To help you with identification, throughout this book we

DID YOU KNOW?

Elaine Z. Jennerich (1974) was a pioneer in the library field in recognizing the value of microskills training for the reference interview. She conducted a major study to evaluate the effects of teaching library school students those microskills that are most useful for public service.

have provided many examples of the skills as they were used in real interviews, so that you can see how they work in the reference interview. Reading about the skill and how it works and being able to define it and recognize it, although necessary, are not enough. You won't really understand the skill and its function until you practice it yourself. So the next level in learning a skill is basic mastery, in which you practice the skill in a sheltered environment such as a role-playing situation. After that comes the level of active mastery in which you demonstrate the appropriate use of the skill in a real-life setting, such as the reference desk. In the final level, which is teaching mastery, you are ready to pass on the skill by teaching it to others.

For Allen E. Ivey, perhaps the most important concept in microtraining is "intentionality." Intentionality has to do with choice: once you have learned the skill and how it works, you need to be able to judge when the skill is appropriate and what effect it is likely to have. From a range of responses that you could make in a particular situation, you are choosing the response that is potentially the most helpful. In short, you are choosing to use a particular skill *intentionally* in order to accomplish some particular goal in the interview. You need to understand the function of each skill so that you can use it intentionally, as a choice among a range of options, and not by rote. Intentionality means flexibility: the ability to use a range of skills and to improvise.

A corollary of the principle of intentionality is that every rule can be broken—*if* there is a good reason. However, before breaking the rule, it is important to know what the rule is and how it is supposed to work.

2.4.2 NONVERBAL ATTENDING SKILLS: EYE CONTACT, SMILING AND NODDING, PAUSING, POSTURE

Inappropriate body language can keep a reference interview from ever getting started. Looking down at work on the desk rather than up to catch the user's eye says, in effect, that the librarian is too busy to be approached. On the other hand, putting aside the materials you are working on, looking up, smiling, and using eye contact communicate a readiness to help. Nonverbal messages are conveyed by behavior such as eye contact, tone of voice, facial expression, posture, gestures, positioning of arms and legs, style of dress, or your distance from another person. Researchers have distinguished various dimensions of nonverbal behavior:

- **the way we use our bodies**: head, arms, and legs, as well as facial expression, posture and movement
- **the way we use interpersonal space**: the distance we stand

A QUICK TIP

TO LEARN A MICROSKILL

Focus on learning and practicing just one skill at a time. Eventually you will integrate all the microskills into one seamless interview. But when you are first learning a skill, you should focus your attention on that one skill. Schedule a specific time when you are on the reference desk to practice a new skill. Promise yourself that, for this time period, you will use one skill—acknowledgment (section 2.4.3), for example—in every interview.

from another person; body orientation such as leaning forward or turning aside

- **how we say something**: the pitch, rate, loudness, and inflection of our speech
- **the way we time our verbal exchanges**: the way we manage turn taking; duration of turns and duration of pauses
- **the way we look**: the formality or casualness of clothing styles; the use of accessories and cosmetics

These nonverbal cues are what is missing from electronic reference interviews that are exchanges of typed text. In face-to-face communication, people rely very much on nonverbal cues to convey emotion. Moreover, they are experts at detecting any discrepancy between spoken words and nonverbal cues. Your words may intend to signal interest when you say, "How may I help you?" but if you frown and speak in a flat, bored tone, users will not perceive you as being interested in helping.

You should think of the nonverbal attending skills as the foundation for the rest of the interview. In the Library Visit study, users emphasized the importance of body language in establishing contact and encouraging them to ask a question in the first place. "He looked up from his work right away and smiled," said one satisfied user. On the other hand, the absence of appropriate eye contact was often mentioned as a discouraging factor that could persist throughout the reference transaction: "She did not look me in the eye but looked at the ceiling, as if the information was there." It is important to be aware, however, that body language is culture-specific. Eye contact, for example, is understood in western cultures as a sign of attentive listening, but in some eastern cultures it may be taken as a sign of disrespect.

When library staff members didn't smile and use appropriate eye contact, users interpreted this failure as a lack of interest in them and/or in their question: "She didn't seem interested in medical questions and acted as if I were wasting her time." In more extreme cases of unwelcoming body language, users felt the library staff considered their question an annoying nuisance: "She looked puzzled and pursed her lips and rolled her eyes. From her expression, she seemed to be saying, 'Why did I get stuck with this question?'" When another librarian was asked for materials on contemporary music, she "started to grimace or wince and let out an 'ooooow.' I was not sure if her reaction reflected a dislike of the topic, her recognition that materials on that topic would be scarce, or a combination of both factors and perhaps others." Tone of voice can be more important than what is actually said. In one case, the staff member eventually looked up from her com-

---

DID YOU KNOW?

Body language in the interview situation often expresses perceptions of status and power. In an interview between people of different cultures, it's important to pay attention to body language. For a discussion of communication between black students and white librarians, see Errol R. Lam, 1988.

DID YOU KNOW?

In her analysis of the "first words" of a reference transaction, Joan Durrance reported that in 5 percent of her 486 observed transactions, the staff member initially "responded to questioners' opening queries without words, but instead used grimaces, guttural sounds, facial expressions, or silence for an awkward period of time" (1995: 250)

A QUICK TIP

SHOWING AN INTEREST

Librarians who show interest in users will generate higher levels of user satisfaction. The librarian demonstrates interest with the following nonverbal behaviors: faces the user when speaking or listening; maintains or reestablishes eye contact throughout the transaction; establishes a physical distance that appears to be comfortable to the user, based on the user's verbal and nonverbal responses; signals an understanding of the user's needs through nodding of the head; appears unhurried; focuses his or her attention on the user. (Adapted from ALA's "Guidelines for Behavioral Performance," 1996.)

puter screen and said, "Can I help you with something?" The user noted, "Her tone implied I was taking her away from something very important, although a quick survey of the library indicated I was the only one in there."

If the goal is to cut down on service and reduce the number of questions asked, here's how to do it: The staff member should avoid eye contact; look very busy with the work on the desk; turn away from the user and become very absorbed with the computer screen. These behaviors confirm the users' common concern of being a bother to the librarian. If the user musters the courage to ask the question anyway, additional discouragements can be added, as happened in the case of a user of a large central public library who said, "I'm looking for some information on polling companies." According to the user's account, the librarian "turned away, narrowed her eyes, and, after wincing for five seconds, proclaimed, 'I don't think we have anything.' I think she hoped I would be satisfied and leave." These librarians whose body language was interpreted as unwelcoming may indeed have been thinking hard about the user's question and doing their very best to help. They may have thought they were looking both serious and professional. Whatever their intention, however, their body language conveyed a message that discouraged users from expecting help.

Eye Contact

Eye contact is an attending skill that people learn in childhood. Culturally appropriate use of eye contact is one of the most powerful cues for opening and maintaining communication. Middle-class, white Anglo-Americans communicate that they are listening by looking at the other person. Without eye contact, they may feel that no communication is occurring. Children who are resistant to parental messages communicate their unreceptiveness by looking pointedly away, hence the adult reprimand, "Look at me when I'm speaking to you." In the reference context, making eye contact is the most important way that you can signal to the user that you are approachable and available to help.

We can powerfully influence how much another person talks by our use of eye contact. Looking at the person who is talking to you usually indicates warmth, interest, and a desire to communicate. Frequent breaks in eye contact are usually interpreted as inattention, lack of interest, embarrassment, or even dislike. Therefore, looking down at the floor, up at the ceiling, or over at a file will get the other person to stop talking. Maintaining appropriate eye contact indicates interest and encourages the other person to continue talking.

A QUICK TIP
LOOK UP AND SMILE

When Marie Radford (1996) asked users how they decided which staff member to approach, they said they chose the staff member who used welcoming body language: eyebrow flash; eye contact; smiling and nodding. Eye contact was found to be the most important behavior for signaling availability, even if the librarian was otherwise busy. Negative nonverbal indicators included lack of immediate acknowledgment of user, no change in body stance as user approaches, covering the eye with the hand, reading, tapping fingers, twitching mouth, and pacing.

DID YOU KNOW?

According to experiments on behavior in the online search interview, effective pausing is more difficult to learn than one might think. Pauses longer than ten seconds may confuse the user, who becomes unsure whether the interviewer is still listening. Very short pauses tend to be unnoticeable. It seems that some librarians habitually pause while considering what the user has said or deciding what to do next. But pausing too often or too long is awkward. (See Auster and Lawton, 1984.)

But what is appropriate eye contact? Too much can be as bad as too little. An unwavering stare can seem hostile, rude, or intrusive. Prolonged eye contact can seem threatening. Appropriate eye contact involves neither staring nor avoiding. The time spent looking directly into the other person's eyes, however, is actually very brief. Your eyes will move from eyes to chin, hairline, mouth, and back to the eyes. Listeners and speakers tend to adopt an alternate pattern of looking and looking away. Moreover, the looking times of speaker and listener are not symmetrical: in mainstream North American culture, listeners spend twice as much time looking as do speakers.

Smiling and Nodding

Looking impassively with a "still face" at the other person discourages communication. Smile and nod occasionally to reassure the other person that you are friendly, interested, and listening. In conversation, smiling and nodding function as minimal encouragers (see section 2.4.4). In most cultures, smiling is understood as a sign of warmth (but sometimes—in Japan, for example—smiling may indicate discomfort or even hostility). Nodding the head up and down is also a positive signal, although in some cultures the side-to-side nod means agreement and the vertical nod means disagreement. If you usually listen impassively, try nodding occasionally. Don't overdo it. An occasional single nod of the head encourages people to say more; successive nods get them to stop because they think you want to interrupt.

Pausing

Pausing is really a kind of nonverbal behavior, although it is often combined with speaking and listening skills. A pause can take the place of a conversational turn. Pausing is defined as intentional silence in place of a statement or question. For example, when it is your turn to speak, you wait, saying nothing until the other person speaks again.

The effect of pausing varies according to culture. In some cultures, lengthy and frequent pauses are taken as a sign of inattention and boredom. In other cultures, such as some Native American cultures, pauses are a sign of respect, an indication that the listener is taking the speaker's last statement seriously and considering a worthy answer. It is important to know what effect your pauses can have in different situations. In mainstream North American culture, effective pausing enhances an interviewer's listening skills and conveys attentiveness to the interviewee. A pause may function as an encourager or a probe. It says to the interviewee, "I'm listening" and "Go on." Because the interviewer re-

EXERCISE

WHAT'S WRONG?

Harold Garfinkle is a social scientist who encourages his students to investigate taken-for-granted social norms by sending them out on assignments wherein they deliberately break these norms. For example, having them stand in an elevator so that they face the inside wall instead of facing the door. Use a version of the Garfinkle technique to investigate the power of the nod during a social interaction (for this exercise, pick someone whom you can trust not to be permanently offended). While a friend is telling you a story about something completely uncontroversial, shake your head from side to side in a tiny but perceptible movement. Keep this up. Watch the effect that it has on the other person's ability to continue with the story.

EXERCISE

SILENCE IS GOLDEN

A common problem in the reference interview is asking a perfectly good open question and then spoiling it by rushing in with the answer instead of waiting for the user to reply. For example: "What kind of legal information do you want? Is it criminal law?" Try this experiment. For a period of, say, a half hour on the reference desk, make a conscious effort to use pauses. Ask a question and then wait. One or two seconds of blank air time may seem endless to you, but you are not on the radio. So just wait. Some people need more time than others to think about what they want to say. Note what happens after the pauses. How, if at all, do these interviews differ from ones in which you are not making a conscious effort to wait for the user's answer?

ANALYZE THIS REFERENCE TRANSACTION

Case 4: Wait for the answer

User:	Hi.
Librarian:	Hi.
User:	I'm doing a project on social problems in undeveloped regions. And I've looked under the different social problems—like divorce and suicide and robbery—and all I could find is case studies.
Librarian:	OK. (minimal encourager)
User:	And I have to relate this topic to native—native people.
Librarian:	Native people. (acknowledgment) OK, what have you done so far? Where have you looked? Just in the catalog? (two open questions followed by a closed question)
User:	Mm-hmm.
Librarian:	This topic is going to be more in magazines, as opposed to books, OK? [Shows the user how the periodical index works.]

Dewdney, Native People

Comment: The librarian asked an excellent question—What have you done so far?—and then got panicky and started answering the question herself, instead of pausing and waiting for the answer. Notice that narrowing the question down finally to the closed question "[Have you looked] just in the catalog?" (see section 3.2.1) ended up producing no useful information.

---

linquishes her turn at the conversation, the interviewee is likely to expand on what he has previously said. For example:

Librarian:	Tell me about your research.
User:	Well, my field is geography.
Librarian: . . .	(pause, combined with encouraging body language such as smiling and nodding)
User:	The project I'm working on right now is a stratigraphy of a particular area on the shoreline of Lake Superior.
Librarian: . . .	(pause, plus nodding)
User:	And you see, what I'm really looking for is [explains].

When librarians are first practicing the skill of effective question-asking (see section 3.2.1), a common problem is remembering to pause long enough to give the interviewee time to formulate an answer. Hence they may ask an open question, "What sort of thing are you looking for?" and then answer it themselves "A reference book?" Pause after you ask your question and wait for the answer. Used correctly, pausing is a skill that helps reduce the common mistakes of talking too much, cutting the user off, interrupting, and answering one's own question. The skills that supplement pausing are restatement, encouragers, and nonverbal skills that show attentiveness.

A QUICK TIP

TRUNK LEAN

To convey relaxed attentiveness during a conversation, stand or sit so that you are leaning slightly toward the other person. This is called "trunk lean."

Posture

Your posture, or the way you hold your body, signals your mood and attitude. Slumping is read as a sign of fatigue, discouragement, or boredom. Rigidity suggests nervousness or disagreement. Closed postures, such as crossing your arms or orienting yourself away from the other person, tend to convey detachment or disagreement, regardless of your actual words. On the other hand, a symmetrical mirroring of the other person's posture or orientation conveys approval or agreement. When you send mixed messages, people believe your nonverbal cues more than what you say.

Whenever possible, it is a good idea to be at eye level with the user. This may mean standing up and moving toward a user. Or it may mean inviting a user to sit down beside you at the computer terminal as you demonstrate how to use an index or find something in the catalog.

2.4.3 ACKNOWLEDGMENT

Acknowledgment is a skill that involves restating or "playing back" the content of what the other person has just said. You restate a key part of the previous statement, using either the same words or a paraphrase. This restatement encourages the other person to confirm, correct, or explain further. Thus you might respond to the request "Do you have anything on lupus?" by repeating "Lupus, uh-huh" or "You want material on the illness lupus." This gives the user the chance to make a correction if you misheard: "No, lupines, the flower."

EXAMPLES

User: I need some information on transportation.
Librarian: We have quite a bit of information on transportation (or simply, Transportation, uh-huh).

User: I need some information on Vitamin D.

EXERCISE

ACKNOWLEDGMENT

Remember that acknowledgment involves repeating, or sometimes paraphrasing, the keyword(s) of the user's question to make sure that you have heard and understood. What could you say to acknowledge a user who asks:

1. Where are your travel books?
2. Where is the Globe? [a newspaper]
3. I'm looking for something on China. [Check your own mastery of the skill of acknowledgment: Was your response useful in clarifying what kind of china is wanted? If not, what could you say instead? Look again at the shingles example.]
4. Do you have recent information on viruses? [Are you sure you know what kind of viruses are meant?]

Librarian:	Vitamin E, uh-huh.
User:	No, actually Vitamin D. I'm doing a project on additives to milk and their role in reducing rickets.
User:	Have you anything on shingles?
Librarian:	Shingles for roofing? (paraphrasing to ensure a shared understanding and to give the user a chance to correct. The skill of acknowledgment will help you distinguish between homonyms such as Wales/whales or Tolkien book/talking book.)
User:	No, viral shingles; it's a disease.
User:	I'm doing a study on transcription factors related to adipocyte differentiation. I'm especially interested in any recent research on the role of Wnt.
Librarian:	Uh-huh. You're doing research on transcription factors related to—what was that again? (With complicated statements, the librarian may catch only part of what's been said. That's OK. The procedure is to repeat what you can and ask for repetition on what you missed. In really complex statements it could take two or three attempts before you have the whole statement. You might also need to ask for the spelling of unfamiliar terms such as Wnt.)

Most people already use acknowledgment in certain situations, such as repeating a phone number that they have been told. So it is not a question of learning an entirely new skill but of using consciously a skill already employed in other communication contexts. Use the skill of acknowledgment routinely, especially at the beginning of the reference interview as your response to the user's initial question. Restatement is an excellent quick way to indicate that you have been listening (see section 2.4.5), and it helps to establish a good climate of communication. In acknowledging, follow these guidelines:

- Be brief. A phrase or even just one word is often enough. You don't want to parrot back everything that's been said.
- Use a matter-of-fact, accepting tone. Responding with an upward intonation ("Vitamin E?") may convey amazement or even disapproval about what has just been said.
- If there is any ambiguity in what is being asked for (e.g., Turkey, Chile, *Grease*), then provide a paraphrase to clarify between different meanings, such as "Turkey, the country?" or "Chili, the sauce?" or "*Grease*, the musical?" In

ANALYZE THESE REFERENCE TRANSACTIONS

Case 5: Acknowledgment

User 1: They say you're an expert on symbols.

Librarian: They must have been lying. [laughs] What exactly would you like? (open question)

User: Are you familiar with the Roman symbol for authority—the battle-axes and staves, bound into a bundle?

Librarian: You said it was a Roman symbol. (acknowledgment) Mythological? (closed question)

User: No. The real thing.

Librarian: And it's a battle symbol, is it? (acknowledgment)

User: No, it's a symbol of authority that they displayed in the Senate of Rome. They carried it in front of official parades. It's the symbol of authority in ancient Rome.

From Dewdney, Roman symbols

User 2: I want recordings of church bells.

Librarian: Actual church bells playing? (acknowledgment)

User: Yes.

Librarian: Do you have something specific in mind? (the librarian might have hoped that the user would understand this as an open question, "What do you have in mind?" but the user interprets it literally, as a closed question.)

User: No.

Librarian: Just the sound of church bells playing? (acknowledgment)

User: Yes, anything to do with bells, actually, would be OK.

Librarian: Anything to do with bells. (acknowledgment) OK. Let me just check the call number. Oh—handbell music. Chimes at dusk. Wedding Chimes.

User: All right!

From Dewdney, Church bells

Comment: In both interviews, the librarian repeats the skill of acknowledgment through several turns. In the first case, acknowledgment allows the librarian to correct his erroneous deduction that the user wanted a battle symbol. Although he has not recognized the user's description of the Roman fasces, he now has a very good description in the user's last statement and the new clue, "symbol of authority." In the second case, the librarian repeats the initial restatement "just the sound of church bells playing" and is rewarded by an expanded definition of bells. Acknowledgment is especially effective at the beginning of an interview.

ANALYZE THIS REFERENCE TRANSACTION

Case 6: With minimal encouragers, a little goes a long way.

User:	I'm looking up Noranda Mines.
Librarian:	Mm-hmm. (encourager)
User:	And trying to find an address for it.
Librarian:	OK, anything else? (encourager)
User:	I'm looking for pulp and paper companies. There are two companies, but the second one is missing [from this directory]. There's another pulp and paper mill missing.
Librarian:	Mm-hmm. (encourager)
User:	I don't know the name of the second one. Maybe it's not here. And they just recently changed the name.
Librarian:	Oh. OK. (encourager)
User:	So I'm not sure. I think it's called the James Bay Project. This mill was going under, so the company bought them out and changed the name to the James Bay Project.
Librarian:	Where was it located? (open question)
User:	Near Marathon.
Librarian:	Near Marathon. OK. (acknowledgment) [Librarian finds contact information for Noranda Mines and also for a second pulp and paper mill just outside Marathon.]

Comment: The user wants to know whom to contact because he wants to apply for a job in these two pulp and paper mills. This librarian got a lot of mileage from using minimal encouragers and letting the user talk. She needed to use only one open question, "Where was it located?" to fill in a gap. All the rest of the information was volunteered by the user.

From Dewdney, Noranda

these cases, it is not enough simply to repeat Turkey or *Grease*.

2.4.4 MINIMAL ENCOURAGERS

In conversations, there is a tacit rule that people should take turns speaking, but a very brief remark will count as a turn. When you are conducting an interview, your turn can be very short. You do not need to respond at length to every statement made. Examples of useful minimal encouragers are short phrases such as:

EXERCISE

ATTENDING SKILLS

Find a partner with whom you can role-play a conversation. Ask your partner to talk about a topic in which he or she is personally interested. Your role is to listen and to encourage your partner to say more by sticking as much as possible just to the attending skills of eye contact, smiling, nodding, and minimal encouragers. Which of these skills do you feel comfortable doing? Which ones need more practice? Change roles. How does your partner's use of attending skills affect your role as speaker?

EXERCISE

DON'T LISTEN

With a partner, role-play a conversation in which your partner is describing an event that happened recently and you play the role of the worst listener that you can possibly be. Recruit a third person as an observer who records all the ways in which you show poor listening behavior. Here are some possibilities: interrupting, changing the subject, fidgeting, looking away, drumming your fingers, yawning, looking at your watch, remaining impassive, and making no response to what was said. After three minutes, stop and ask the observer to report all the poor listening behaviors recorded. Ask your partner how these behaviors made him or her feel. Trade roles, so that all three people have a turn with each role.

Uh-huh.
I see.
Go on.
That's interesting.
Tell me more.
Anything else?
Can you give me an example?

These phrases, which encourage the other person to say more, are nonjudgmental and free of content. Let the other person describe the problem, and use encouragers, along with appropriate body language, to indicate that you are interested and are listening.

EXAMPLE

User: I'm trying to find some books for my neighbor.
Librarian: Yes, uh-huh (in an interested tone).
User: You see, she's just broken her ankle and can't get out, but she needs some mysteries to read while she's stuck at home.
Librarian: Mysteries, I see. (Here the librarian uses *acknowledgment* followed by an *encourager*.)
User: Yes, she especially likes mysteries written by women.
Librarian: Right. (Here the librarian *nods*, along with using a *minimal encourager*.)
User: And of course Patricia Cornwell is a favorite, but she's read all of Cornwell. I know she doesn't like those cozy English mysteries. She finds them too tame.

2.4.5 LISTENING

Good listening is the foundation of all oral communication. A good listener is always engaged in selecting, interpreting, remembering, making guesses and trying to confirm them, coming to conclusions, and checking out the conclusions by playing them back to the speaker. Naturally, listening is crucial throughout the interview, but it is especially important in the first 30 seconds when you are setting the foundation for the rest of the interview.

Effective listening involves a variety of things that are interconnected:

1. You actually have to be listening, not just pretending to be listening. Listening is not the same thing as not talking. Instead of really listening, people who are not talking might be daydreaming, waiting for their turn to

DID YOU KNOW?

Middle-class Anglo-Americans tend to think you are not listening unless you look at them. However, Native Americans generally avoid steady eye contact. African-Americans tend to make more eye contact when speaking but will not have such a steady gaze at someone they are listening to.

A QUICK TIP

SHOW AN INTEREST

Users in the Library Visit study responded negatively when they felt that the staff member did not treat their questions as important. Here are some comments from users:

> "She did her job, but not in a way that made me feel the question was important."
> "He did not seem especially concerned with my needs."
> "The reference worker did not help me to find the answer I was looking for and seemed completely uninterested in looking for it."

The staff members in these cases may in fact have been very interested, but unfortunately did not convey this interest to the user. The appropriate use of attending skills can go a long way toward reassuring users that you are interested in the question and are paying attention.

WHAT USERS SAID ABOUT NOT LISTENING

She assumed I wanted a child's book on turtles because my 12-year-old son was with me. Even when I asked her questions, she was more preoccupied with searching than with paying any attention to what I was saying. . . . What was not helpful was her indifference to any comments I made.

I felt she had not listened to what I had said. . . . I was usually interrupted before I could actually complete most of my sentences.

[When I asked for books on papermaking], she asked, "Are you interested in recycling?" I said, "No, I want to make paper." She said, "We don't have too much on papermaking. I think you'll find more in recycling books. I'll give you two call numbers." . . . Under call number 696 (pulp and paper technology) were books on making anything but paper. Under call number 363.7282 were books on toxic waste and pollution.

—From the Library Visit study

---

talk, or thinking about something else, such as sources or search tactics, or, for that matter, what they are planning to cook for dinner.

2. You have to let the other person know that you are listening. This is where nonverbal attending skills come in, such as eye contact, nodding, acknowledging, and using minimal encouragers.

3. Allow time for the user to answer your question. Don't be afraid of silence (see section 2.4.2 on pausing).

4. Listen for what is important to the user. When a user describes a complex information need, you may feel overwhelmed by the amount of detail that you get. Skilled interviewers use active listening techniques to focus on the elements of the situation that the user considers most important.

5. Ensure that you have heard and understood by restatement, followed by a question to confirm (see section 3.2.4). For example you could say, "So what you really need is a table showing the breakdown of domestic wine production by year, is that right?"

6. Don't interrupt or try to speed things up by finishing the user's sentence. You might think that you have heard the question before and that you know what is wanted,

but you could be wrong. Interrupting is a way of exercising power, especially over people considered of lower status. It is not a good way of showing respect.

2.5 ANNOTATED REFERENCES

2.5.1 GENERAL

American Library Association, Reference and Adult Services Association. 1996. "Guidelines for Behavioral Performance of Reference and Information Services Professionals." *RQ* 36, no. 2 (winter): 200-203. Includes techniques for showing approachability and interest, listening/inquiring, searching, and providing follow-up. Available on the ALA Web site at www.ala.org/rusa/standard.html.

Auster, Ethel, and Stephen B. Lawton. 1984. "Search interview techniques and information gain as antecedents of user satisfaction with online bibliographic retrieval." *Journal of the American Society for Information Science* 35, no. 2: 90–103.

Durrance, Joan, C. 1989. "Reference Success: Does the 55% Rule Tell the Whole Story?" *Library Journal* 114, no. 7 (April 15): 31–36.

———. 1995. "Factors that Influence Reference Success: What Makes Questioners Willing to Return?" *The Reference Librarian* 49/50: 243–65.

LaGuardia, Cheryl. 1996. *Teaching the New Library: A How-To-Do-It Manual for Planning and Designing Instructional Programs.* New York: Neal-Schuman. For a discussion of helping users in the electronic arcade, see pages 109–34.

Massey-Burzio, Virginia. 1998. "From the Other Side of the Reference Desk: A Focus Group Study." *The Journal of Academic Librarianship* 24, no. 3: 208–15.

Radford, Marie L. 1996. "Communication Theory Applied to the Reference Encounter." *The Library Quarterly* 66 (April): 123–37.

Swope, Mary Jane, and Jeffrey Katzer. 1972. "Silent Majority: Why Don't They Ask Questions?" *RQ* 12, no. 2 (winter): 161–66.

Westbrook, Lynn. 1984. "Catalog Failure and Reference Service: A Preliminary Study." *RQ* 24, no. 1 (Fall): 82–90.

2.5.2 MICROTRAINING

Ivey, Allen E., and Mary Bradford Ivey. 1999. *Intentional Interviewing and Counseling: Facilitating Client Development in a Multicultural Society.* 4th ed. Pacific Grove, Calif.: Brooks/Cole. This classic textbook on microcounseling provides a structured approach for learning the hierarchy of microskills.

Jennerich, Elaine Z. 1974. "Microcounseling in Library Education." Ph.D. diss. University of Pittsburgh Graduate School of Library and Information Sciences.

2.5.3 NONVERBAL BEHAVIOR: GENERAL

Adler, Ronald B., and Jeanne Marquardt Elmhorst. 1996. *Communicating at Work: Principles and Practices for Business and the Professions.* 5th ed. New York: McGraw-Hill. Includes an expanded consideration of culture and gender. Chapter 2, "Communication, Culture and Work," provides an excellent overview of diversity in the workplace, broadly interpreted. Chapter 3, "Verbal and Nonverbal Messages," deals with personal space and distance, appearance, and the physical environment, as well as body language.

Birdwhistell, Raymond L. 1970. *Kinesics and Context: Essays on Body Motion Communication.* Philadelphia: University of Pennsylvania Press. A classic work on body language, originally published in 1940.

Burgoon, Judee K. 1994. "Nonverbal Signals." In *Handbook of Interpersonal Communication,* edited by Mark L. Knapp and Gerald R. Miller. 2d ed. Thousand Oaks, Calif.: Sage Publications. An overview of scholarly research, with an extensive bibliography.

Burgoon, Judee K., and Laura K. Guerrero. 1994. "Nonverbal Communication." In *Human Communication,* edited by Michael Burgoon, Frank G. Hunsaker, and Edwin J. Dawson. 3d ed. Thousand Oaks, Calif.: Sage Publications. A scholarly review.

Giles, Howard, and Richard L. Street Jr. 1994. "Communication Characteristics and Behavior." In *Handbook of Interpersonal Communication,* edited by Mark L. Knapp and Gerald R. Miller. 2d ed. Thousand Oaks, Calif.: Sage Publications. A scholarly review of research on individual differences (e.g., gender, culture, socioeconomic status, and psychological variables) and communication behavior.

Hall, Edward T. 1959. *The Silent Language.* Garden City, N.Y.: Doubleday. A classic book on cross-cultural differences in the way cultures experience time and space.

Hunt, Gary T. 1985. *Effective Communication.* Englewood Cliffs, N.J.: Prentice-Hall. Chapter 5 on nonverbal communication includes exercises and questions for discussion.

Ivey, Allen E., and Mary Bradford Ivey. 1999. *Intentional Interviewing and Counseling: Facilitating Client Development in a Multicultural Society.* 4th ed. Pacific Grove, Calif.: Brooks/Cole. This latest edition is particularly good on how culture and gender affect nonverbal behavior.

Tannen, Deborah. 1990. *You Just Don't Understand: Women and Men in Conversation.* New York: William Morrow. A popular, easy-to-read book by an expert on gender differences in communication.

———. 1994. *Talking from 9 to 5: How Women's and Men's Conversational Styles Affect Who Gets Heard, Who Gets Credit, and What Gets Done at Work.* New York: William Morrow. Popular follow-up to *You Just Don't Understand.*

2.5.4 LISTENING

Jaffe, Clella Iles. 1995. *Public Speaking: A Cultural Perspective.* Belmont, Calif.: Wadsworth. Chapter 6, "Listening," includes a section on active listening and also explains cultural differences in expectations about listening.

Rogers, Carl, and Richard Farson. 1973. "Active Listening." In *Readings in Interpersonal and Organizational Communication*, edited by Richard Huseman, Cal M. Logue, and Dwight L. Freshley. 2d ed. Boston: Holbrook Press. This article introduced the term *active listening*.

Smith, N. M., and S. D. Fitt. 1982. "Active Listening at the Reference Desk." *RQ* 21, no. 3: 247–49. Brief but still useful introduction to this important skill.

Wolvin, Andrew, and Carolyn Gwynn Coakley. 1992. *Listening*. Dubuque, Iowa: Wm. C. Brown. A basic textbook.

2.5.5. INITIAL CONTACTS AND NONVERBAL BEHAVIOR IN THE LIBRARY CONTEXT

Eichman, Thomas Lee. 1978. "The Complex Nature of Opening Reference Questions." *RQ* 17, no. 3 (spring): 212–22.

Jennerich, Elaine Z., and Edward J. Jennerich. 1997. *The Reference Interview as a Creative Art*. 2d ed. Littleton, Colo.: Libraries Unlimited. Includes a brief discussion of nonverbal skills.

Kazlauskas, Ed. 1976. "An Exploratory Study: A Kinesic Analysis of Academic Library Public Service Points." *Journal of Academic Librarianship* 2, no. 3 (May): 130–34. An early study of nonverbal behavior in libraries.

Lam, R. Errol. 1988. "The Reference Interview: Some Intercultural Considerations." *RQ* 27, no. 3 (spring): 390–93.

Radford, Marie L. 1989. "Interpersonal Communication Theory in the Library Context: A Review of Current Perspectives." In *Library and Information Science Annual*, edited by Bohdan S. Wynar. Vol. 5. Englewood, Colo.: Libraries Unlimited.

3 FINDING OUT WHAT THEY REALLY WANT TO KNOW

In this chapter . . .

3.1 SOME COMMON PROBLEMS

After you establish contact, you still have to find out what the person wants to know. The next stage in the reference interview involves the use and integration of specific skills that will be considered in this chapter: open and closed questions; avoiding premature diagnosis; sense-making questions; paraphrasing and summarizing; and closure. A good reference librarian uses these skills intentionally and combines them in order to advance the purpose of the interview.

The use of the skills discussed in this chapter provides a solution to most of the commonly recurring problems identified in the reference interview. A small number of recurrent problems accounts for a large proportion of failed reference transactions. Elimination of these commonly occurring problems will go a long way toward getting beyond the notorious 55 percent success rate. The following example from the Library Visit study illustrates many of these common problems. In this transaction, the user wanted information on jet lag. Here is her account of what happened as she reported it to a student interviewer from the same reference class:

User:	I was trying to look normal—to take a normal user's approach to the library. . . . So I said that I was looking for some books on flying. She [the staff member] just turned around and started punching on her terminal. . . . After a few minutes, I realized she wasn't going to ask me anything more, and I knew I'd get sent to the wrong section. So I said, "Well, actually, I'm looking for jet lag, but I don't know if it's in 'flying' or not." She just kept punching, but I intuited that she was getting another subject heading. And then she said that there's nothing on jet lag. Then she wrote down a number and tore it off the paper and gave it to me. . . . The specific number she gave me was a book on how to fly a light aircraft.
Interviewer:	Did you ask again?
User:	No, I didn't feel like going to her again. I was too upset.
Interviewer:	Did you tell her anything?
User:	No.
Interviewer:	How did you feel?
User:	I felt like dropping out of [library school]. . . . I thought, if that is the experience that the general public gets, they can't be getting the books they want, because I didn't get anywhere near my subject.

This case highlights four common problems with the staff member's role in the transaction:

1. **Failure to establish contact** by using appropriate attending skills (see section 2.4.2). In this case, the terminal was a physical barrier. The staff member didn't speak to the user but spent her energy "punching on her terminal." The user's impression was that "her job was to punch on the machine . . . just somebody typing. It was just like getting an airline ticket—just like saying, 'I want to go to London,' and they start punching at the desk. . . . There was me and the machine, and she was the thing that punched in."

2. **Bypassing the reference interview** and accepting the initial question at face value (see section 1.2).

3. **An unmonitored referral,** which is what happens when the staff member refers the user to a source, either inside or outside the library, without taking any steps to check whether or not the user eventually gets a helpful answer. In this case, the user later reported, "We had to go back— my little girl had lost her toy—we went past her desk several times, but she didn't even ask if we'd found a book. I don't think she'd recognize me."

4. **Failure to pay attention** to cues from the user that the transaction was going off track. In this case, when the user realized that she was going to be packed off to the wrong section, she volunteered further clues about the information she wanted in order to get the staff member to search a different subject: "Well, actually, I'm looking for jet lag, but I don't know if it's in 'flying' or not." However, the librarian was too busy punching to hear.

5. **Lack of knowledge of appropriate sources.** Searching the library catalog for a keyword from the user's question should not be the default search strategy for every question. In this case, it would not have been difficult for the staff member to use a periodical index to find a couple of articles written at various levels of specialization.
(Reported in Dewdney and Ross, "Flying a Light Aircraft," 1994)

This reported reference transaction was an epitome of almost every possible deficiency: the staff member didn't smile or use appropriate eye contact, didn't conduct a reference interview (in fact spoke only one sentence in total), didn't listen, and didn't use a follow-up question to invite the user to return if the source provided wasn't satisfactory. In the next sections, we look in more detail at some of these common problems.

3.1.1 "WITHOUT SPEAKING SHE BEGAN TO TYPE"

In about one-quarter of the Library Visit transactions, users reported that as soon as they asked their initial question, the staff member silently started to perform some mysterious activity, without asking any questions or providing any explanations. Most often, the silent activity was typing keywords from the user's initial question into a catalog search statement. After encountering so many observations in the Library Visit accounts along the lines of "She didn't speak to me after I asked my question but just started punching the keys" or "He turned to the computer without explaining to me what he was doing," we began to think of this response as the "without speaking she began to type"

DID YOU KNOW?

"Without speaking, she began to type . . ." is a common complaint of library users. Librarians need to acknowledge the user's question and explain that they are going to check the catalog before they begin to enter the search. Otherwise, users feel that the librarian may not have heard their question, because they don't know what the librarian is doing. For more examples from the user's point of view, see Dewdney and Ross (1994).

maneuver. Quite possibly, the staff member was being very efficient in executing a search strategy. But the user doesn't know that and isn't learning anything about the search process. And, of course, the staff member has started searching before doing anything to clarify the real question.

In public libraries especially, the following scenario was a common occurrence, as reported by users in the Library Visit study. The user asked an initial question: Do you have information about the best scuba diving spots/information about optical character recognition/books about how to buy a dog/books on Richard Wagner/instructions on how to plant a pine tree? Then, without asking any questions or providing any explanation, the staff member searched the catalog by typing the keywords of the user's initial statement: scuba diving/optical character recognition/dogs/Richard Wagner/pine trees. By fixating on the catalog, the staff member in effect translated the user's request for "information" on a topic into a request for a book on that topic. A frequent automatic response, whatever the initial question, was to use the keywords from the user's initial question as a catalog search statement. Unfortunately, this routinized response prevents the staff member from thinking of other sources, often more appropriate, such as encyclopedia entries, periodical articles, vertical file materials, or Web pages.

In the Library Visit study, the user sometimes did end up with an acceptable answer when the librarian bypassed the reference interview, typed some keywords into the catalog search statement, and provided an unmonitored referral (see section 3.1.4). This strategy has a chance of being successful in certain cases in which the following conditions apply: the requested information is addressed by a whole book on the topic and not by, say, a section within a book on a broader topic; the keywords in the user's initial statement happen to match the title of a book in the catalog; the book is on the shelf. For example, the person wanting to buy a dog was given a call number that got her within browsing distance of *The Puppy Report: How to Select a Healthy, Happy Dog*. In contrast, the staff member who was asked for information on optical character recognition was unsuccessful at finding anything in the online catalog through a keyword search and blamed the topic itself for being too technical. The user provided this account:

> I stood there for several minutes while she searched. I could not see the screen and she did not ask me any questions. The silence grew a little awkward as I watched her mutter and purse her lips as her searches seemed to render negative results. Finally she said, "This may be too technical."

A QUICK TIP

GET TO THE BOTTOM LINE

In the Mental Models study, an experienced librarian described a transaction in which the user's initial question was "Do you have any information about Canadian universities?" The librarian reported that when she heard this initial question her first thought was "That's not the bottom line. I had no idea what the real question was at that point." The rest of the interview went like this:

Librarian: Can you be more specific?

User: I'm looking for information on Middle East graduate studies.

Librarian: What kind of information on Middle East graduate studies do you need?

User: Scholarship information. The two programs I'm interested in are at Toronto and McGill.

When asked how she would explain or describe this type of reference situation to a new librarian who was just learning about reference service, the experienced librarian said, "Keep sitting in your chair until you figure out the bottom line of the question. I could have spent a lot of time looking for Middle East programs. This type of [initial] question is the next level down from 'Where are your science books?' but is still too broad."

In the case of the optical character recognition topic and a number of others, the online catalog did not produce a match between the keywords of the user's request and the title of a book, and the user was told either that the information didn't exist at all or that it didn't exist in this library and the user would have to go elsewhere: to another type of library, to another city, or to another type of institution altogether. A very frequent occurrence in public libraries, especially branch libraries, was that a match would be found between a keyword in the user's question and a book in the catalog, but it would turn out that the book in question was not available within the particular library; it was at another branch or it was out on loan. At this point the staff member would offer to recall the book or to have the book sent from another branch to be picked up later. This way of handling the transaction got rid of the user for the time being, but it entailed additional work for the library system to handle the recall or transfer and additional work for the user to return to the library to pick up a book that still might not answer the question. Remember that the librarian in these cases has chosen not to conduct a reference interview and therefore has no way of knowing what kind of material is really needed to provide the help that the user requires. Conducting a proper reference interview is especially crucial when the user has to make a special return trip to pick up the requested material, transferred from another location.

(Reported in Ross and Nilsen, "So Has the Internet Changed Anything in Reference?" 2000)

3.1.2 BYPASSING THE REFERENCE INTERVIEW

Reference interviews are conducted only half the time, a figure that has scarcely varied over 25 years of reported research. Only 50 percent of the users in the Library Visit study (Ross and Nilsen 2000) reported that they were asked one or more questions intended to elicit further information about their information need. As we saw in section 3.1.1, instead of conducting a reference interview, the staff member often latches on to a keyword in the user's initial query and uses it as a search term in the catalog. Far from saving time, this practice often wastes time. In the Library Visit study, a user who had asked for books about Richard Wagner returned to say that none of the books on Wagner contained the desired information. At that point, the librarian discovered belatedly that the user needed a plot synopsis for all of the Wagner operas and recommended an opera guide. The librarian admonished, "You could have saved a lot of time if you had just asked for that initially"—a good example of blaming the bad-guy user (see section 1.7).

DID YOU KNOW?

In addition to wasting time, the failure to ask any questions to pinpoint the user's real interest can end up leaving the user irritated and dissatisfied. In the Library Visit study, one public library user who asked for "anything on the subject of the paranormal" observed that "unfortunately . . . I was presented with a multitude of information, some of it pertinent and some of it peripheral to my question. The broad range of information I received would have taken me weeks to wade through." Another remarked, "I was irritated that the librarian did not try to ascertain what I was asking her. She didn't understand me and didn't try to—she just fit my question into her frame of reference, without consulting me, and tried to answer me that way."

3.1.3 TAKING A SYSTEM-BASED PERSPECTIVE

Even when the library staff member does conduct an interview, a common problem is that too many of the librarian's questions relate to the library system, not to the context of the user's information need. In the Dewdney transcripts, librarians asked a lot of questions such as "Did you check the catalog?" "Have you used this index before?" "What were the indexing elements?" "Did you come up with some call numbers?" "Have you checked the 282s?" and "I suppose you've checked our circulating collection?" Sometimes these system-based questions were *all* that they asked.

Why is it a bad idea to take a system perspective? Well, library professionals obviously feel comfortable talking about the system, which is their home ground where they are the experts. They are the ones who know all the acronyms, understand the difference between a bibliography and biography or a keyword and an assigned subject heading, and are very fluent in the specialized vocabulary of information systems. However, you should remember that for many users, entering a library is like going into a foreign country, where a foreign language is spoken. So rather than asking users to use *your* language and fit their questions into your systems, you should ask them questions that allow them to describe their information need in their own terms and in *their* native language.

Brenda Dervin was one of the first to turn away from the system perspective in favor of a user-based perspective. Her colleague Douglas Zweizig provided a succinct summary of this perspective in a 1976 article called "With Our Eye on the User." The main point is that taking a user's perspective requires a transformation in the way in which we think about library services. Instead of looking at the user in the life of the system, Zweizig argues that we should be looking at how our services fit into the life of

EXERCISE

302.2 WIN

Consider this example from the Library Visit study. The user asked for information on the impact of technology on literacy. The librarian did a search, found two promising titles, and copied out the call numbers on a slip of paper. The user commented, "At this point I wondered why the librarian did not give me any directions to find the shelves. I guess maybe she thought I was familiar with the physical layout of the library. I thought that was a lot to assume, and making assumptions like this might be a hindrance to a shy patron using the facility for the first time. . . . People who are versed at using the library system might take the organization of information for granted in the library, but for the novice it could be a devastating experience. I was thinking that if I had not known the meaning of the call number 302.2 WIN that I would be embarrassed to ask for an explanation. The librarian assumed that the symbols she had written on the paper were meaningful and helpful to all."

In this instance, the librarian took for granted a number of things about the user's familiarity with the library's layout and the classification system. What could the librarian have done to take a more user-centered approach?

the user. Once we shift the focus of our attention from the system to the user of the system, the types of questions we ask in the interview change and become more user-centered.

Instead of asking a system	Ask a user-centered question
Have you looked in the catalog/looked at the author field in the MARC record/ checked the shelves?	What have you done so far?
Do you know the subject heading/search terms/ keywords?	What would you like the book/ article to cover? What would you like your map to show?
Do you want a directory?/ encyclopedia/biographical dictionary?	How do you plan to use the information?
Do you want books or articles?	What format would help you most?
That particular book is out right now. Do you want us to put a hold on it?	Perhaps we have another book available that will cover the same topic. What specifically were you hoping that book would include?

ANALYZE THIS REFERENCE TRANSACTION

Case 7: What's wrong with this picture?

The following account described what happened when one of the users in the Library Visit study visited a branch of a public library:

At the desk, I asked, "I was wondering if you could help me find some information about degenerative muscle diseases." The librarian reacted to my question by grimacing somewhat. She was not responding in a negative way, but rather in a way which indicated that this question would be tricky. She did not comment at all, however, which I found rather awkward. She began typing at her monitor and continued to type quite a long time without saying a word. . . . I felt so silly standing there silent that I finally spoke when she stopped typing for a moment. I said, "Are you searching for the subject Degenerative Muscle Diseases?" She said, "Yes, but I'm not finding anything with those terms." . . . Then she said that the only thing she could suggest I do would be to go to the stacks and try looking at the medical books. She told me the medical books were assigned the number 610.

In the stacks, I did manage to locate a dictionary of medical terms. The entry for Lou Gehrig's Disease indicated that it is Amyotrophic Lateral Sclerosis (ALS). I took this book to the desk and informed her that I had located [a possibly useful search term]. She told me that it really wouldn't be helpful to search using a term of such technical specificity. . . . Then she said nothing and seemed to be indicating that our search was at a dead end. I told her that none of the books in the stacks looked helpful for my particular interest. I asked if there might be books anywhere else that I could look at now that I knew the name of the disease. Her response was to say, "The only other place that you might find something would be the reference section over there. You can look up the same number, 610."

(Reported in Ross and Dewdney, "Negative Closure," 1998)

Comment: Despite the fact that the user rated the answer that she obtained as a 7 ("very helpful") on a 7-point scale, the user reported that she was "not sure" whether she would return to the same staff member with another question. A clue to the user's dissatisfaction is that she revised the question of the questionnaire, "How helpful was the answer given in terms of your own needs?" She deleted "answer given" and wrote in "answer obtained." Assuming that the user's report is accurate, how justified was she in finding the librarian unhelpful since, after all, she did find the information she wanted? What specific problems can you identify in the librarian's handling of this transaction? What could she have done instead?

WHAT USERS SAID ABOUT TAKING THE QUESTION AT FACE VALUE

- What was least helpful about the service I received was the few questions they asked me when I first approached them. If they had clarified what it was that I wanted, the search might not have taken as long.
- On hearing only part of my question, he dashed off into the stacks.
- He didn't ask me any questions about what I was looking for, and his manner was quite severe. I felt that he was rebuking me for asking for help rather than looking for the information myself.
- I asked the librarian for materials on the stock market. She entered "stock market" into the subject search of the library computer catalog. When the result came up, she swung her screen around and showed me what results she had found . . . . I found the books listed on the computer, but I did not feel I understood the stock market. I did not have all the information I wanted but I did not know what additional questions to ask. I did not want to seem like a pest. However, I did not think that the librarian had done that much for me. She looked up the information on the computer, but I could have done as much on my own. I remember thinking that there was little point in having librarians if they did not do anything for the users that they could not do for themselves.

(From the Library Visit Study)

3.1.4 THE UNMONITORED REFERRAL

One surprising finding in the Library Visit study was how often users reported unmonitored referrals. An unmonitored referral is our term for the situation in which the reference librarian gives the user a call number or refers the user to a source within the library but does not follow up or check to make sure that the source is not only found but also actually answers the question. The unmonitored referral routine too often immediately follows after the "without speaking she began to type" maneuver described earlier.

In general, the pattern for the unmonitored referral goes something like this: The user starts the reference encounter by asking for information on some topic. Often without conducting a reference interview, the staff member does a catalog search using

A QUICK TIP

AVOID THE CATALOG QUESTION

You might worry that if you don't ask, "Have you used the catalog?" that people will expect you to do all their work for them. But how much work you do versus how much the user is expected to do independently is a policy question. You are still free to follow your library's policy if, instead of asking the question about catalog use (which many users dislike), you ask, "What have you done with this question so far?" If the user says, "Well, actually, nothing really," you can still say, "The best place to start with this question is with the online catalog. Are you familiar with how our catalog works?"

However, the user may tell you something quite useful that will guide your handling of the question, as, for example, "Well, first I asked the staff member on the other side of the library, and he asked if I had checked the catalog. And then I looked in the catalog and I got these numbers. But then, when I went to the shelves, none of the books I found contained what I want." Now you can ask, "What specifically did you want the books to include?"

ANALYZE THIS REFERENCE TRANSACTION

Case 8: A system question or a user-centered question?

User: I checked the catalog but couldn't find what I was looking for.
Librarian: Not on the shelf? (acknowledgment)
User: No.
Librarian: What is it that you wanted? (open question)
User: The books.
Librarian: Yes, but what type of information? (open question)
User: It's on body work.
Librarian: OK. (encourager)
User: I'm helping a friend.

Dewdney, Auto body

Comment: Users are so used to being asked system-based questions in libraries that sometimes they misinterpret a user-centered question as a system question. In this case, the librarian had to rephrase her question "What is it that you wanted?" which produced a system-based answer, "The books." By persisting and asking, "Yes, but what type of information?" she ended up uncovering the user's situation. An even better question would have been, "Books, OK. But what were you hoping to find out?" We recommend that you avoid the term information when possible, because it has now become a system word.

---

terms from the user's initial question, gives the user a call number, points to some shelves, and recommends browsing, saying something along the lines of "I suggest you just browse the shelf around the call numbers I have given you." Sometimes the librarian points the user in the right direction, but not always. For example, one user asked for information on cellulitis, which is a skin infection, and was given a call number for a book on unwanted fat: "I found the book (not quite in its right place). It was called *Cellulite: Defeat It through Diet and Exercise*." In another case, a public library user who wanted information on endangered species was told, "Well, they seem to run from 591 to 599" and was given a slip of paper with 591-599. An academic library user who wanted the names of five U.S. corporations that had closed their corporate libraries was advised to "try Lexis/Nexis." When the user asked in what she called her "ignorant undergradu-

DID YOU KNOW?

According to Marie Radford, librarians often experience a particular reference transaction very differently from the way in which the user experiences it. She gives the example of a student who asked for help finding journal articles on psychology. The librarian directed her to a computer terminal and briefly showed her how to use PsychLit on CD-ROM. When asked about the transaction, the student said, "I felt like she couldn't help me on my subject. [It] isn't that she didn't know the answer, but I felt that she didn't want to [help]. . . she looked like she did not know what I was talking about, a blank stare and also almost like irritated." On the other hand, the librarian reported the same transaction this way: "I think it went all right from my viewpoint because I didn't have to really interact too much. She seemed capable, she seemed to know what she was doing. I felt she had found what she wanted because she said she had what she needed. She seemed to be capable of handling it on her own" (1999: 4).

DID YOU KNOW?

In a study of academic reference services, Murfin and Bunge (1984) reported that when the librarian was busy and made unmonitored referrals, the average success rate dropped from 69 percent to 22 percent in the five libraries studied. They concluded that the practice, policy, or necessity of directing the user rather than of accompanying the user on the search was a factor that caused these libraries to perform far below their potential. Nonprofessional staff were affected to an even greater extent by this adverse factor.

ate" tone, "Lexis/Nexis?" the staff member said, "That's one of the databases" and departed. The implication is that a list of call numbers or a URL or the name of the database is all the help to be expected and that users are on their own to sink or swim. That is, instead of providing an answer, the librarian provides a slip of paper and some call numbers. Usually no authors' names or titles are provided, which makes finding the actual book tricky for novices.

In "Reducing Failures in Reference Service," Douglas has classified six types of reference failure identified in studies that support the 55 percent rule. One of these is "Referral to a source within the library (e.g., another service point) or referral to a printed source but not actually locating the answer for the patron" (1988: 97). Although Douglas stated that this type of failure was not often mentioned in the studies he reviewed, we have found it to be a frequent occurrence. The unmonitored referral was reported in somewhat more than one-third of the Library Visits accounts—in 96 out of 261 accounts (Ross and Nilsen, 2000). When we examined these accounts to see what happens after an unmonitored referral, it turns out that some users are able to succeed on their own, but too often they do not and are left feeling dissatisfied. The user who was given a range of call numbers when she wanted information on endangered species remarked, "The librarian seemed to feel her job was done, but I felt quite unsatisfied with her assistance."

Another user who asked for information on fibromyalgia was told, "The best place to look would be Medline, which you can access from our computers here in the library." The staff member gave the user a piece of paper with the URL for Medline and said, "When you type this in, it'll bring up Medline. Then all you do is type in 'myofascial-fibro' or whatever and it will bring up the citations." In reflecting on this experience, the user said, "I felt that if he had helped me to use the database, I might have found some useful information. But as it was, I only tinkered with the database for a little while and then left empty-handed." There seems to be a high rate of search failure when users are not interviewed, are given minimal instructions, and are left on their own.

This doesn't mean that all the users who were given an unmonitored referral and who then found little of use left the library empty-handed. Some of them returned to the same librarian for help or pursued other strategies, including starting over again with a second librarian. In some cases the user took a proactive approach by explicitly asking for help in using the database and was more likely to get useful information. For example, a user who said she wanted to know how to find "information

---

WHAT USERS SAID ABOUT THE UNMONITORED REFERRAL

- Without saying anything, she handed me the piece of paper with the books listed on it and automatically assumed that I knew where to locate them. I asked her, "Where do I search for these books?" feeling that I better ask, since she was not going to tell me. She said, "Oh, right over there."
- She took for granted that I would be able to figure out for myself how to use the Book Review Index, as she offered me absolutely no guidance.
- The reference staff member wrote two call numbers down and handed them to me. . . . It bothered me that she did not take the time to point me in the right direction. As it was, the two books were found, but they were of no use to my topic.
- The librarian handed me a yellow piece of paper [listing call numbers]. I looked down at the numbers and asked, "Where do I find these books?" She replied, "They're over there in that direction," pointing to some place past the reference desk. . . . [The user found 9 of the 11 books listed.] None of them mentioned [the topic the user had asked about].
- She looked up something in the computer, wrote down a number, and said, "Try this," but didn't even give me a title.
- She did not explain to me what she was doing. She handed me a slip of paper with numbers scrawled on it and pointed me towards the stacks along the far wall. . . . I went to the stacks and found the call number for the book she had recommended. She had not written down the author or the title of the book on the slip of paper and, since the subject of the book was not evident by its title, I was not sure if this was the book I was searching for. I glanced through the book and it seemed inadequate. I headed back towards the reference desk to ask about medical journals, but she was gone. I suppose it was her coffee break."

(From the Library Visit study)

---

on a certain person," was immediately told, "the best bet is to use Biobase." The user commented, "I think he expected me to know what that meant and to get going on my way. So I explained that I was new to this library and didn't know *what*, let alone *where*, Biobase was." This user ended up getting excellent help, but other novice users who were less assertive were on their own and often missed out on finding information because unassisted they were unable to navigate through the library resources (Ross and Nilsen, 2000).

3.1.5 NEGATIVE CLOSURE: HOW TO MAKE USERS GO AWAY

In busy libraries, staff members face the practical problem of processing an endless stream of questions and sending users out of the system. Of course, the best way to do this is to provide an answer that is helpful. Highly rated librarians in the Library Visit study faced with a challenging question showed no inclination to give up, but instead said things like, "OK, let's not get discouraged. There are other places we can check" or "Here are some more things that you can try. Make sure you come back if you don't find what you need." But less highly rated librarians too often gave the impression that their goal was to get rid of users. Users made comments such as, "I think she hoped I would be satisfied and leave" or "I felt she would be glad if I went and found the materials for myself" or "He made it clear that he didn't want to be bothered with me when I came back to say that the first suggestion hadn't worked." Here are ten strategies, apart from providing a helpful answer, that some librarians used for getting rid of the user. We call this phenomenon *negative closure*.

1. **The librarian provides an unmonitored referral.** In the unmonitored referral, the staff member gives the user a call number or refers the user to a source without taking any steps to make sure that the source is found and answers the question (see section 3.1.4). This is not to say that making a referral is always unhelpful; in fact, staff members should probably be doing *more* referral both inside and outside the library. The key here is to build into the referral process some way of checking that the source being referred to is both available and appropriate. Referral is a strategy of negative closure only when the librarian doesn't know enough about the real question to have any reasonable confidence that a user who follows the advice will find an acceptable answer. In the Library Visit study, the unmonitored referral was used less often in academic libraries than in public libraries. Because academic libraries are strongly committed to providing bibliographic instruction, the staff member more often works together with the user to consult a source and therefore gets immediate feedback when the source is inappropriate.

2. **The librarian immediately refers the user somewhere else, preferably far away**—to another floor within the library or to another agency altogether. When asked for information on the relationship between homicide rates and capital punishment, the librarian immediately said, "That would be on the third floor." The librarian on the third floor said, "Have you tried the criminology library at University X [in another city]?" When this strategy of referral elsewhere is used *before* the library staff member has conducted a proper reference interview, the distant information provider often is *not* the appropriate place to answer the user's question, and the user is referred elsewhere yet again.

3. **The librarian implies that the user should have done something else first before asking for reference help.** When a user asked for information about good mystery writers, the librarian said in a manner that was "quite severe: 'Well, of course you've already checked in our catalog under authors' names to see if there is any information there.' . . . I felt he was rebuking me for asking for help rather than looking for the information myself." Questions such as "Have you checked the catalog?" feed into users' anxiety about asking for help; as one user wondered, "Was it irresponsible of me to seek assistance without first having done any searching myself?"

4. **The librarian tries to get the user to accept more easily found information** instead of the information actually asked for. When a user refused to accept the answer that there are no fiction writers in Newfoundland (see negative closure strategy 9), the librarian "pointed out all kinds of information that she *could* find . . . reference books for French Canadian literature, the literature of Canadian women, Western Canadian writers, etc." Whether the suggestion to switch to a more readily answered question is negative closure or an offer of genuine help in finding an acceptable answer depends on the context and what else the librarian knows about the user's information needs. Librarians may offer more readily available material because they assume the user is working on a school project and could change the topic, but they should ask.

5. **The librarian warns the user to expect defeat** because the topic is too hard, obscure, large, elusive, or otherwise unpromising. Asked for information on how carnival glass is made, one staff member typed in "carnival" and got sixty entries dealing with carnivals and fairs. She typed in "glass," found glass manufacturing, and said repressively, "This is

quite large." Another user commented, "She seemed to imply that this was going to be a long-drawn-out process and that probably nothing would be found." "Your question is rather elusive," warned another librarian. This strategy blames the anticipated failure to get an answer on the supposedly intractable nature of the question itself rather than on ineffective search skills.

6. **The librarian encourages the user to abort the transaction voluntarily.** When a user asked for the educational background of Camille Paglia, the librarian "rolled her eyes and said 'Oh, her,' and then said, 'Is it really necessary to find out her major(s)? Why do you want to know?'" Strategy 6 is often preceded by strategy 5, as users are more likely to say that the search is not worth pursuing if they expect that it will end in failure. (See section 3.2.3 for a discussion of why staff members should not ask "Why?" directly.)

7. **The librarian signals nonverbally that the transaction is over** by tone of voice, by turning away, or by starting another activity. Users said variously: "I knew from the tone of her voice that this was her final offering." "She was obviously finished with me at this point because she turned away and began shuffling through some papers."

8. **The librarian states explicitly that the search has reached a dead end.** Examples are: "I'm not sure what other information we might have on that" and "I am sorry. This is everything we have in our catalog under the entry *[City name] in art*." An international student who wanted to understand health insurance coverage was told that, apart from an out-of-date pamphlet, "I'm not sure what other material we might have available that would be of use." When a user wanting literary criticism of Margaret Atwood's novels returned after an unsuccessful unmonitored referral to ask for help finding material on the Internet, the staff member said, "Well, we're very busy right now, but if you come back later, someone will be available." In this case, the user noted that there was no one else in line and there was another librarian behind the desk reading a newspaper.

9. **The librarian claims that the information is not in the library or else doesn't exist** at all. When a user presented the initial question "I need some information on archaeology," the immediate response was that there was "not much material available at the library on this subject." In another case, when the user asked for help in finding the names of some fiction writers from Newfoundland, the librarian "reg-

---

DID YOU KNOW?

Sometimes the answer that there is no published material on a particular topic is a helpful response. For example, a student doing a literature review for a proposed area of thesis research finds it useful to be told that a thorough search of the relevant databases has found little or nothing of relevance on the topic. The negative search result differs from negative closure strategy 9 because it comes after a thorough search; it is not a strategy to avoid doing a search, which, had it been done, would have found quite a lot of relevance to the question.

UNHELPFUL BEHAVIORS IDENTIFIED IN THE LIBRARY VISIT STUDY

The staff member didn't smile/nod/look at me when I approached the desk/during the reference encounter.

Seemed to be using the desk or the terminal as a barrier.

Didn't listen. Cut me off when I tried to explain.

Made assumptions about what I wanted or why I wanted it (e.g., for a school project).

Seemed uninterested in/indifferent to me or my question.

Treated my question as unimportant or bothersome. Made me feel that I was inconveniencing the library staff and wasting their time.

Took a judgmental stance toward the content of the material I was looking for.

Didn't ask me anything about my question. Didn't find out why I needed the information and so gave me information that was too general.

Didn't try to understand my question but just fitted my question into his or her frame of reference.

Without speaking, he or she just began typing at the computer.

Looked up something in the computer, wrote down a call number, and said, "Try this," but didn't give me a title or author's name.

Was unwilling to move out from behind the desk to help me find material.

Made me feel that I shouldn't expect to get an answer to a question like that/that the question was too technical/that there probably were no reliable answers.

Made me feel it was not the librarian's job to answer questions about anything but the resources that were in the immediate library.

Made me feel stupid.

Said, "I suppose you've done the obvious and tried X?"

Didn't let me see the screen/the index as he or she was doing the search, so I couldn't tell how to do it myself next time.

Didn't explain what he or she was doing and left me wondering if I should follow her or wait.

Didn't explain how to use the catalog/indexes/microfilm reader/ library interface.

Made me feel left out of the search.

Just said, "No, we don't have it" and made no effort to suggest anything further to do.

Seemed impatient or vexed by my question and anxious to have me leave. Seemed to be trying to get rid of me.

Made no effort to follow up or verify that I had found what I was looking for.

Seemed more interested in time management than in helping me find an answer.

(Reported in Dewdney and Ross, "Flying a Light Aircraft," 1994)

istered that this was a very difficult question" and then, without consulting anything, said "that she didn't think there were any."

10. **The librarian tells the user he's going away to track down a document but then never returns.** One user reported that after the librarian said, "I'll go and see what I can find," she waited for 45 minutes but "never saw the man again, neither at the desk nor with the promised document." Another said, "I waited at the shelf for a while, but she did not come back." In a variant of this tactic, another staff member advised the user to go home and wait for a call with the requested information, but no one ever called back. Joan Durrance (1995) has described this phenomenon as the "Disappearing Librarian."
(Reported in Ross and Dewdney, "Negative Closure," 1998)

A QUICK TIP

IMAGINE THE TITLE

Here's an open question that often works when all else fails in the reference interview. Ask the user to imagine the title of the perfect source: "If you could have the perfect article (book, solution, help, etc.), what would it be called?" Be sure to give the user a few minutes to think about this. Often the imaginary title contains most of the keywords or concepts that you need to do the search. (Thanks for this suggestion to one of the trainees at our Reference Interview Workshop in Fredericton, New Brunswick.)

3.2 SKILLS FOR NEGOTIATING THE QUESTION

When most people think of interviewing, they think of question-asking. In this section we consider various kinds of questions and how they work. We also consider some related skills that need to be used in conjunction with questioning skills: summarizing, avoiding premature diagnosis, and closure or the skill of keeping the conversation on track. The eventual goal, of course, is to integrate all these skills into one seamless interview that moves smoothly from acknowledgment to an open question or two to a summary to a concluding statement that includes a follow-up question and an invitation to return. However, when learning a new skill, you should focus on one skill at a time to start with. After you feel comfortable using the single skill, then you can think about the integration of skills, a topic we discuss in section 4.2.

3.2.1 OPEN AND CLOSED QUESTIONS

You can ask questions in different ways. The form in which you ask the question determines the sort of answer you are likely to get. Research involving tape-recording reference transactions in real settings has found that, without training, library staff tend to ask a certain type of question, as in this example:

ANALYZE THIS REFERENCE TRANSACTION

Case 9: It just depends on what you want.

Librarian: Hi.

User: Is there a listing of companies and addresses and stuff like that?

Librarian: We have different manufacturers directories. (acknowledgment) Is that what you're after? (closed question to confirm)

User: Yes.

Librarian: Companies? (acknowledgment) OK. Now are you looking for any specific area in—. Is it American companies you're looking for? (closed question)

User: Yes. American.

Librarian: Are you looking for a special area, like a city? (closed question that functions as a polite version of the open question "What specific geographic area are you looking for, if any?")

User: No, no. Definitely not a specific area, but maybe like engineering and stuff. Manufacturing.

Librarian: OK. OK. Now these [pointing to some print sources] are industrial directories. For manufacturers. The companies actually have to produce a product. It's not going to be like ABC Insurance Company. (bibliographic instruction)

User: Right.

Librarian: OK. What we have here is a Trade Index, OK? [She explains how it works and shows him other sources. She describes how some directories have more information of different kinds.] It just depends on what you need.

User: See, what it is, is that I'm going to be sending out résumés and job applications. I just need the company names and what they do—and addresses—that's all.

Librarian: Yeah. You know what's good, though, is to have a name of a person, rather than just sending it to the company. Some of these do include personnel. [She explains.]

User: OK, thanks a lot.

Dewdney, Manufacturing (Job search)

For discussion:

How successful do you think this interview was overall? Which questions seemed to work best? Which not so well?

How might this transaction have turned out had the librarian treated this as a directional question and said, "Our company directories are over there."?

Is there anything that the librarian could have done to get to the user's real information need sooner?

Look closely at the two questions in which the staff member asks about "specific area." What happens in terms of the way the staff member phrases the question? In terms of how the user responds? Did the staff member get the answer he or she was hoping for?

Take a second look at the statement "It just depends on what you need." It's not formally a question. How does it function in this exchange?

In the interview that the researcher conducted with the user just before he left the library, this user said that he was very satisfied with the results of his conversation with this librarian and would definitely be willing to return to this same staff member for help.

User:	Do you have anything on computers?
Librarian:	Have you checked the catalog?
	Is this for a class project?
	Would you rather have books or articles?
	Are you interested in hardware or software?
	Do you want to buy a computer?

These are all *closed questions*—that is, questions that require a yes/no, this/that response. A closed question requires the other person to choose from the options provided. It works best in circumstances in which there exists only a small set of options known in advance. For example, at the coffee bar, the clerk might ask, "Small, medium, or large?"

In situations in which there may be many options that can't be known in advance—the usual case at the reference desk—open questions are more useful, especially at the beginning of the interview. *Open questions* differ from closed questions in both function and effect. Unlike a closed question, an open question allows people to respond in their own terms. A handy way of recognizing whether a question is open or not is to look at the way it begins. If it begins with Who, What, Why, Where, When, or How, the question is probably open. "What format do you want for the information?" and "How did you hear about this particular computer virus?" are examples of open questions. The less restrictive structure of open questions invites elaboration and longer answers. When you ask open questions, you give up some control over what gets talked about. Instead of specifying the aspect of the topic to be discussed ("Do you want hardware?"), you ask the other person what aspect of the topic concerns him or her ("What did you want to know about computers?"). The user might possibly say hardware. But chances are he will mention something altogether different that you would never have been able to guess, such as listings of local continuing education courses on designing Web pages. Guessing "Is it this? Is it that?" can be risky and sometimes offensive because it involves making assumptions. Open questions make no assumptions.

To summarize, closed questions restrict the user's response and furthermore restrict it to aspects of the topic that concern the librarian but not necessarily the user. Many commonly asked closed questions are attempts to relate the user's request to the library system and its methods of organizing, retrieving, and providing information (see section 3.1.3 on taking a system-based approach). Hence a staff member in an academic library may ask, "Are you a student here?" because access to licensed databases require passwords available only to students and faculty of that

EXERCISE

EVALUATING QUESTIONS

This exercise can be done on your own or in a group discussion with either small breakout groups or a large group.

1. Look closely at the list of CLOSED QUESTIONS provided in the bipolar disorder case. Closed questions usually involve assumptions. For each closed question, specify what the assumption is. How confident should the librarian be that this assumption is right?

2. To ask a closed question, you need background knowledge. One kind of background knowledge concerns the library system, how information is collected, organized, retrieved, and stored. The other kind is subject knowledge about the user's topic. For each closed question, specify the kind of background knowledge needed to generate the question.

3. Now look at the list of OPEN QUESTIONS. How do they differ in terms of assumptions made and knowledge needed about the topic?

4. Suppose another user asks, "Do you have any information on fish?" How many of the listed open and closed questions could you use again with this new user by replacing references to bipolar disorder with references to fish? (e.g., "Do you want recent research articles on fish?" "Do you want the contact number for a fishing organization?"). What conclusions can you draw from this exercise about the generalizability of open and closed questions. If you could ask only one question and had to use it in every reference interview, which one of these open and closed questions would you pick?

institution. Usually closed questions elicit very short answers. Sometimes short answers are wanted, so there is a place for closed questions in the reference interview. Closed questions are effective in focusing wandering conversation and can also be useful, especially at the end of the interview, to verify that the librarian understands what really is needed (e.g., "So all you want to know is the name of the archaeologist who discovered the Crystal Skull?"). But at the beginning it is usually preferable to get users talking, and this can be done best by asking open questions ("What do you want to know about the Crystal Skull?" or "How did you hear about the Crystal Skull?" or "I'm not familiar with the Crystal Skull. What can you tell me about it?"). Asking open questions encourages the user to say in his or her own words what is wanted. Compare these two sets of questions.

Closed Questions

User: Do you have any information on bipolar disorder?
Staff: Is this for a school project?
Do you want books or articles?
Have you checked the catalog?
Do you want information about drug treatments?
Do you want recent research articles on this disorder?
Do you want firsthand accounts of living with bipolar disorder?
Do you want the contact number for a support group?

Open Questions

User: Do you have any information on bipolar disorder?
Staff: What would you like to know about bipolar disorder?
What aspect of bipolar disorder are you most interested in?
We have material on bipolar disorder in different areas of the library. Perhaps if you could tell me what aspect interests you, I could help narrow things down. [Not, strictly speaking, a question, but this statement functions as a question, inviting the user to say more.]

So if open questions are so good, why does it seem to be second nature to ask closed questions? Mary Jo Lynch reported that an analysis of the 366 reference transactions recorded in four public libraries in New Jersey in the late 1970s showed that 10 percent of all questions asked were either open questions or functioned as open questions and 90 percent were closed, such as "Do you need pictures of frogs or material about them?" (1978: 131). In Dewdney's study, before providing training in specific skills,

A QUICK TIP

YOU DON'T HAVE TO KNOW EVERYTHING

As a library professional, you are supposed to be an expert on how to find sources of information; you are not expected to know everything on every subject. If the user asks about a person, place, or thing that you are unfamiliar with, don't try to fake it. Ask the user to tell you what he or she knows about it.

In the Mental Models study, a user asked for "information on Sheridan." (She was doing a college project on the eighteenth century British playwright Richard Sheridan and wanted to find criticism on School for Scandal.) The librarian reported that when he heard this initial question he thought, "It's a name, but I don't know who this is. My immediate reaction was that it must be the Civil War general. I was stalling until I could figure it out—it didn't ring any bells with me. So I showed her how to walk through the catalog search. I got her to type in the name Sheridan. She was very quiet, so I didn't want to ask her too many questions. I was hoping to pick up some cues from off the screen about whether Sheridan was an author or politician or whatever."

Instead of hoping for cues to appear magically on the screen, why not say at the outset, "I'm not sure I know which Sheridan you mean. What can you tell me about him or her?" or "I'm not familiar with Sheridan. If you could tell me a bit about this topic, I would do a better job of searching." If it turned out that the user wanted calendar information for Sheridan College available on the Web, then the catalog would not have been the best place to search.

Dewdney recorded and transcribed 166 reference interviews to establish a baseline of interview behaviors. She found that in about 80 percent of transactions, either no open questions were asked or the open question was immediately converted to a closed question, as in, "What would you like to know about antique dolls? The prices?" (1986: 109). Often, as we have seen, closed questions are system-based. Although system-based questions are logical to the library staff member, they often put the user on the spot by asking for information the user doesn't know, as in this example:

Staff: You're looking for a song, "The Lamplighter's Serenade." Do you know if it was written recently? (*closed question*)
User: No, I'm afraid I don't.
Staff: Was it written by an American?" (*closed question*)
User: Sorry, I don't know.
Staff: Is it a popular song? (*closed question*)
User: I think so. No, I'm not sure. I shouldn't really bother you about this. I can come back later.

As this example illustrates, staff members often ask closed questions that are related to the way that information is organized in reference tools (by time period, geographical region of origin, type of song, etc.). But unfortunately, when users don't know the answers to these closed questions, the interview can seem like a game of twenty questions. Worse, users may be left with the impression that they should have researched the topic far more thoroughly before bothering the librarian. Instead of asking a series of closed questions that the user can't answer, the staff member could have asked, "What can you tell me about this song?" Although it is sometimes argued that busy staff don't have time to listen to long stories elicited by open questions, the fact is that open questions save search time.

A frequently asked question raised by prospective and practicing librarians and reference workshop participants is: "Won't it take too long to ask open questions and use all these other skills?" Well, no. You can conduct short interviews by taking the user's initial question at face value and answering it literally ("Sorry, all our copies are out"), but is that real service? Our answer is that asking open questions might take a little longer (although often it won't). But extra time spent at the beginning to clarify what the user really wants saves time in the long run, time that would otherwise be wasted searching for the wrong thing or transferring the wrong book from another branch. For example, one librarian reported going to the cookery section with a user who had asked for a book on carving game birds. It turned out that

QUICK TIP

SOMETIMES IT'S BETTER TO BE INDIRECT

In some cultures, direct questions (either open or closed) may be interpreted as too direct or even impolite. Instead of asking: "What do you want to know about X?" you may want to rephrase your question as a statement, such as:

- I may be able to help you better if you could tell me more about X.
- We have a lot of different materials on X in various parts of the library. I may be able to help you better if you could tell me more about X.
- Perhaps if you tell me a bit about how you plan to use this information, I could help you locate some relevant articles.

These statements work because they let the user know why the librarian needs more details from them, but at the same time, the librarian is being respectful by not demanding an answer.

ANALYZE THIS REFERENCE TRANSACTION

Case 10: Closed system-based questions

User: Excuse me, but I'm looking for some poems.

Librarian: Some poems. What poems are you looking for? (acknowledgment followed by an open question)

User: Love poems.

Librarian: Love poems. (acknowledgment) OK, is there anything in particular? By anybody—American, Canadian, British—does it matter? (a question that is open in its function—meaning "anybody in particular?"—gets turned immediately into a closed question)

User: No, just a project on love poems.

Librarian: OK, do you know how to use the catalog here?

User: No.

Librarian: OK. [Explains the catalog.] Did you want books that you can take home or is it all right to work here? (closed question)

User: Mm-hmm. No.

Librarian: Do you know how to work the index? (closed question)

User: No. [Librarian explains the index.]

Dewdney, Love Poems

Comment: After a good start with the open question "What poems are you looking for?" the librarian switched to closed questions related to the library system and its organization and retrieval tools: authors classified by nationality because that's the way the library classification system organizes them; books divided into circulating or reference because that's how the library works; the user's familiarity with the library's catalog and indexes because the user is expected to use these tools. Because these questions focused on library-related areas that the user didn't know anything about, rather than on areas related to the user's own interests and purposes, the information produced was minimal.

What else could the librarian have done here? After the response "just a project on love poems," more useful information would probably have been elicited by an open question such as "What kind of project are you doing on love poems?" or "What are the requirements of your project?" or even "What did your teacher tell you about this project?"

DID YOU KNOW?

An analysis of Library Visit accounts indicates that users often misinterpret closed questions such as "Are you a law student?" (or music student or whatever other subject area), "Are you a student here?" and "Is this for a course or for personal interest?" The users did not see these questions as part of the librarian's attempt to help them find useful and suitable materials. They thought that if they were students here, then they would be expected to find the answers themselves and not ask for help. And if they weren't students here, or were students asking a question for personal interest, then they thought they might be told they had no business taking up the librarian's time. For example, one student was asked if his question about earthquakes was for a course or for personal interest. His interpretation of the staff member's question was: "Do you really need this information or are you just wasting my time?"

DID YOU KNOW?

In a posting to LIBREF on the topic of "Why don't they ask for what they want?" Dr. Diane Nahl emphasized the need for practice: "My students always have trouble learning to use open questions. [Asking open questions] is unnatural, somehow, and must be focused on and practiced explicitly . . . . For 10 years I have taught reference interviewing in a professional library school and I have always emphasized finding out what the person really wants through role plays, analysis of real interviews, and through fieldwork at real reference desks in which students analyze their live interviews" (Nahl, 1997, used with permission).

SOME USEFUL OPEN QUESTIONS

To find out what a person wants in order to supply the need:
What sort of thing are you looking for?
What information would you like on this?
What sort of material do you have in mind?
What requirements do you have (for the project, design, etc.)?

To get a description of a problem or event:
What have you done about this question so far?
Where did you hear about this?
What did your teacher/boss tell you about this topic [for the "imposed question"]?

To encourage the person to elaborate:
What aspect of X concerns you?
What else can you tell me about X?
Perhaps if you tell me more about this problem/project, I could make some suggestions.

To get clarification:
What do you mean by X?
What would be an example of that? Can you give me an example? Please give me an example.
Can you help me to understand X?

(Adapted from Brenda Dervin)

---

he didn't want to carve cooked fowl for the dining table; he wanted to do wood sculpture. An open question such as "What would you like to know about carving game birds?" would have saved the librarian time and embarrassment. In contrast, another librarian reported her success using open questions with a young user who had asked, "Do you have cookbooks from different lands?" An open question elicited the further information, "I have a grade seven project on special Christmas recipes and I'm supposed to do *bûche de Nöel*." The librarian's summary of the transaction: "We had two books for her in one minute." Open questions usually save time because they give users the chance to focus immediately on whatever is important to *them*.

ANALYZE THESE REFERENCE TRANSACTIONS

Case 11: Closed questions that are intended to function as open questions

1. **User:**   Do you have a section on true-to-life murders that have been committed?
   Librarian: Yes we do. Is there—are you just interested in general reading?
                There isn't a particular murder that you heard . . . ?
   User: Yes. No.

   Dewdney, Murders

2. **User:**   I have a list of publications. [reads from paper.] I don't know if those are magazines
                or journals or . .
   Librarian: [Looks at list.] They're all magazines. . . . Are you looking at a particular topic?
   User: Yes. I'm looking at wage restraint in the federal government.

   Dewdney, Wage restraint

3. **User:**   Where would I find the U.S. phone books?
   Librarian: They're over here. We've just got the major cities. Were you looking for one in particular?
   User: No, two. Cleveland and San Mateo, California.

   Dewdney, San Mateo Clinic

4. **User:**   Where would you have books on credit cards?
   Librarian: Books on credit cards? (acknowledgment)
   User: Yes.
   Librarian: OK. How to manage credit cards? The history of credit cards? Or . . .?
   User: I'm doing an essay on credit cards.

   Dewdney, Credit cards

Comment: In each case the librarian asked a question that is technically a closed question—it can be answered by a yes or no. However, the librarian intended the question to function as an open question. Sometimes the user understands what is intended. Sometimes the user misunderstands, as in the first case, in which the user takes the questions literally. In the second case, the user interpreted the closed question, as intended, to mean, "What topic are you looking at?" The third user initially answered "Were you looking for one in particular?" as if it were a closed question, responding, "No, two." But then he continued on as if the question had been "Which one(s) in particular were you looking for?" In the final case, the librarian used two closed questions that were intended to say in effect, "We have a lot of material on credit cards, from managing them to the history of them. It all depends on what you need." Note that two closed questions followed by "or?" to suggest an open-ended menu of possibilities work differently than a single closed question, "Do you need something on how to manage credit cards better?" The user responded as intended by explaining the context for the question. However, closed questions can be tricky to use because they involve assumptions, and sometimes the assumptions can be offensive. (The user might think indignantly, I can manage my credit cards just fine right now, thank you very much.)

3.2.2 AVOIDING PREMATURE DIAGNOSIS

Premature diagnosis is another term for jumping to conclusions. Some examples of premature diagnosis:

> A young adult who is wearing running shoes, jeans, and a T-shirt asks for some material on eating disorders. The librarian asks, "Is this for a school project?"

> A woman in her thirties asks for pictures of Scandinavian costumes. The librarian asks, "Is this for your child—a costume to make for your child?"

> An elderly man asks for books on entomology. The librarian asks, "Are you trying to get rid of ants?"

In each case, the librarian assumed something about the user's situation and asked a closed question that made the assumption explicit to the user. Sometimes the librarian is right (the elderly man *did* want to get rid of carpenter ants), but that's just good luck. When the librarian is wrong, the user could find the explicit assumptions offensive (the woman who was asked if the Scandinavian costume was for her child thrust out her ringless left hand indignantly and said, "Does this look like I had a child?").

Premature diagnosis is one of the commonest causes of communication accidents in libraries; try to avoid it. You can't help making assumptions, but you can avoid making these assumptions explicit to the user. Instead of guessing and asking a closed question based on your guess, ask an open question that makes no assumptions.

Compare the following ways of handling the same question:

User:	Do you have an elementary math book?
Librarian:	Is this book for a child?
User:	No, I want it for myself.
Librarian:	You must be teaching in the adult basic education program then.
User:	No, I'm not a teacher.
Librarian:	Oh, I thought you were. A lot of teachers come in asking for basic books for their courses.
User:	Is that so?

User:	Do you have an elementary math book?
Librarian:	We have books of that sort in both the children's and the adults' sections. How do you plan to use this book?

EXERCISE

ASKING OPEN QUESTIONS

This exercise provides practice in distinguishing between open and closed questions. It can be done individually or as a group exercise, with participants divided into small groups of three to five people. **Library user:** "I have to give a speech on Saturday and I'm looking for some books I could use."

1. Write down three possible closed questions that you could ask.
2. Write down three possible open questions that you could ask.
3. Examine your open and closed questions to determine whether your closed questions are really closed and your open questions are really open. (Remember: A closed question limits the response to a yes/no/I don't know or a this/that answer.) Which of your six questions do you think would work best?

If you want the small groups to share their experiences afterward with the larger group, you can assign a different user's question to each group. Think up your own user questions that are typical of ones asked in your setting. Some possibilities: "Do you have information on high technology?" "I'm looking for something on children's reading." "Where do you keep your travel books?" "I would like to find recent research on allergies." "I'm looking for your pet section." "I'd like a book on racing." "Can you help me find some information on milk products?" "Could you direct me to your map section?" "Where are your materials on breast cancer?" "Do you have any books on witchcraft?" "I'm looking for information on plants."

ANALYZE THIS REFERENCE TRANSACTION

Case 12: Jumping to conclusions

Librarian: Can I help you?

User: Do you have a sports section?

Librarian: Yes, we do have a sports section. (acknowledgment) What specifically were you looking for? (open question)

User: Something on golf.

Librarian: Golf? (acknowledgment)

User: I want to learn to play golf.

Librarian: [Librarian walks with user to the shelves and shows him the books on learning to play golf.] You're not introducing golf to your wife, are you? (closed question that makes an assumption)

User: I am single.

Librarian: [laughs]

User: I'd have to find a wife first.

Comment: In Anne Tyler's novel The Accidental Tourist, the central character, Muriel, is a dog-care provider who is interested in starting a relationship with another character, Macon. She angles to find out about his marital status by asking, "Can't you leave [your dog] home with your wife?" so that she won't waste her time on an unlikely prospect. Unlike Muriel, the librarian in this interview transaction may just have been making small talk, but the question about a wife did seem to startle the user and sidetrack the interview. In general, closed questions that make assumptions about the user should be avoided.

From Dewdney, Golf

User:	It's for myself. To brush up.
Librarian:	What sort of thing are you wanting to brush up in?
User:	Pie charts. You see, I have to write a report for my work and need to be able to use pie charts and graphs, but I can't figure out how to make them on the computer.

DID YOU KNOW?

In 1981, in a series of workshops called Turning Public Libraries Around (TPLA), Brenda Dervin began teaching librarians a new strategy for asking questions in the reference interview. During these workshops, she first labeled the strategy "neutral questioning," a term that has been used in the literature, especially in Dervin and Dewdney's article "Neutral Questioning: A New Approach to the Reference Interview" (1986). Although the term sense-making questioning is now being used, the strategy is the same: Ask questions the answers to which help the information-provider understand the context of the information need.

Asking closed questions at the beginning of the reference interview almost always involves the librarian in making assumptions. Often the assumption involved is of the following order: this aspect of topic X is most important to *me* and therefore it must be the most important thing for the user too. Such assumptions, when they are mistaken (as so often they are), lead to questions that are not salient for the user and hence not readily answered. More problematic are personal questions such as "Is this something for your child?" which run the danger of offending the user.

3.2.3 SENSE-MAKING QUESTIONS

Open questions are effective at getting people talking. But what we said earlier about the contextualized nature of people's questions (section 1.4) implies that librarians have to do more than just get users talking. They have to get them to talk about the context of the question. Sometimes asking an open question is all that is needed to encourage the user to talk about contexts, but often users need more guidance. They need to be told what information the staff member needs to know in order to do her job. A good way of guiding the reference interview into useful channels is to ask a special form of open question that we used to call "neutral questions." We now call them "sense-making questions" because this type of questioning technique is derived from Dr. Brenda Dervin's Sense-making theory. Sense-making questions provide more structure than open questions, but are less likely to lead to premature diagnosis than closed questions.

The strategy of sense-making grew out of three decades of Dervin's research on how people seek and use information. Dervin uses the term *sense-making* to refer to her model of information seeking, which really deals with how people "make sense" of the world. According to this model, information needs grow out of specific situations in a person's life. Individuals go through their everyday lives, trying to make sense out of what is happening, seeking certain outcomes, and trying to avoid others. Sometimes people can't achieve particular goals by themselves and turn to other people for help. For example, they have to fill out an income tax form, but they don't understand the difference between an expense and a capital cost, so they go to an accountant. If they are looking for a job and need tips on how to write a résumé, they go to the public library for a book on writing a résumé.

In general, then, people often have some gap in understanding that must be filled in before they can achieve a goal. If it is your job to provide help, you need to know three things: (1) the *situation* the person is in, (2) the *gaps* in his or her understanding, and (3) the *uses* or helps—what the person would like to do as a re-

A QUICK TIP

WAIT FOR THE ANSWER

After you have asked your question ("What would you like to know about endangered species?"), wait for the answer. Don't succumb to the common temptation to turn your open question into a closed question by guessing, "Do you need statistics?"

EXERCISE

CLOSED QUESTIONS ARE NOT FASTER

This exercise can be done with a group. Get a 30-sided die of the sort used in games like Dungeons and Dragons. Throw the die, note the number, and ask group members to find out from you what the number was by asking you closed questions (e.g., "Is it 30? Is it less than 15? Is it an even number?"). Ask one member of the group to keep track of how many questions it took before the correct number was guessed. Then throw the die again and ask the group to find out from you what the number was this time by asking you open questions (e.g., "What is the number?"). The point of this exercise is that guessing is not faster.

sult of bridging this gap. In order to understand the question fully, the librarian needs to know all three of these elements. How do you find out these three things? Ask sense-making questions. A *sense-making question* is a special kind of open question that asks specifically about situations, or gaps, or helps.

To clarify the differences among closed, open, and sense-making questions, consider this situation of a user who asks for information on travel.

EXAMPLE

1. **User:** Excuse me, but can you tell me where to find information on travel?

   Librarian: Would you like a book on travel—a travel guide? (*closed question* that makes an assumption)

   User: Yes, I guess so. Thanks.

   Librarian: Our travel guides are over there [points to shelves].

In this case, the librarian does not discover anything about either the situation or the gap or the uses.

2. **User:** Excuse me, but can you tell me where to find information on travel?

   Librarian: What sort of travel information do you have in mind? (*open question* that encourages the user to say more)

   User: Information on New York City. I'm traveling there next month.

   Librarian: We have several good travel guides to New York City. Here's the *Fodor's Guide*, etc.

In this case, the librarian finds out the situation (making a trip to New York City), but does not discover the gap or the uses.

3. **User:** Excuse me but can you tell me where to find information on travel?

   Librarian: We have quite a lot of travel information in different parts of the library. If you could tell me how you would be using this information, I could help you find something. (*sense-making question* focusing on uses)

   User: I need New York City information. I'd like to read up on plays that will be on in New York next month so that I can order some tickets in advance.

A QUICK TIP

HERE'S WHAT I WANT TO DO

Using the sense-making framework is useful in everyday contexts as well. Jane Houston posted this tip to LIBREF (August 26, 1997): "I finally have learned to tell the hardware store clerk, 'Well, I'm not sure what I want, but let me tell you what I'm planning to do and perhaps you can help me.' Needless to say, it works like a charm." (Thanks to Jane Houston, Reference Coordinator in the Government Information Center in the Idaho State Library, Boise, Idaho.)

EXERCISE

CLARIFYING THE QUESTION

If someone asked you for information on China, what kinds of materials do you think would prove most helpful? The graphic (Jordan, 1986) shows some different meanings the term might have for the user.

DO YOU HAVE ANY MATERIAL ON CHINA?

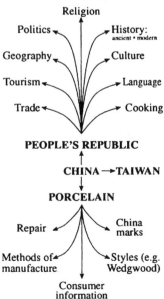

Librarian: OK, you want to learn about what's playing in New York so that you can order tickets. (*acknowledgment*) You'll need really current information for that, and so the Internet would be a good place to look, etc.

In this case, the librarian finds out all three elements: the situation (the user is making a trip to New York City), the gap (what plays will be on in New York during the visit), and the use (the user wants to be able to order theater tickets in advance).

To consider another example, suppose a user asks, "Do you have anything about crime?" The librarian can ask *closed* questions that involve making assumptions and that invite short answers: "Do you want criminal law? Do you want a crime story? Do you want statistics?" The librarian can ask an *open* question that encourages the user to talk: "What are you interested in?" "What more can you tell me about your question?" Or the librarian can ask a *sense-making* question focused on the situation, gap, or use, such as "What are you working on?" "What would you like to know about crime?" or "How would you like the information to help you?"

Answering these sense-making questions, the user might respond, "I've been looking in this index under crime, but I can't find anything on the James Bulger case" or "I want the address of the Crime Writers of America" or "I need statistics of the crime rate in Florida for a school project." Following up with a second neutral question in a process that Dervin calls "help-chaining," the staff member could ask, "If we could find X, how would *that* help you?" This will usually elicit more details about the context of the question: "I'm compiling information on a list of cases involving very young children who have committed homicide" or "I've written a detective story that's sure to be a bestseller if only I can find the right publisher" or "I need to get ready for a debate on the efficacy of capital punishment."

We know from extensive research on people's information-seeking behavior that the kind of answer that is most helpful depends on the use they plan for the information—what it will help them do. Someone writing a short essay on the symptoms of Alzheimer's disease, for example, will need a different kind of material (and hence require a different reference source) than will a person who is trying to find out about the best care for a relative suffering from the disease. Until you know how the user hopes the information will help, you will not be able to make effective use of your knowledge of reference sources. In a Norwegian study that observed and audiotaped the interactions between users and li-

---

SOME SENSE-MAKING QUESTIONS

Here are some examples of good sense-making questions to ask when you want to help someone but must first determine the precise nature of what would help:

To encourage the person to describe the situation:
What are you working on?
How did this question arise?
What happened that you need to know this?

To find out how the person sees his or her situation:
What problem are you having in this situation?
Where would you like to begin?
Where do you see yourself going with this?

To assess the gaps:
What kind of help would you like?
What are you trying to understand?
What would you like to know about X?
Where did you get stuck with this project?

To identify the kind of help wanted (uses):
What would help you?
How do you plan to use this information?
What would you like to see happen in this situation?
What are you trying to do in this situation?
If you could have exactly the help you want, what would it be?

---

brarians during reference transactions, Ragnar Nordlie (2000) noted that only 6 percent of the questions that librarians asked users were concerned with the users' purpose or plan for using the information. In contrast, purpose was the second most frequent theme of users' own voluntary contributions, occurring in 30 percent of cases. When librarians discovered they needed to change the direction of their search, the most frequent cause for modifying the search was discovery of the user's purpose.

When we teach the skill of sense-making questions in workshops, we find that participants sometimes report reservations about asking for the context of a question when the situation might turn out to be personal or embarrassing. Potentially embarrassing situations include, unfortunately, most of the human situations in which people desperately need help: situations of

DID YOU KNOW?

Dewdney and Michell (1997) draw on speech act theory to explain the linguistic reasons that "why" questions are often misinterpreted: It's because the user doesn't understand their relevance. The problem is that the librarian's "why" question does not fit into the user's mental model, such as it is, of a reference interview. The librarian can avoid misunderstandings by prefacing questions about intended uses with an explanation such as, "I could help you better if I knew something more about how you plan to use this information."

WHY NOT ASK "WHY?" DIRECTLY?

Library professionals have long recognized that they can be most helpful if they understand the user's intended purposes. Moreover, most users are quite willing to explain how they plan to use the information if you ask the question appropriately. There are four guidelines for asking this question:

1. Never ask "why?" directly. "Why do you want to know that?" sounds abrupt and possibly judgmental. It runs the risk of the user's responding, "What's it to you why I want to know?" or even "None of your business." Moreover, "why" questions aren't necessarily efficient at eliciting answers about situations or uses because users might not understand why you are asking why. They may say, "Because this library is closest," "Because the teacher told me to ask," or "Because I can't find what I want." If pushed into a corner by a direct "why" question, some users may deliberately conceal their personal interest ("It's for a friend."). (See section 5.3.1.)

2. Make it clear that you are asking about intended uses because it is your business. You are not just prying. You are an information professional who can do the job better and provide more helpful sources if you know how the information will be used. If the user says, "Where do you keep your Alzheimer's information?" you could say, "We have a lot of material on Alzheimer's—it all depends on what you're looking for. Can you tell me a bit about how you plan to use this information?" or "I could help you better if I knew what you are trying to do."

3. Avoid assumptions. A user who looks like a student could be asking the question for personal reasons, while an older, harried-looking person might be trying to get a few statistics for an assignment due tomorrow in a continuing education course. Let users tell you themselves what they are trying to do. Don't guess. Don't ask, "Is this for a school project?"

4. Leave the user in control. When you ask a sense-making question like "How do you plan to use this information?" users can say as much or as little they want. They may tell you the whole context, which will help you suggest the most appropriate material. But they might also say, "Oh, I'm just interested," a response that lets you know they don't want to say anything further just now.

EXERCISE

A COSTLY MISUNDERSTANDING

The user of a branch library asked for "a book on bats." "Bats as in the animal? not baseball bats?" asked the librarian, using acknowledgment to solve the homophone problem (see section 1.4.1). "Bats that fly, yes," confirmed the user. So the librarian ordered the book from the central library and within a week was pleased to present the user with a new natural history book with a hundred color plates and everything you could possibly want to know about bats. But not quite everything; the user was very disappointed. "I wanted to know how to get rid of them," he said.

1. What could the librarian have asked the user to avoid this misunderstanding?
2. What could be the economic consequences of this misunderstanding? Might there be other consequences? How serious are they from the viewpoint of the user? from the viewpoint of the branch librarian? from the viewpoint of headquarters?
3. If you were the headquarters librarian and had received this request for a book on bats, what would you have done? What training or procedures would help to avoid this problem in the future?
4. What are the policy implications of this example?

bereavement, serious illness, and approaching death; situations of family problems, sexual dysfunction, divorce; situations of job loss and economic hardship. Something worth asking parenthetically is this: Whose embarrassment are we as library professionals really concerned about—the user's embarrassment in revealing something personal about himself or our own in hearing it? If it is our own embarrassment, then we will be more comfortable *not* asking sense-making questions and simply saying to the user, "We have some materials on crime/health/small businesses over there, and if you just look through those you might find something." The downside to this hands-off approach is that it deprives the user of your professional help in finding the appropriate source.

But if it is the user's embarrassment that solely concerns us, it may be reassuring to remember that sense-making questions leave the user in control. In response to a sense-making question, the user can say as much or as little as he chooses. He can say, "My niece has just been diagnosed with Non-Hodgkin's Lymphoma and I want to read about treatment and survival rates." But he doesn't have to. He could say, "Oh, I'd like to just browse in the medical books, thanks." He need not say any more about his situation than he feels comfortable revealing. You could respond with, "Here are the medical books along these shelves. But if you don't find what you're looking for, let me know because we have additional information in other places, including in electronic sources." This way, the user can return later if he has not been able to find the information on his own.

Librarians do not normally ask sense-making questions as a matter of course. But they can learn to use this skill and they can use it intentionally, as Dewdney (1986) demonstrated in her doctoral thesis, "The Effects of Training Reference Librarians in Interview Skills." Twenty-four practicing librarians in three relatively large public libraries volunteered to participate in a field experiment. One-third received no training, one-third were trained in microskills, and one-third were trained in the use of neutral, or sense-making questions. Before and after the training period, tape recordings were made of 332 interviews between each librarian and the adult users who presented an information need. In addition, 236 of these users were interviewed afterward by a research assistant, who asked what kind of help was wanted and how helpful was the answer provided. Users received significantly more helpful answers from librarians trained in sense-making questioning, in comparison with librarians trained in microskills and with untrained librarians.

SOME QUICK TIPS

PRACTICE AND PERSIST

Any new skill takes practice before it can be used with confidence. As a way of getting started using this skill, pick two questions from the list SOME SENSE-MAKING QUESTIONS and use them until you feel comfortable with them. Observe what happens when you ask these questions. This experience in real situations will help you understand the function of sense-making questions.

Be prepared to ask more than one question. If the first sense-making question you ask doesn't produce enough information for you to recognize whether a source would be helpful, follow it up with a different one.

In our workshops on the reference interview, a frequently asked question is "When someone asks for something specific, do I still need to conduct a reference interview?" As is well known, people often ask for a particular title or reference tool such as Charles Dickens's *A Christmas Carol* or the *Encyclopaedia Britannica*. A reference interview might seem redundant because the user obviously knows what's wanted. But are you sure? Our advice is that if the requested item is easy to provide, then by all means give it to the user along with the follow-up "If this doesn't have everything you need, make sure you come back" (see section 4.1.3). However, if the specific source or person asked for is unavailable or hard to access, a good rule of thumb is *not* to say, "Would you like us to recall that book?" or "Come back in three weeks when our German specialist has returned from her vacation." The user, not familiar with the whole range of sources available, might have asked by name for the one source he happens to know about, but the library may have additional or better sources.

When you find yourself about to suggest an interlibrary loan or about to refer the user to another library or agency, try saying this first: "Perhaps there's something else that would help you. What sort of information are you looking for?" In the case of *A Christmas Carol*, for example, it turned out that all copies were out. But the librarian was able to determine that the user wanted to put on a play with her grade seven class and was thinking of making a play out of Dickens's Christmas story. The librarian was then able to provide a collected edition of Christmas plays for children that included a dramatic version of *A Christmas Carol*. When the reference transaction has been most successful, users have been helped to achieve whatever goal it was that brought them to the library.

EXERCISE

SENSE-MAKING QUESTIONS

Try this exercise in pairs. Before starting, copy each scenario onto a separate card. Make up more scenarios of your own. For the exercise, one person plays the role of the user and is given one of the scenarios below. The other person is a librarian who asks sense-making questions to find out what the user really wants to know. The librarian should have close at hand the list SOME SENSE-MAKING QUESTIONS, and should keep asking sense-making questions until the user is satisfied that the question is really understood.

Scenario 1: User is a student who has to write an English essay, which is to be "a close analysis of the text" of some American colonial poem. He doesn't have a fixed topic in mind, and his first problem is that he doesn't know what is meant by "a close analysis of the text." He asks, "Where is the section on American poetry?"

Scenario 2: User is planning to take the Police College entrance exam and wants to prepare himself as much as possible in advance. He has heard that there is often a question about proverbs. He says, "I'm having trouble with this catalog."

Scenario 3: User has a neighbor who is building an addition to his house right up to the property line. The user wants to find out whether there are any building codes that would prevent this building from going up. She asks, "Where is your law section?"

Scenario 4: User wants to write a letter to a local author, saying how much she enjoyed the author's most recent book. She thinks that current information about where the author lives may be on the book jacket. She says, "I'm looking for [recent title] by [fairly well-known author] but it's not on the shelf. (In this scenario, the person taking the user's role should use the name of an author who comes from the local region.)

Scenario 5: User thinks that ingesting caffeine could be causing ringing in his ears. Therefore he wants to be able to identify foods containing caffeine so as to avoid them. He already knows that coffee, tea, chocolate, and certain soda drinks contain caffeine, but he wants to know if there are any other foods that he should avoid. He asks, "Where is your section on drugs?"

Scenario 6: User is worried about a change in her daughter Laura's behavior that has happened recently. Laura used to be a straight A student in her high school, but recently her grades have dropped. She has stopped seeing her previous friends and is hanging out with a group of kids that are not doing well in school. She has become uncommunicative and rebellious. The mother has heard that drugs can cause behavior changes. She asks, "Where is your section on drugs?"

EXERCISE

PLAYING TWENTY QUESTIONS

This role-playing exercise can be done as a group exercise, with two volunteers playing the parts of the user and librarian and the rest of the group as observers. Before the exercise begins, cards must be prepared for the users' roles. Each user card includes a single initial question that the user asks, plus a scenario that gives some background information about the question. Some examples are presented here. Think up scenarios of your own for additional cards.

SCENARIOS

Initial question: "Where is your agriculture section?" The user wants to know what makes Mexican jumping beans jump.

Initial question: "I'm interested in information on Disney." The user is taking a leisure studies course and has to write a short assignment on Disney theme parks. Specifically, the user needs to know about the Disney theme park in France: how long it has been open, how many people on average visit it, and any special features about it.

Initial question: "Where is your literature section?" The user is a member of a book group who wants to bring to the next meeting a list of local authors who write adult fiction. The user is interested in both literary fiction and popular fiction in any genre.

Initial question: "Do you have information on snow conditions?" The user wants to know what the skiing is like in Colorado in February.

Initial question: "I was looking for something by Barbara Kingsolver, but I can't find it on the shelf." The user has read all of Barbara Kingsolver's fiction and would like to read High Tide in Tucson, a collection of essays.

ROLES

User role: The user presents the initial question and thereafter answers only closed questions, responding "yes," "no," "this," or "that." The user must be careful not to volunteer any information and not to answer if, by mistake, the librarian asks an open question before the three-minute time limit is up.

Librarian role: The librarian is instructed to find out as quickly as possible what this user wants to know, using only closed questions.

Observer role: Observers watch to make sure that all questions are closed, to count the number of closed questions asked, and to call time if the librarian does not discover the true query in three minutes. If the query is not fully negotiated in three minutes, the librarian may at this point ask open questions and the user improvises answers according to the scenario on the card.

DISCUSSION

After each role-play, the group leader may ask the observers to analyze what happened in the interview: which questions worked, which didn't, what was the difference between asking open questions and closed question, etc.

3.2.4 REFLECTING CONTENT: PARAPHRASING AND SUMMARIZING

After you have asked some open or sense-making questions, it is good practice to summarize what you have understood, just to make sure that you have a complete and accurate picture. Reflecting content is a way of communicating that you have been listening. Moreover, like acknowledgment, this skill gives you a chance to check that your understanding is correct. When you reflect content, you are not supplying any new information of your own. You are mirroring back to the user what you have understood. If you have gotten something wrong or left something out, the user has a chance to provide a correction. The two major ways to reflect content are *paraphrasing* and *summarizing*.

PARAPHRASING

Paraphrasing feeds back what has been said in the previous comment. In the reference interview, paraphrasing is prepared for by an introductory clause such as:

> So you're looking for . . .
> What you need is . . .
> You mean . . .
> As I understand you . . .

plus a concise summary giving the essence of what you think was meant.

Example of paraphrasing:
User: All the leaves are falling off my poinsettia and I need some help.
Librarian: So you're looking for plant care information for your poinsettia? Is that it?

Tips for paraphrasing:
  Be concise. Usually a short pithy sentence is enough.
  Feed back the essence by restating what you understand to be the main idea of what was just said.
  Try not to add to or change the meaning of what you have heard.
  You may want to use a checkout such as, "Is that what you wanted?" or "Was that it?"

SUMMARIZING

Summarizing is like paraphrasing except that it covers a larger span of conversation and requires you to distill the essence of what was said over the course of a longer series of questions and answers. It may be used as a good conclusion to an interview before you start looking for sources.

Example of summarizing:
Librarian: So you are doing a project on the tobacco industry for your media studies course. And you would like to find some analyses of recent class-action lawsuits against tobacco companies. You also want to know if there has been any recent legislation that is relevant to tobacco advertising. You need it soon because your project is due on Friday. Have I got that right?

Tips for summarizing:
Synthesize the gist of what was said in the course of a number of previous statements.
Condense.
Go for the big picture.

3.2.5 CLOSURE

Closure is the art of the tactful ending. It really consists of a cluster of skills that are used to signal leave-taking. We are all familiar with some of the ritualistic nonverbal skills that signal the end of any conversation: changes in body orientation, such as moving away from the other person, or changes in eye contact, such as looking toward an exit or a clock. Sometimes, however, these nonverbal cues give the other person a feeling of being suddenly cut off. To return the topic of discussion back to the purpose of the interview or to wrap up a conversation smoothly, you may want to use the verbal skills of closure. Some functions of closure are:

- to indicate that discussion of a topic has been completed, at least for the moment,
- to focus the participant's attention on what has been achieved in the discussion,
- to establish a good communication climate so that the other person looks forward to the next encounter (Hargie, Saunders, and Dickson, 1994: 162–63).

In the reference interview, you should use closure when the conversation is wandering, bringing the talk back to the purpose of the interview. Don't make the mistake of cutting the other per-

A QUICK TIP

CLOSURE THAT HELPS

Closure can also be used when you realize you're going to have to refer the user to someone else. For example: "This sounds like a pretty technical topic, so what I'd like to do is find our science and technology librarian." The difference between this use of closure and the unmonitored referral, which is a strategy of negative closure (section 3.1.5), is that here you are monitoring the referral by making sure that the science and technology librarian is available and is in fact the person who can help.

son off midsentence or of changing the subject abruptly. Not only will you be perceived as impolite, but the other person may, despite appearances, have been telling you something that is important to your understanding of the problem. However, when it is apparent that the conversation is clearly off track, you can get back to the point tactfully by acknowledging what the other person is saying and then moving quickly back (not pausing) to the main purpose of the conversation. You might say, "Yes, it sounds like your daughter's graduation dress will be very suitable. Now about your genealogy project—what information are you interested in today?" Knowing the effect of the questions you ask enables you to choose an appropriate questioning style—using open questions to encourage the reticent person to talk about what concerns her but practicing closure to focus digressers.

The second way to use closure is to signal the end of an interaction. If the conversation has been brief, perhaps all that is necessary is a one-phrase summary or a comment to suggest future steps, such as, "So now you know how to request an interlibrary loan" or "Next time you'll know that we have other material that's not in the catalog." In almost all reference transactions, it's a good idea to use a follow-up question (see section 4.1.3) that will provide you with a chance to confirm that the user has gotten what she or he wanted, as well as to close the conversation: "If you find that you can't get logged on, please be sure to come back and ask again."

The skill of closure is a way to be helpful and keep the interview on track. This skill should not be confused with what we call negative closure, which is a way to get rid of the user without providing a helpful answer (see section 3.1.5).

3.3 ANNOTATED REFERENCES

3.3.1 COMMON PROBLEMS IN THE REFERENCE INTERVIEW

Bunge, Charles A. 1985. "Factors Related to Reference Question Answering Success: The Development of a Data-Gathering Form." *RQ* 24, no. 4 (summer): 482–86. Identifies factors that lead to success and failure.

Dewdney, Patricia, and Catherine Sheldrick Ross. 1994. "Flying a Light Aircraft: Reference Evaluation from a User's Viewpoint." *RQ* 34, no. 2 (winter): 217–30. Describes user reactions toward librarians' use of acknowledgment, questioning skills, giving instructions, and making referrals.

Douglas, Ian. 1988. "Reducing Failures in Reference Service." *RQ* 28, no. 1 (fall): 94–101.

Durrance, Joan. 1995. "Factors that Influence Reference Success." *The Reference Librarian* 49/50: 243–65.

Lynch, Mary Jo. 1978. "Reference Interviews in Public Libraries." *Library Quarterly* 48, no. 2 (April): 119–42. Lynch reports her research done for her doctoral degree at Rutgers in which she tape-recorded reference transactions in public libraries.

Murfin, Marjorie, and Charles Bunge. 1984. "Evaluating Reference Service from the Patron Point of View: Some Interim National Survey Results." *The Reference Librarian* 11: 175–82.

Ross, Catherine Sheldrick, and Patricia Dewdney. 1994. "Best Practices: An Analysis of the Best (and Worst) in Fifty-two Public Library Reference Transactions." *Public Libraries* 33, no. 5 (September/October): 261–66. Contrasts the best and worst and provides some practical suggestions for improving service.

———. 1998. "Negative Closure: Strategies and Counter-Strategies in the Reference Interview." *Reference and User Services Quarterly* 38, no. 2 (winter): 151–64. Examines ways that librarians get rid of the user, apart from providing a helpful answer.

Ross, Catherine Sheldrick, and Kirsti Nilsen. 2000. "So Has the Internet Changed Anything in Reference? The Library Visit Study, Phase 2." *Reference & User Services Quarterly* 40, no. 2 (winter): 147–55.

Zweizig, Douglas L. 1976. "With Our Eye on the User." *Drexel Library Quarterly* 12, nos. 1/2 (January/April): 48-58.

3.3.2 WORKS OF RELEVANCE TO THE REFERENCE INTERVIEW IN GENERAL

American Library Association, Reference and User Services Association. 1996. "Guidelines for Behavioral Performance of Reference and Information Services Professionals." *RQ* 36, no. 2 (winter): 200-203. Also available online at www.ala.org/rusa/stnd_behavior.html [17 February 2002]. Includes techniques for showing approachability, interest, listening/inquiring, searching and providing follow-up.

Hargie, Owen, Christine Saunders, and David Dickson. 1994. *Social Skills in Interpersonal Communication.* 3d ed. London: Routledge. The authors use a skills-based model to describe basic interpersonal strategies.

Ivey, Allen E., and Mary Bradford Ivey. 1999. *Intentional Interviewing and Counseling: Facilitating Client Development in a Multicultural Society.* 4th ed. Pacific Grove, Calif.: Brooks/Cole. The latest edition of this classic work focuses more on solution-centered and person-centered interviewing and relates these to microskills. It includes an expanded section on listening skills and a new emphasis on solution-oriented interviewing. The *Instructor's Resource Guide* is published separately.

Jennerich, Elaine Z., and Edward J. Jennerich. 1997. *The Reference Interview as a Creative Art.* 2d ed. Littleton, Colo.: Libraries Unlimited. Using a metaphor of reference interview as dramatic production, this book discusses verbal and nonverbal skills for the reference interview in a chapter called "The

Actor's Tools." This book builds on the pioneering work done by Elaine Jennerich in her doctoral dissertation, "Microcounseling in Library Education," University of Pittsburgh, 1974.

Lesikar, Raymond V., John D. Pettit Jr., and Marie E. Flatley. 1996. *Lesikar's Basic Business Communication*. 7th ed. Chicago: Irwin. Useful sections on speaking skills.

Malbin, Susan L. 1997. "The Reference Interview in Archival Literature." *College and Research Libraries* 58, no. 1 (January): 69-80. A review essay on the writing about reference from within the archival field. Malbin concludes that the reference interview and communication skills for successful query negotiation have not been studied or taught within the archival setting, to the detriment of service to the user.

Nolan, Christopher W. 1992. "Closing the Reference Interview: Implications for Policy and Practice." *RQ* 31, no. 4 (summer): 513–23.

Ohio Library Council. 2000. *Ohio Reference Excellence (ORE) on the Web* [online]. Available: www.olc.org/ore/2intro.htm [17 February 2002]. The Ohio Library Council has produced a very useful Web-based training program on the Reference Interview, which it calls "the key to the reference process." Skills covered in the ORE program include paraphrasing, asking open questions, clarifying, verifying, following up, and ending the interview.

Radford, Marie L. 1999. *The Reference Encounter: Interpersonal Communication in the Academic Library*. Chicago: Association of College and Research Libraries. Finds that users and librarians have different perceptions of what is happening in the reference transaction.

———. 1996. "Communication Theory Applied to the Reference Encounter: An Analysis of Critical Incidents." *The Library Quarterly* 66, no. 2 (April): 123–37.

White, Marilyn Domas. 1998. "Questions in Reference Interviews." *Journal of Documentation* 54, no. 4 (September): 443–65. Categorizes the types of questions asked in a presearch interview before delegated online searching, and finds that about half the questions were verification questions such as "Have you looked at *Psych Abs* yet?"

———. 1989. "Different Approaches to the Reference Interview." *The Reference Librarian* 25/26: 631–46. Distinguishes between two models of reference interview behavior: the Needs-Oriented Model and the Question-Oriented Model.

Whitlatch, Jo Bell, ed. 1995. "Question Classification." In *The Reference Assessment Manual*. Ann Arbor, Mich: Pierian Press.

3.3.3 QUESTIONING SKILLS

American Library Association. 1992. *Does This Completely Answer Your Question?* Produced by Library Video Network. 16 min. Videocassette. Shows how to use questioning, paraphrasing, and follow-up skills. Useful for stimulating discussion with new or experienced librarians.

Dervin, Brenda, and Patricia Dewdney. 1986. "Neutral Questioning: A New Approach to the Reference Interview." *RQ* 25, no. 4 (summer): 506–13. Explains the theory and practice of sense-making questions. Readers who want to find out more about Brenda Dervin's Sense-making Methodology can find articles, papers, and commentaries on sense-making at http://communication.sbs.ohio-state.edu/sense-making/ [17 February 2002].

Dewdney, Patricia H. 1986. "The Effects of Training Reference Librarians in Interview Skills: A Field Experiment." Ph.D. diss., University of Western Ontario. (Microform, National Library of Canada.) Reports a field experiment in which 24 experienced reference librarians from three Ontario public libraries were observed both before and after training in specific listening and questioning skills.

Dewdney, Patricia, and Gillian Michell. 1997. "Asking 'Why' Questions in the Reference Interview: A Theoretical Justification." *Library Quarterly* 67, no. 1 (January): 50-71. Explains the linguistic reasons that "why" questions are often misinterpreted and suggests other strategies for finding out "why." This article is a good starting point for references on research on question-asking from the literature of linguistics as well as from the library literature.

Dyson, Lillie Seward. 1992. "Improving Reference Services: A Maryland Training Program Brings Positive Results." *Public Libraries* 31, no. 5 (September/October): 284–89.

Gers, Ralph, and Lillie J. Seward. 1985. "Improving Reference Performance: Results of a Statewide Study." *Library Journal* 110, no. 8 (November 1): 32–35.

Gothberg, Helen M., ed. 1995. "Communication and the Reference Interface." In *The Reference Assessment Manual*. Ann Arbor, Mich.: Pierian Press.

Isenstein, Laura. 1992. "Get Your Reference Staff on the STAR Track." *Library Journal* 117, no. 7 (April 15): 34–37. Describes a program for training reference staff to use open questions, paraphrase, and follow-up.

Jordan, Peter. 1986. "Training in Handling Library Users." In *Handbook of Library Training Practice*, edited by Ray Prytherch. Aldershot, Hants, England; Brookfield, Vt.: Gower.

King, Geraldine B. 1972. "The Reference Interview: Open and Closed Questions." *RQ* 12, no. 2 (winter): 157-60.

Lynch, Mary Jo. 1978. "Reference Interviews in Public Libraries." *Library Quarterly* 48, no. 2 (April): 119–42. Analyzes 309 reference interviews recorded in public libraries in order to find out how often a reference interview occurs and what proportion of the questions asked by the staff member are open or closed.

Nordlie, Ragnar. 2000. "Conversing with the Catalogue: How the Reference Interview Can Inform Online Catalogue Searching." *Scandinavian Public Library Quarterly* 33, no. 2: 22–27. This study used two sets of data gathered in Norwegian public libraries—transaction logs of end-user searches, and audiotaped and transcribed reference transactions—to see what online catalog designers could learn from reference interactions.

Ross, Catherine Sheldrick. 1986. "How to Find Out What People Really Want to Know." *The Reference Librarian* 16 (winter): 19-30. Theory and practice of open and sense-making (neutral) questions.

Ross, Catherine Sheldrick, and Patricia Dewdney. 1986. "Reference Interviewing Skills: Twelve Common Questions." *Public Libraries* 25, no. 1 (spring): 7–9.

3.3.4 REFLECTING CONTENT AND FEELING

Dickson, David A. 1997. "Reflecting." In *The Handbook of Communication Skills*, edited by Owen D. W. Hargie, 2d ed. London and New York: Routledge. This scholarly overview of verbal and nonverbal reflecting behavior may be useful to trainers.

Evans, David R., Margaret Hearn, Max Uhlemann, and Allen Ivey. 1998. *Essential Interviewing: A Programmed Approach to Effective Communication*. 5th ed. Monterey, Calif.: Brooks/Cole. Chapter 4 in this workbook deals with reflecting feeling; Chapter 5 deals with reflecting content.

3.3.5 CLOSURE

Ross, Catherine Sheldrick, and Patricia Dewdney. 1986. "Reference Interviewing Skills: Twelve Common Questions." *Public Libraries* 25, no. 1 (spring): 7–9.

3.3.6 INCLUSION

Michell, Gillian, and Roma M. Harris. 1987. "Evaluating the Reference Interview: Some Factors Influencing Patrons and Professionals." *RQ* 27, no. 1 (fall): 95-105. Reports an experiment in which the level of inclusion was varied in videotaped reference interviews that were evaluated by both public library users and librarians.

White, Marilyn Domas. 1981. "The Dimensions of the Reference Interview." *RQ* 20, no. 4 (summer): 373–81. Describes how the librarian can increase the coherence of the reference interview by explaining to the user what is happening.

4 MOVING BEYOND NEGATIVE CLOSURE

In this chapter . . .

4.1 SKILLS FOR WORKING TOGETHER

In *Information Ecologies*, Bonnie Nardi and Vicki O'Day describe librarians as a "keystone species"—one of the species in an ecology whose loss leads to the extinction of other species in the ecosystem. They say, "We believe that the diverse services available in the library are still important and useful, and we believe that the increase in online information presents more opportunities to leverage the skills of professional librarians than ever before. Through our fieldwork in libraries, we have identified librarians as a keystone species." They argue that the work of librarians is not well understood (or appreciated) because so much of it is invisible work. One of the most valuable and unrecognized services that they identified is "to help clients understand their own needs—a kind of information therapy" (1999: 85).

What they are talking about, of course, is the reference interview, a creative problem-solving process that is collaborative. Few library users, even experienced ones, have ever heard of the reference interview or know that they are being interviewed. But through the questions they answer during a well-conducted reference interview, they are able to clarify in their own minds what their question really is. This narrowing and clarifying process is most evident in situations such as school assignments for which the user often has no idea of how much is available in a particular area. The librarian's questions help the user narrow a topic (e.g., plant adaptations) to a manageable topic for a science project (e.g., the carnivorous diet of the pitcher plant as an adaptation to life in an acidic bog). At the end of the process, the library professional and user, by working together, have achieved a new understanding that neither could have arrived at individually.

A good reference interview is a collaboration. User and staff member are equal partners in the search, with different areas of expertise. The user is the expert in the question itself and knows how the question arose, what necessary information is missing in her understanding of the topic, and how the information will be used. The staff member is the expert on the library system and the organization and retrieval of information. Both need to work together. The staff member can't find the most appropriate sources without the user's active collaboration, and vice versa. By asking questions to clarify the real information need and working with the user in checking what is available, the staff member can help the user clarify in her own mind what information is wanted, but the user needs to be kept engaged in the process.

It is important to emphasize the user as active agent because, in so much of the published literature on reference service, the user's question is considered largely as an "input" into the system. As one user in the Library Visit study lamented, "I felt that once I had handed over my question, the question developed a life of its own apart from me and I was no longer of interest to the librarians. Only the question was of interest. Neither of them asked me any questions concerning my question." In this construction of the user role as passive bystander, the user gets the ball rolling by asking the initiating question, but after that it's the librarian who takes charge, asks the questions during the reference interview, finds the sources, evaluates the sources, gives directions and advice, and so on. The user is there mainly to tag along, answer the librarian's questions during the reference interview, and receive the answer at the end.

In contrast, our research on users has led us to construct a picture of an active user energetically pursuing goals. In successful transactions, the staff members help the users achieve their goals; in unsuccessful transactions, staff members are obstacles and stumbling blocks that users have to work around. In the latter cases, when users experience negative closure, they often adopt strategies of their own to elicit more help from library staff and keep staff from giving up too soon. Users in general want to be accepted as active partners in the search and are most satisfied with their experience when library staff members take steps to involve them. In the next section we consider three skills for getting beyond negative closure by making the user an active partner: inclusion, bibliographic instruction, and the follow-up.

DID YOU KNOW?

According to Nardi and O'Day, librarians are able to be helpful because they start with a more accurate mental model of the information system and, during the course of the reference interview, develop a more or less accurate model of the user's needs: "The librarian contributes to the client's activity and to do so effectively, creates a representation of the activity that guides and focuses the search. This representation goes beyond understanding the client's task, simplistically conceived, to a broader contextual sketch of the client, including the client's preferences, constraints, and environment" (1996: 75).

DID YOU KNOW?

In a controlled experiment conducted by Michell and Harris (1987), librarians who demonstrated the skill of inclusion in the reference interview were judged to be more effective information providers under certain conditions. This study suggests that males and females may perceive the use of inclusion differently.

4.1.1 INCLUSION: TELLING PEOPLE WHAT YOU ARE DOING

You can prevent many communication accidents from happening simply by telling the user what you are doing. Inclusion, or telling people what you are doing, is especially important when users can't see you (e.g., in a telephone interview) or when users can't tell what you are doing from observation alone. Inclusion is an attending skill: It maintains the communication process between two people when one person must perform a task that does not, in itself, require interpersonal communication or when one person must do something that might otherwise signal an interruption or termination of the conversation. This skill works because it helps to answer unspoken questions: Are you still there? Are you still working on my problem? Why are you doing something that doesn't seem related to my problem?

In the Library Visit study, users often reported feeling confused and left in the dark when staff members didn't explain what they were doing or what they expected users to do. Users said things like "He left me standing there and didn't tell me where he was going or how long he would be," "I wasn't sure whether I should be following her or whether I should wait at the desk for her to return," and "I couldn't tell if he heard me."

Inclusion reassures the person you are helping and is an easy solution to the "without speaking she began to type" problem described in section 3.1.1. If you have to focus your attention on the computer screen to search for information on the user's topic, you should explain what you are doing—checking a special database or looking for other subject headings or whatever. Instead of silently abandoning the user, explain, "I'm going to check the shelves for you and will return in a minute." Inclusion is a way of making the user a partner in the search and not a bystander. And users like it. "I did wish," said one user, "that she explained what she was doing and included me more." It doesn't take any longer to explain things to the user as you are doing them.

In addition, inclusion often has an instructive function. Describing and explaining your behavior helps the observer learn how to replicate that behavior. So the librarian could say, "Often a good place to start with this sort of question is with the catalog. I am going to search for books on your subject by using the term *Technological innovations—Social aspects.* And when the librarian says, "What I am doing now is looking for other headings we could use," the user learns that an index may have synonymous or alternate terms.

Inclusion is a skill that is particularly useful in these situations:

- When the other person cannot see what you are doing. On the telephone, always describe behavior that interrupts

A QUICK TIP

INCLUDE THE USER

In general, users in the Library Visit study reported far greater satisfaction with the process when they were able to see the screen and follow what was going on. This principle of letting the user see what you are doing applies not just to the computer screen but also to book-based resources. For example, one user said approvingly, "She did the search while tilting the book towards me, so that I could see what steps she was taking." An additional advantage with letting the user see is that the user sometimes notices that the search process is going off track and can volunteer a correction or supplementary information. For example, one user who wanted biographical information on the naturalist F. W. Kortright saw that the librarian was searching under C and intervened to say, "Kortright is spelled with a K, not a C." Obviously this opportunity for user feedback and correction can occur only when the user has some way of following what the librarian is doing.

normal conversation. For example, "I'm going to put you on hold for a minute while I check an index for you" or "I'm writing this down as you speak" or "I'm looking in our directory of community services." It is especially important to use inclusion with blind people: "I'm going over to the other desk for a minute to ask Marge if she knows the name of the organization you were asking about. She is our in-house expert on business questions."

- When the relationship between your behavior and the problem is not immediately apparent to a layperson. For example, a library user may expect you to answer his question off the top of your head, but you need to check a reference book to be sure. Say, "I want to be sure so I'm verifying this in the current directory."

- When you want to instruct the user (and the user wants to be instructed). Explaining precisely what you are doing helps the user learn the procedure. "I'm going to look in a medical database called Medline. Here it is . . . and I'm looking under the heading Anorexia Nervosa . . . I see ten items . . . one called, 'Researchers study causes . . . .'"

- When you ask a question or make a request that may seem unrelated or inappropriate to a library user. Users sometimes do not understand that it is necessary for you to determine the scope of their query and may think you are prying. For example, instead of asking, "Why do you need this information?" you can use inclusion to introduce your question: "The library has a great deal of material on this topic. We'll have a better chance of finding the best sources if you can tell me a little bit about how you plan to use the information." (See section 3.2.3.)

- When the other person will have to wait, because the task takes a few minutes, or you need to concentrate on the task without talking, or you are going to be out of sight. People usually do not mind waiting, as long as they know what to expect. If there's a waiting line, people become less impatient when you acknowledge them, even if you can't immediately help them. For example, "I'm going to help this man, and I have a telephone call waiting, and then I will be right with you" or "I'm going to my office and will be back in about three minutes" or "This will take me some time to check because I have to call the university library. Would you like to wait while I do that or would you rather do some other work and come back in five minutes?"

- When you are instructing large groups in the use of a particular information resource during a bibliographic instruction session, since not everyone can see exactly what you are doing.

Inclusion involves four basic steps:

1. Acknowledge. Restate the problem or otherwise indicate that you are listening so that your next action will be seen to be related. "So your parrot's feathers are falling out and you want a book on what to do about it."
2. Describe briefly what you are doing (or have done or are just about to do). "I'm looking under 'Parrots—diseases' in our catalog, to see what books we have on this subject." If you want to instruct the user about the difference between subject headings and keyword searching, you can provide more detail.
3. Explain briefly why you are doing it. State the reason for your behavior, or summarize the advantages. For example, "This could be in the biology section or it could be in the pet books. The catalog will tell us all the places we should look and it might also tell us what else to look under."
4. If appropriate, indicate how much time the task will take. Be specific. Say, "I should be able to call you back this afternoon" rather than "I won't be able to call back right away" or "This may take a while."

4.1.2 BIBLIOGRAPHIC INSTRUCTION

Most of the library literature on bibliographic instruction (BI) concentrates on the formalized instruction that happens in the classroom, lab, or workshop, or on a library tour, when instruction is the main purpose. In this section we consider instead the incidental instruction that happens one-on-one at the point of use, when the main purpose of the interaction is finding information. In the broadest sense, in every reference transaction a library user learns something about the library. And every interaction produces a change in the user's mental model of what a library is and does. As noted in section 1.4.1, when users get help in libraries, they learn at minimum that the library is the right place to come for help with information problems and that they are more likely to be successful if they ask a staff member for help. In addition, if the library staff uses inclusion to describe or explain a procedure as it is carried out, the user develops a more sophisticated understanding of how the catalog or indexes or particular bibliographic tools work. In the BI situation, as elsewhere, the basic attending skills of nonverbal behaviors (section 2.4.2), acknowledgment (2.4.3), minimal encouragers (2.4.4), and listen-

A QUICK TIP

FOCUS ON USER'S GOALS, NOT THE SYSTEM

An experienced librarian from the Mental Models study said that he never says he's going to explain how the computer works; instead he focuses on the user's end goal of finding information: "I find that if you start telling people you're going to explain the computer to them, it turns them off. Once you say, 'how the machine works,' they get intimidated. I just say, 'Well, this is how you can find it.'"

A QUICK TIP

EASY FOR LEONARDO

Don't assume. When a user in the Library Visit study asked for information on Saudi Arabian women, the librarian directed her to a database, saying, "Well, the system is quite straightforward." However, systems that seem straightforward to experts are often far from straightforward to novices. The user reported, "I found the Women's Resources International database very useful but not as 'straightforward' as the librarian said it would be."

QUESTIONS FOR ONE-TO-ONE INSTRUCTION

To assess the need:
What are you working on? [not Is this for a term paper/Is this a science project?]
What have you done so far? Where have you looked? [not Have you looked in the catalog?]
What happened? What stopped you? [not Are you having trouble with the headings?]

To assess the gap:
What do you want to find out? [not Do you want a review article?]
What do you already know about this index? [not Do you know how this index is arranged?]
What don't you understand about it? [not Do you know how to limit by date?]

To assess the help required:
What do you want this index/database/search engine to do for you? [not Do you want abstracts?]
What would help you most?
What other help do you need to do this? [not Do you need to know how to operate the machine?]

---

ing (2.4.5) are the foundations that help establish a good communication climate.

In the context of the reference interview, bibliographic instruction often involves working step-by-step with the user who is using an information source for the first time. When the reference desk is so busy that the staff member has to send the user off on his own, bibliographic instruction consists of giving the user some specific advice on how to get started, plus an invitation to return for more help if he gets stuck. In the Library Visit accounts it was clear that, even in academic libraries, staff members tend to err on the side of overestimating the users' expertise and underestimating the difficulty of navigating the information resources. For example, a user who wanted to know how many times the work of a particular author had been cited in the research literature was given a piece of paper on which the librarian had written "Web of Science" and was told to click on the Web of Science icon in the library gateway. When the user accessed the Web of Science as directed, he discovered to his confusion that he "was confronted with many choices, as it appears Web of Science is actually a collection of various databases." The user commented,

---

ANALYZE THIS REFERENCE TRANSACTION

Case 13: If it's an R

User: Can you tell me where to start? I have things to look up in, like, the files?

Librarian: Yes. (encourager)

User: Where do you start if you want to look up . . . ?

Librarian: Are you looking for a particular book? Or . . .? (closed question that functions as an open question)

User: Yes. A book on mortgages.

Librarian: On mortgages, OK. (acknowledgment) So what you're looking for then is a subject.

User: Right. Yes.

Librarian: Right? You use the subject listing. If you were looking for a particular title, you'd very obviously use the title listing and ditto authors. [Explains more how the catalog works.] This will tell you what books we have under that subject [mortgages] and it will tell you where to find them on the shelf and what departments and branches have copies . . . and whether or not it's a reference or a circulating book.

User: Oh. OK.

Librarian: Now when there's no letter-number combination after it, that means it's a circulating book. When it says CE SC, that means it's Special Collections and it means that it's noncirculating. Or if it's an R, same thing.

User: What I wanted was the chart for amortization tables, which shows various interest rates.

Librarian: OK, now when you see that number, it means the book is just at the [branch] library reference, OK?

User: Oh.

Librarian: But it's unlikely that the branch would have something where there's not something similar here. Most of these items seem to be in the same general area.

User: OK, 332, yeah.

Librarian: They're all going to be basically in two areas. You should look in the 330s, which is economics, just the first two aisles over there. And then there is 511, which is mathematics, right down there, OK?

User: Thanks very much for your help.

Dewdney, Mortgages

Comment: Evaluate the bibliographic instruction provided in the context of the six quick tips provided earlier. Consider:
1. How well do you think the librarian understood what the user really wanted?
2. What proportion of this interview is devoted to finding out the user's needs?
3. Where did this reference interview start to go wrong? What could the librarian have done instead?

A QUICK TIP

BEWARE

In the Mental Models study, an experienced librarian described what happened when a user came to the desk and said, "Is music listed in the computer?" It turned out that, for a 50th wedding anniversary party the next day, he wanted to borrow a recording of a popular song with the word "dream" in the title. When asked how she would explain or describe this type of reference situation to a new librarian who was just learning about reference service, the experienced librarian said, "I would tell the new staff person to beware. Often you can tell users the whole way music is set up, when all they want is a particular song. I stopped doing that [launching into system descriptions]. I was taught years ago to say, 'What exactly are you looking for?'"

"It would have been very useful if the librarian had specifically directed me to search the Science Citation Index once I had accessed the Web of Science." A generalization that can be drawn from examples such as this is that nothing should be taken for granted about the user's level of information literacy and search skills. The default position should *not* be that everyone knows how to use the Art Index or Medline unless the user explicitly declares otherwise.

Quick Tips for Providing BI in the Context of the Reference Interview

- **Conduct a proper reference interview** so that you are sure that the tool you are providing instruction about is actually going to help the user find a helpful answer. The user might ask an initial question "Where are your encyclopedias?" Before you launch into an explanation about online encyclopedias, specialized subject encyclopedias, etc., find out what the user wants to know. Maybe he really needs a directory to find an address, in which case instruction in encyclopedias is wasted. Bibliographic instruction is effective only when the user comes to understand that the tool has actually saved him time.
- **Get at eye level** with the user, if possible. If you are showing a user how to use an electronic resource, it works best if the two of you are sitting side by side so that you can see the screen and also each other.
- **Guide users through the process,** while letting the user do the work. Said one user, "What I found most helpful was that the librarian let me perform each step myself." Users who have been guided through the steps in this fashion are more likely to be able to do it on their own the next time. And of course, it immediately becomes clear where the user is running into trouble.
- **Don't set a pace that is too fast.** In not one of the Library Visit accounts did anyone say that the library instruction was performed too slowly. On the other hand, there were frequent comments about the process being too quick to follow.
- **Provide instruction in stages** as needed. The first step might be instructions to help a user begin using an index. Later the librarian might be involved in providing help with narrowing down a search or evaluating the sources found.
- **Leave the user in control** concerning how much or how little instruction is wanted. Some users just want the an-

A QUICK TIP

I ALREADY KNOW THAT

Find out how interested the user is in receiving instruction before launching in. In the Mental Models study, some users observed that the librarian's need to instruct considerably exceeded their own need to be instructed. One user said, "He sat me down in front of the microfiche reader and showed me how to use it. I already knew about the index and how to use it, but he wanted to show me anyway."

ANALYZE THIS REFERENCE TRANSACTION

Case 14: Putting the user in the driver's seat

A user in an academic library wanted information on the physiological effects of silicone in human blood. The librarian took the user to a computer terminal and provided instruction in logging on. Then she said she would be back in two minutes to help with Medline, after she had finished with another person she was helping. When she returned, she began to explain the features of Medline. Here's how the user described what happened next:

> Although she suggested I type in "silicone," she also insisted that I be the one doing the typing and clicking, since, she said "that would be the only way" I would learn. I really appreciated this gesture, as I have encountered librarians who have taken over the search project and zipped through the reference sources, leaving me unsure of how the results were actually obtained.
>
> She then took the seat beside me because it became available. I felt more comfortable that she was sitting beside me rather than standing behind me as before, because it enabled us to make eye contact so that we could see if we understood each other. . . . Above all, she did not just climb into the driver's seat. She allowed me to interact with the database. [The librarian next provided instruction on how to limit the search.] At this point, she said she would leave me alone and let me complete the search. I appreciated the fact that she respected my autonomy. She also sincerely invited me to come and ask her more questions "if [I was] not finding what [I was] looking for."

From the Library Visit study

Comment: In this transaction, the user was very happy with the help she got. Make a list of all the specific behaviors that this librarian performed that contributed to making this bibliographic instruction so positive for the user. How many of these things are within the control of the individual librarian? How many of these things could be done in your own library setting?

A QUICK TIP

A SECOND CHANCE TO HELP

Most people will only ask their question once, unless they are invited to return for further help. Therefore, follow-up questions are especially useful when you are too busy to do a complete reference interview or to provide further help right away.

A QUICK TIP

ELECTRONIC FOLLOW-UP

Try adding this follow-up question to your signature line when you answer reference questions by e-mail: "If this answer doesn't help you, please send us another message and we'll try again."

DID YOU KNOW?

Despite advice to include the follow-up question as a matter of course in every transaction, librarians are still not using this skill as often as they should. In the Library Visit study, the follow-up question was reported as occurring in slightly more than one-third of all transactions. One user said, "I remained in sight of the desk for ten minutes as I tried to sort through the periodical index to find the articles I needed. As it turned out, none of the citations dealt with [my topic]. She did not bother to check with me to see how I was doing. I decided to try again with someone else."

swers—they don't want to know about the different algorithms that various search engines use to retrieve Web pages or why you are using Google; they just want the Web page for, say, the White House. Other users treasure their independence and prefer to work on their own, at least initially. Use your attending skills of listening and reading body language to determine how much instruction a particular user wants. If in doubt, ask.

4.1.3 FOLLOW-UP QUESTIONS

Research has shown that asking follow-up questions is one of the most important skills you can use in the reference interview. Make the follow-up question a standard part of every (well, almost every) interview. It is especially useful at the end of a reference interview. Staff members who routinely ask, "Did you find what you needed?" or "If you don't find what you are looking for in that section, make sure you come back" automatically have a second chance to get it right. In many cases, a follow-up question can make the difference between a satisfactory experience for the user and a frustrating series of events. The follow-up question is so useful because it allows you to discover, and repair, communication accidents before the user leaves the library. Gers and Seward have said that the follow-up question "may be the single most important behavior because it has the potential for allowing one to remedy lapses in other desirable behaviors" (1985: 34). Lillie Seward Dyson's influential article "Improving Reference Services" (1992) provides statistically significant evidence that asking follow-up questions enhances your chances of giving a correct answer. There are two kinds of follow-up questions: those that invite the user to ask for additional help if needed and those that allow users to tell you whether they got the kind of help they were really hoping to get.

Users in the Library Visit study commonly expressed their appreciation of the follow-up question, when it was used. For example, a user wanting articles on Toni Morrison and motherhood said that the librarian ended the transaction "by welcoming me back if I had more questions, saying 'If you have any other questions, come on back.' I felt very relieved to hear this and felt like it would be OK to come back if I got stuck in my search."

A word of warning, however. Users may have good reasons for not answering a follow-up question by saying they didn't find what they were looking for. For example they may fear "losing face" if they acknowledge that they couldn't use a particular tool or find something in an online database. Moreover, in some cultures, it is considered a lack of respect to say that the service pro-

DID YOU KNOW?

Users need help sorting out reliable sources of medical information from the not so credible. Jana Allcock (2000) recommends that librarians take bibliographic instruction beyond showing users how to use health databases such as EBSCO's Health Source Plus. She says that the explosion of health information on the Internet has created a new need to help users distinguish between trustworthy and questionable Internet sites.

DID YOU KNOW?

The computer monitor can be a powerful barrier to communication. In the Library Visit study, users reported that sometimes staff members directed their attention to the screen and not to them.

SOME FOLLOW-UP QUESTIONS

To invite the user to ask for additional help:
> If you don't find what you are looking for, please come back and ask again.
> Is there anything else I can help you with today?

To discover if the need has been met:
> Does this completely answer your question?
> Is that the kind of help (information, material, direction) you were hoping to get?
> Will this help you?
> Are you finding what you are looking for?

---

vided has not been helpful, particularly as a response to a person presumed to be an authority, such as a teacher or a librarian (see section 5.5.1). Hence when you ask some international students if the material you provided was helpful, they may say "Yes" out of politeness, even if it was not at all helpful, in order to help *you* save face. To interpret the response, first watch for nonverbal signs of hesitancy or dissatisfaction, then try another way of finding out what is needed, perhaps avoiding direct questioning. For example you could say, "If that is not exactly what you are looking for, I would be glad to look for some more material."

The good news is that follow-up questions are easy to ask. Here are some questions asked by librarians in Dewdney's study, in which she tape-recorded real reference questions in public libraries. The specific words used are different, but all of these statements have the same function, which is to reassure the user that it is OK to ask again:

> OK, if that doesn't work, come back and I'll see what else.
> If you need further help, let me know.
> Double-check the shelf with those numbers, and if the books aren't there come back to the desk.
> If you find that's not enough, there's another alternative. You can come back and use the encyclopedia.
> If you need more, come looking for me and I'll pursue it further if necessary. [Gives name.]
> Start with this. If you're not happy with what you find, come back to the desk, OK?
> Take a look through those books. If they don't help you, come back and we'll try again.

4.2 INTEGRATING REFERENCE INTERVIEW SKILLS

When librarians first attempt to apply new interviewing skills in an intentional, integrated way, they often wonder about the appropriateness of some skills, about the effect of the skill on the user, or whether they will ever be able to use the skill without awkwardness. It may be that the first time you use a skill that you *will* sound awkward, but more awkward to yourself than to the user. If possible, try out the skill in a role-played situation in which you practice a single skill with another staff member or trainee. You will find that the skill becomes more natural with practice. Eventually you will feel comfortable making the skill work for you in a variety of situations, and the skill will become part of your normal behavior.

Skills must be learned individually, but together they form a repertoire from which the helper can draw spontaneously, selecting one skill in a certain situation, adapting another skill to supplement, trying yet another skill if the first one doesn't work. Intentionality means flexibility—the ability to use a range of skills and to improvise. It means not depending on one skill or always using the same skill in similar situations. As mastery of skills increases, so does intentionality, which is not limited to verbal skills. The intentional helper also becomes adept at using nonverbal skills as the need dictates.

We recommend that initially you focus on these separate skills, one at a time. But it is a simplification to think of these skills as separate—a fiction used to make the initial learning easier. Eventually when used in a real library setting, the skills are combined, each one supporting the rest in a smooth and seamless integration in the service of a larger purpose, which is to help the user. As you develop mastery, you will see how one skill can be substituted for another and how several skills can be integrated to achieve specific purposes in the process of communication.

Sometimes when library staff are introduced to new communication skills, they might react by saying that they're being taught to manipulate their own behavior in order to manipulate others. Some trainees say that they feel deceptive when they try to make the transition from practicing a skill in a training setting to using the skill in a real-life setting. Suppose, they say, that it's not natural to me to use encouragers or ask open questions to get people to talk. But I learn these skills and use them, and hey—presto—people open up and tell me things. Isn't there something deceptive and manipulative about this? Well, there might be, depending on your motive. Any skill can be abused. But in the service of shared goals, these skills facilitate communication and allow you to be more helpful.

4.2.1 TIPS FOR PRACTICING

There's no substitute for real practice. Changing your communication behavior is hard work—it's not easy to break old patterns of response. But unless you practice your new skills, you'll lose them. Here are ten tips to help you through the learning process.

1. Make a commitment. Promise yourself that for a specified period of time—for the next hour or on Thursday afternoons—you will consciously use one of your new skills.
2. Start immediately. Begin practicing the skill right away. Remind yourself by taping a photocopy of SOME SENSE-MAKING QUESTIONS (section 3.2.3) to your desk. At first you might feel awkward, but practice anyway. Most library users respond positively when they see that you are trying hard to help.
3. Practice one skill at a time. Best results come from practicing one skill over and over. Don't try to use all the skills at once. A good skill to start with is acknowledgment or restatement. An easy sense-making question to use is "What kind of help would you like?"
4. Use support groups. Practice with a coworker who has made the same commitment. Give each other feedback and share experiences. Or set aside time at regular staff meetings to discuss your progress.
5. Learn from missed opportunities. Each time you do *not* use one of these skills, think about the situation afterward. Would acknowledgment have helped prevent a misunderstanding of what the user meant by "books on Wales"? How could you have used a follow-up question to find out sooner that the information provided was not useful?
6. Develop your own style. There is no magic list of open questions and no perfect sequence in which to use your skills. Adapt your behavior in a way that is comfortable for you in the situation at hand. Use words that function in the same way as the examples, even if the exact words differ.
7. Learn from communication accidents. When you are first learning these skills, you might find that they do not always work. If the user seems puzzled, you might have had a communication accident. Recover by explaining to the user what you are trying to do. For example: "I asked you that question because I can help you more if I know a little

BEHAVIORS THAT HELPED

When student participant observers in the Library Visit study were asked to reflect on librarians' behaviors that had helped them, it turned out the same factors emerge repeatedly in accounts of successful reference transactions. Fortunately, all these factors are communication behaviors that are within the control of the individual staff member and not dependent on external changes in the system. Here are some "best practices."

The staff member:
smiled/nodded/moved out from the desk/used eye contact.
was friendly/warm.
took the initiative by approaching me and offering help.
appeared interested.
accepted my question as important.
responded to my initial question by saying, "What do you want to know about X?"
asked questions that helped me clarify in my own mind what information I wanted.
included me as a partner in the search and seemed interested in my suggestions.
didn't just point or give directions, but took me to the shelves/ indexes/reference tools and made sure that the answer was there.
pulled out several books for me to look at while he checked something else.
explained what he was doing/where he was going/what he expected me to do.
left me with some leads and didn't close off the search.
was very knowledgeable about the sources of information.
introduced me to some helpful starting points for my search.
didn't get discouraged easily but was willing to investigate further.
didn't overwhelm me with too much information.
invited me to come back if I didn't find the answer.
came over and asked, "Did you find the information you were looking for?"

(Reported in Dewdney and Ross, 1994)

bit about what you plan to do with the information" or "I want to make sure I understand what you're looking for." Users hardly ever become angry in such situations, but if they do, recover simply by saying, "I'm sorry" and explaining.

8. Practice off the job. Microskills work in any situation in which your help is being sought: by family, friends, even strangers asking directions. Practice these skills in your daily life; you may be surprised at how much everyday communication improves.

9. Observe others. Notice how others use microskills: the salesperson who restates your request, the talk show host who asks open questions, the physician who encourages you to describe your problem, the consultant who is trying to find out what features the new system software needs to include. Pay particular attention to those people you like dealing with; chances are they are using microskills.

10. Teach someone else. After you have learned a skill and practiced it, pass it on to someone else. Teach a coworker one skill that you have found to be particularly effective. Your ability to teach someone else demonstrates that you have really mastered the skill.

4.3 ANNOTATED REFERENCES

4.3.1 GENERAL

Allcock, Jana C. 2000. "Helping Public Library Patrons Find Medical Information—The Reference Interview." *Public Library Quarterly* 18, no. 3/4: 21–27.

Nardi, Bonnie A., and Vicki L. O'Day. 1996. "Intelligent Agents: What We Learned at the Library." *Libri* 46, no. 2: 59–88.

———. 1999. *Information Ecologies: Using Technology with Heart.* Cambridge, Mass.: The MIT Press. With the combined skills from the domains of anthropology, computer science, and special librarianship, the authors examine what they call "information ecologies," which they define as a system of people, practices, values, and technologies in a particular local environment.

4.3.2 INCLUSION

Michell, Gillian, and Roma M. Harris. 1987. "Evaluating the Reference Interview: Some Factors Influencing Patrons and Professionals." *RQ* 27, no. 1 (fall): 95–105. Reports an experiment in which the level of inclusion was varied in videotaped reference interviews that were evaluated by both public library users and by librarians.

White, Marilyn Domas. 1981. "The Dimensions of the Reference Interview." *RQ* 20, no. 4 (summer): 373–81. Describes how the librarian can increase the coherence of the reference interview by explaining to the user what is happening.

4.3.3 FOLLOW-UP QUESTIONS

Dewdney, Patricia, and Catherine Sheldrick Ross. 1994. "Flying a Light Aircraft: Reference Evaluation from a User's Viewpoint." *RQ* 34, no. 2 (winter): 217–30. Reports the first phase of the Library Visit study.

Dyson, Lillie Seward. 1992. "Improving Reference Services: A Maryland Training Program Brings Positive Results." *Public Libraries* 31, no. 5 (September/October): 284–89. Persuasively makes the case that the follow-up question is one of the most important skills for the reference interview.

Gers, Ralph, and Lillie J. Seward. 1985. "Improving Reference Performance: Results of a Statewide Study." *Library Journal* 110, no. 8 (November 1): 32–35.

Ross, Catherine Sheldrick, and Kirsti Nilsen. 2000. "So Has the Internet Changed Anything in Reference? The Library Visit Study, Phase 2." *Reference and User Services Quarterly* 40, no. 2: 147–55.

5 EXPLORING SPECIAL CONTEXTS FOR THE REFERENCE INTERVIEW

5.1 INTRODUCTION TO SPECIAL CONTEXTS

In this chapter we consider the reference interview with a difference. In the special reference contexts considered here, you still need the same attending skills, questioning skills, and summarizing skills discussed in Chapters 2 and 3. But in addition there are extra considerations. These result variously from differences in the media of communication (e.g., the telephone interview versus face-to-face); special considerations needed for a particular client

DID YOU KNOW?

Decades ago, Robert Rohlf (1958) wrote an article advocating that libraries do a better job of keeping up with the "new machines and methods" employed in the "technological world of today." He recommended the introduction of a separate telephone reference department so that both remote and in-house users got optimum service.

group served (e.g., users with an imposed query, children, or adults with special language-related needs); or special purposes (e.g., readers' advisory or tricky questions such as those dealing with legal or medical issues). In the sections that follow, we focus on what makes these contexts special and how to adapt the reference interview for these special circumstances.

5.2 THE TELEPHONE INTERVIEW

Users who called the reference desk by telephone were the original remote, interactive real-time users. Although electronic reference (see Chapter 6) will replace telephone reference service for some users, there are others who prefer to communicate by talking rather than by typing. Users without easy access to computers or the Internet and users who are uncomfortable using computer technology will continue to call. Sometimes, even when the question is presented originally using e-mail or electronic chat, participants find it easier to switch to the telephone to complete the negotiation of a complex question or to communicate detailed explanations. And of course, some users simply like to talk to a real person in real time using the simple and familiar technology of the telephone. Admittedly, digital reference services involving e-mail and chat can be expected eventually to integrate interactive audio applications as an option for complex questions and instructions that are hard to communicate in a text-only environment. But just as other older technologies such as radio and film have found their own niche and have not been replaced by television and video, we predict that telephone service will remain a valued aid that will complement the evolving new forms of remote reference.

The rationale for telephone reference is to offer a service that saves the user time. Many libraries and community information centers have developed telephone reference service into a specialty that stresses short answers and convenience, marketing it under names such as Quikfacts. Traditionally, telephone reference has focused on ready reference questions with answers that don't take long to read over the phone. In an article from the 1930s, "Reference Service by Telephone," Emily Gannett explained that most libraries declined to provide information over the telephone on the following topics: "genealogy, identification of insects, plants, paintings, coins, etc., long lists of names and addresses, patent information, definitions of words unsuitable for relay over the

DID YOU KNOW?

telephone. Most libraries will not read long articles or poems" (1936: 909–11). However, fax machines have now extended the options beyond the limits of data that the voice can convey in a few minutes. A faxed page can contain a map, a graphic symbol, a table of numbers, a mathematical formula, or a highly technical text passage.

The special constraints of the telephone reference interview are by-products of the technology used: You and the user can't see each other or rely on visual cues; you can't use the physical setting as a prop for the interaction or work through a problem by showing the user a book or resource and getting her feedback; you can't very easily provide bibliographic instruction. But on the other hand, a plus for the user is that you can't just say, "Have you checked the catalog?"

5.2.1 INTERVIEW SKILLS FOR THE TELEPHONE

The telephone reference interview heightens the need for good interviewing skills and attentive listening. You lose all visual cues when you conduct a telephone reference interview: You can't see that look of annoyance, the shrug, the unsure or worried expression, or the look of doubt in the eyes. And you can't see the look of pleasure and appreciation when a user gets exactly the answer needed. Users also are at a disadvantage, because they don't see your welcoming smile and they can't know what you are doing unless you tell them. On the plus side, neither you nor the user is quite so likely to leap to conclusions based on age, physical appearance, or clothing (see section 3.2.2). Unlike the electronic interview, you *can* get nonverbal cues that can be conveyed through sound. You can hear the enthusiasm, interest, affirmation, annoyance, or insecurity expressed through the voice. Moreover, in the interactive real-time environment, you have the chance to ask clarifying questions immediately, while the caller is on the phone.

In this section we focus on the skills you need to conduct an interview over the telephone and take the appropriate action. Sometimes the staff member who picks up the phone does not answer the question but must make a referral. At other times, when the question cannot be answered over the phone, the user must be advised to come to the library in person. But before you can make appropriate referrals or recommendations, you must still find out what the user really wants to know. Users with telephone questions are even more likely than face-to-face users to ask questions that are too broad or too specific or to ask obvious questions (e.g., after the staff member answers the phone with "Riverbridge University Reference Department," the user asks, "Is this the reference department?"). Because they can't see you

A QUICK TIP

SMILE

Smile when you're on the phone, even though the user can't see you. Smiling conveys warmth in your voice (Walters, 1994).

there at the reference desk, they need to be reassured that their phone call has reached the right place and that you won't be transferring the call elsewhere. Use PACT (section 2.3) to establish contact and reassure the user that you are indeed the right person to be answering his or her question.

Be sure to acknowledge the user's question promptly by restating at least part of it. Since the user cannot see you, it is often a good idea to explain what you are doing. Rather than leaving her to wonder if you have forgotten her, use inclusion (section 4.1.1) to explain that you are working on her question, that you are just checking the online catalog, or that you are going away for a moment to get a city directory. As with the face-to-face interview, open questions and sense-making questions work well (see sections 3.2.1 and 3.2.3). Some librarians feel that the user's anonymity over the phone makes it easier to ask how the information is expected to help. But the guidelines for asking about intended uses remain the same as they are for an in-library user: Explain that you are asking this question so that you can be more helpful, and don't make any assumptions. Because your caller cannot see your nodding and smiling over the telephone, you should pay special attention to vocal qualities and verbal skills. For the caller at the other end, your voice represents the whole library. You are literally the front line. Here are some suggestions:

Develop a pleasant speaking voice. Monitor how you sound over the phone. Is your tone interested and courteous? Do you speak slowly and clearly enough to be easily understood? Do you sound as if you welcomed the caller's question? Or does your tone imply that you experience the call as a nuisance or an interruption of other more important work?

Identify yourself. When you answer the phone, your greeting should identify your library and your role or name, but most important, it should indicate your willingness to provide service. Instead of saying Yes or Hello, try something like this:

> Reference Department. Ahmed Hassan speaking.
> The Legal Information Center. This is the librarian, Mimi Holland. How may I help you?

Volunteer your help. Don't force the caller to pry help out of you. If the caller asks, "Is Mrs. Lopez there?" don't just say no. Say, "Mrs. Lopez will be back at one o'clock. If you'd like to leave a message, I'll make sure she gets it when she returns" or "Mrs. Lopez is not here right now. Can someone else help you?"

Acknowledge (see section 2.4.3). Be sure to acknowledge the caller's question promptly by restating at least part of it. If you didn't quite catch the question, repeat what you did understand and let the caller fill you in on the rest.

> Yes, I'd be happy to check that for you in *Books in Print*.
> Sherry Turkle. And that's spelled T-U-R-K-E-L? . . . OK, so it's L-E.
> Uh-huh, so it's the Cairo Trilogy. What was that first title again? . . . OK, *The Palace Walk* . . . And you just wanted to know if the book was in?
> So you want the phone number for the local Asperger Syndrome support group?

Use minimal encouragers (see section 2.4.4). Minimal encouragers like "Uh-huh," "Go on," "That's interesting," and "Anything else?" are especially important over the phone as cues that you are listening. Without these encouragers, the caller is apt to wonder if you are still there.

Listen. Listening skills (see section 2.4.5) are even more important than in a face-to-face interview because you have no visual clues that could let you know that things are going off track. After your initial greeting, give the caller a chance to explain what is wanted. Don't interrupt. Initially, don't do much talking yourself except for minimal encouragers.

Clarify the question or request. Use open questions (section 3.2.1) or sense-making questions (3.2.3) to find out what kind of help the caller wants. For example:

> How may I help you?
> What information would you like on that?
> What aspect of X are you interested in?
> What kind of help would you like?
> How would you like this information to help you?
> How would you be using that information?

As in the face-to-face interview, it might take several questions before you think you understand the question well enough to begin to look for an answer. You can say, "I'm not familiar with X. What more can you tell me about it?" or "Is there anything more you can tell me about your requirements?"

Verify. After the user responds to your clarifying questions by telling you what he wants, repeat and verify the key facts before you rush off to find the answer or before the phone connection with the caller is ended (see section 3.2.4).

Write it down. Write down the question while the caller is still on the phone. Check spellings, dates, and other particulars with the caller. As you are writing it down, you may realize that you don't really understand what the caller really wants to know about migration patterns in Wales (or was it whales?). You can ask another question to clarify before you start to look for sources—a step that can avert the need to call back to get more of the context of the question.

Explain. Remember that the caller cannot see you. If you are going to ask people to wait, don't just say, "Hang on" or "OK, I'll look," and then go away. The caller won't know what you are doing or how long to expect to wait. Studies show that people can cope better with frustrating experiences if they are told ahead of time what to expect. Therefore, explain what you are doing. Say, "I'll check that for you in the index. It will take about two minutes. Would you like to wait or should I call you back?" If the problem turns out to be unexpectedly difficult, return immediately to the phone to give your waiting caller a progress report. Say, "I haven't forgotten you. I'm checking that information and will have it for you in a minute."

Refer. If you can't answer the question yourself, don't say, "No, I don't know anything about that program" or "That's not our department." Instead you could say something like this:

> If you would leave your number, I'll find out about that program and call you back within a half hour.
> Let me transfer you to our reference librarian who specializes in legal materials.

But don't make an unmonitored referral (see section 3.1.4). Invite the user to call back if the referral is not successful, and provide your name again so that the caller can ask for you.

Call back. Don't leave people on hold. If finding an answer will take longer than a minute or so, offer to take the number and call back or e-mail or fax the answer. Often things take longer than expected or other interruptions occur. Rather than stranding your user on the phone and tying up your phone line, it is often better to offer to call back. Ask what would be a good time to call. But make sure that you *do* call back within the agreed upon time, even if you have not been able to find the answer.

Don't be what Joan Durrance has called the "disappearing librarian." And if you are about to end your shift and someone else will make the call back, be sure to tell the user what to expect.

Identify the caller accurately. If you are going to call back or send an e-mail response, restate names and telephone or fax numbers as you write them down (see section 2.4.3). This will give the caller a chance to correct errors. Standard message forms are helpful and save time. Even if you are going to send the answer by e-mail, it's a good idea to ask for the phone number as well in case your message bounces back. With telephone interviews, you can ask for the user's name: "Who should I ask for when I call back?"

Follow-up. After you have provided the answer, don't forget to follow up (section 4.1.3). Say, "Did this completely answer your question?" or "Is there anything more you would like to know?" If you have referred the user to an outside source such as a Web page, agency, or another library, be sure to monitor the referral. Say, "If this source doesn't completely answer your question, make sure you call back and we can try something else."

Indicate the source of the answer. Since you can't show the source to the user, explain which source(s) you used. If you used a printed source, give the patron the author, title, date, and page number. If you used an electronic source, provide the name or other information about the source. Provide the URL, if the user wants it.

Keep a record. Especially if the question is likely to require a follow-up by someone else later, keep a record of the question and the sources found, so that a second staff member doesn't have to start over from scratch.

ANALYZE THIS REFERENCE TRANSACTION

Case 15: Telephone reference

User: Is this the reference department?
Librarian: Yes, it is. How can I help?
User: I'm trying to track down information on a book by an author, Beerbohm.
Librarian: Beerbohm. Hmmm. The name I've seen; I just can't connect it with anything.
User: I think he's English.
Librarian: Uh-huh.
User: The title I'm looking for is Zuleika Dobson.
Librarian: When . . . approximately what time period?
User: I'm not sure exactly. Maybe the 1930s?
Librarian: What field is Beerbohm associated with?
User: He writes novels.
Librarian: Oh, OK. Hold on a minute then. Let me just check something right now.
User: OK, thanks.
Librarian: I thought I might be able to tie it down. I thought of a couple of things that listed works, but it didn't list that particular one. Let me take your name and number and we'll call you back.
(Adapted from an unpublished telephone interview recorded by Mary Jo Lynch and used with permission.)

Comment: This telephone transaction has been adapted from an interview recorded by Mary Jo Lynch as part of her pioneering dissertation research on reference transactions in public libraries. Which skills do you think this librarian used successfully? Which additional ones could have been used?

   Next consider the librarian's conversational turns. Consider each turn separately. What is the librarian trying to do in each case? Categorize each turn according to its primary function by assigning one or more of the following codes:

Code	Intended function
1	Establishing rapport (opening communication, reassuring, demonstrating availability, and listening)
2	Gathering information from the user (questioning, clarifying, confirming)
3	Giving information (explaining sources, policy, procedures; explaining what is being done)
4	Giving instructions or directions (e.g., how to use an index)
5	Giving opinions (e.g., assessing the likelihood of finding an answer, evaluating the problem)
6	Other (specify)

   You can use these same codes to analyze other reference transactions presented in this book. Which functions would you expect to find more often in a telephone interview than in a face-to-face interview? Which functions would you expect to find less often?

ANALYZE THIS REFERENCE TRANSACTION

Case 16: I didn't have a pencil handy.

User: I'm looking for information on caffeine.

Librarian: Uh-huh. On the effects of caffeine? (acknowledgment)

User: Yes. Caffeine.

Librarian: Did you call us earlier this week? (closed question)

User: Pardon?

Librarian: Did you call us earlier this week?

User: I did. Yes.

Librarian: You did. (acknowledgment) And what did the gentleman tell you? (open question) Because I remember he was working on it.

User: I didn't have a pencil handy and I didn't write it down, and with me it's gone. I should have said "Excuse me" while I got something.

Librarian: Yes. You don't remember what he told you? Because he spent some time on it.

User: Something about a digest or something. Something like that. You see, I want to avoid things with caffeine in it.

Librarian: Mm-hmm. (encourager)

User: Because it was making me deaf—I'm getting noises in my ears.

Librarian: So you want to know which foods contain caffeine? (acknowledgment to restate the librarian's understanding of the question)

User: No, I want to know the deleterious effects of caffeine.

Dewdney, Caffeine

Comment: Users sometimes ask their question more than once, with the result that several people within the library system have worked on the same question. If the answer provided by the first librarian has not fully answered the question, the user may start over, as happened here. The earlier transaction with the male librarian was hampered by several features of the telephone as a communication medium. Unlike in face-to-face transactions, in which users can be shown materials or be given photocopied pages, in the telephone transaction everything depends on the ear (clearly not this particular user's strong point). And because users are never sure when the staff member may call back, they may not be prepared to record the answer. To fend off this problem, the librarian could ask, "Do you have paper and pencil handy?" and then could spell out words or names that are likely to be misheard or misspelled.

EXERCISE

EVALUATE YOUR VOICEMAIL SERVICE

Using the criteria listed for a good voicemail system, prepare an evaluation checklist that could be used to evaluate your service. Call your library's phone number yourself from home and evaluate the voicemail service of the library as a whole and of the reference department in particular. Then ask three friends who are not connected with the library in any way to do the same. Compare the evaluations. Are there differences in the results? What do the results tell you about your library's voicemail service? How might it be improved?

5.2.2 VOICEMAIL

If you can't answer the telephone within three or four rings, the caller should automatically be routed to your voicemail system. The library's voicemail system is the first point of contact between users and the library. Be sure that the initial automated response is pleasant, welcoming, and not too complicated. Voicemail systems can be as simple as the recorded message that invites the caller to leave his or her name and number, or as complicated as a multilevel menu of choices to connect the caller with the right department. Well-designed voicemail systems offer convenience and efficiency to callers, allowing them to leave a message at any time, 24 hours a day, seven days a week. It should be immediately evident to callers which menu choice they need to make if they have a reference question, and they shouldn't have to wait through descriptions of irrelevant services before they can choose the reference option.

Some people, and often the elderly, are put off by automated message answering, especially when faced with an instructional menu that is too long or complicated. For some users, voicemail can be such an obstacle that they simply won't try to get through to a librarian. Some voicemail systems with multilevel menus seem to have been designed as a trial to weed out callers, just like the tests of piling logs in fairy tales that weed out unworthy suitors. Make sure that the voicemail in your library system helps users and is not just another obstacle to service.

Here are some tips for creating an effective automated greeting or menu:

- Keep routine announcements short and simple. Avoid nonessential statements such as "Thank you for calling. The reference desk is not staffed in the evening. . . ." and get to the point: "You've reached the reference desk. Please leave a message or call back. Our hours are . . . ."
- Reduce the time callers have to spend listening to menu options by putting the most frequently used options first and by explaining how to skip the items that are not relevant.
- Simplify actions required of the caller. Break down instructions into manageable steps. Avoid complicated, confusing, or unnecessary directions like "Enter the first three letters of your last name, press the number sign, and then choose 1 to hear our hours of opening, 2 to place a reserve, or 3 to be connected with our circulation desk. Press 4 if you want to talk to someone in Spanish. Press 5 if you want to hear an automated message about our new Home Library service. Press 6 if you want to talk to our reference staff."

ANALYZE THIS REFERENCE TRANSACTION

Case 17: Come to the library in person for our telephone service.

A public library user phoned the library's advertised telephone reference service with what she thought was "a fairly straightforward question." She wanted to know when the premier of Ontario called the 1999 election, and she knew that election day was sometime shortly after May 1, 1999 (it was actually June 3). The response was that she "would have to come down to the library and search the newspapers on microfilm." The user explained that she was "quite amazed, as it would take only a minute or two for someone to check the local paper's front page headlines for three to five days and seven at most. No dice." So then the user found the answer herself within a minute by searching the paper's digital archive online—the answer was in the paper's May 5, 1999, headline. Her evaluation of the service received: "I would give it an F . . . and if I weren't such a strong library supporter, I would certainly go elsewhere next time."

(Thanks to Lynne McKechnie for this example.)

Comment: There was clearly a mismatch between the service that the user expected and the service that she received. Apart from anything else, the library has a public relations problem here. What are the possible factors that could have created the environment in which this situation could happen? Is this a policy problem? A training problem? What else might it be? What could be done to prevent this situation from happening again? Could something like this happen in your library?

- If possible, give callers the option, early in the message, to transfer to a real person if that is their preference.

Answering your messages promptly is an important part of effective voicemail. You should have a policy that calls are returned within a certain period of time—within three working hours, for example.

5.2.3 WHO GETS PRIORITY?

Do callers almost always get a message saying, "The reference staff is busy right now. Please call back or leave a message."? Alternatively, do in-house users get interrupted while you respond to a phone call? Trying to serve two different kinds of users can turn into a juggling act wherein no one is satisfied. In many library policies, the in-house user is given precedence over the telephone caller on the grounds that a user should be rewarded for taking the time and effort to make the trip to the library. On the other hand, it does seem odd to set up a service the whole point of which is to provide convenient access to remote users and then regard these users as second-class—and quite possibly lazy.

The best solution, if staffing levels allow, is to avoid the problem altogether by separating the two services: one staff member gives top priority to an in-house user while another gives top priority to a telephone caller. This way both types of users get the undivided attention of the reference staff. Some libraries combine the telephone reference function with the e-mail reference function, both of which can be handled in a quiet office away from the busy reference desk. A separate telephone reference service with its own name, phone line, and dedicated staff can be advertised and promoted as a service without the concern that callers will swamp regular face-to-face reference service.

A QUICK TIP

QUESTIONS TO TEACH YOUR STAFF

Here are two questions that almost always work:

"What would you like to find out about X?"

"If we can't find X for you, what else might help you?"

5.3 THE SECOND-HAND REFERENCE INTERVIEW

In some situations you cannot communicate directly or immediately with the user who has the question. You receive the reference query secondhand, mediated through a written message or through a second party who may not know the context for the question. For example, you may be expected to do a search from a written request or search form. You might receive an interlibrary loan request by mail or by telephone through an intermediary. You could have just a secondhand account of the information needed ("Marge, I'm leaving now. Would you get some stuff on rock paintings for Mr. Martin? He'll pick it up at six.")

If you feel you don't have a complete picture of what the user wants, try to contact the person who spoke to the user ("Hold it, Santos, tell me more about what Mr. Martin said he needed. What kind of rock paintings?"). If the intermediary didn't do a proper reference interview, you should contact the user directly before you put in a lot of searching time, request an interlibrary loan, or mail out a lot of material. When there's no way of contacting the user, the best you can do is to find one or two examples of what you think might be wanted (as a gesture of good intentions) and

DID YOU KNOW?

With imposed queries, it is more difficult to get useful answers to follow-up questions such as "Does this completely answer your question?" The agent may not know if the question has been answered adequately or not. Melissa Gross cautions, "Even agents who feel confident won't know for sure until the answer is evaluated by the imposer" (1999: 59). However, you can teach the intermediary to ask a follow-up question when she gives the information to the person who will be using it. Suggest that she say, "If this book/video/map isn't exactly what you need, the librarian says that she can find some additional materials if you could explain what aspect of topic X you are looking for and say a bit about how you plan to use the information."

invite feedback through a note asking the user to call or write again if this material doesn't help (a written version of the follow-up question).

A better way to solve this problem is to prevent it. Make sure that everyone who is in a position to receive requests knows the importance of the reference interview and knows how to ask at least one or two basic questions such as, "What would you like to find out about X?" Then ask everyone who might receive a request to write down everything the user says while the conversation is happening; this reduces the chance of premature diagnosis or incorrect interpretation. You can also avoid some communication accidents and save a lot of time by routinely asking the user, "If we have any trouble finding this, do you mind if we call you to get more information?" and take a number. These should be routine procedures for accepting requests, no matter how clear the requests seem to be. You might supplement (but not replace) these procedures with a brief form that is filled out by the user or with the user present.

5.3.1 THE IMPOSED QUERY

For reference librarians, the following scenario might sound familiar: A lost-looking user approaches the desk in an academic library and asks, "Does Eric work here?" After some conversation about staff members that goes nowhere, the librarian finally finds out what the user is trying to do. It turns out that the user is a student in Professor X's class, and this professor has said to the class, "To get background on your topic, you should go to the education library and ask for ERIC." This is an example of what Melissa Gross (1999) has called "the imposed query," a situation in which the question asked at the reference desk was generated by someone else. When questions are imposed and not self-generated, they are very apt to be presented to reference staff as an "ill-formed query" (section 1.4.1) because the person asking the question might not fully understand it. The phenomenon of the imposed query is more common than was once supposed. In a survey of public libraries in southern California, Gross discovered that 74 percent of questions asked at the reference desk were self-generated, and nearly 25 percent of questions asked were "imposed queries." Imposed queries are asked at someone else's request: for example, a wife asks a question on behalf of her husband; a student asks a question that is generated by a school assignment; an employee asks a question to get information for a boss.

Gross, whose pioneering work on the imposed query has established the terminology generally used, calls the person who

A QUICK TIP

SCHOOL PROJECT

Instead of asking, "Is this for a school project?" ask, "How do you plan to use this information?" or "What are you trying to do?" or "How would you like this information to help you?" Then wait for the answer. In one of the interviews recorded by Dewdney, the user asked for information on pregnancy. The librarian responded with a sense-making question, "If you don't mind my asking, what were you going to use this information for?" but then panicked and added, "Like if it's for a school project . . . ." "Oh, no," said the user. The librarian thereafter asked no further questions, except about the search process.

generates the question "the imposer" and the person who asks the question "the agent." The interview concerning an imposed query provides special challenges for the interviewer. Often the agent doesn't know the real context for the question, how it arose, or to what use the information will be put. Gross has pointed out that when the person asking the question is not the person who generated the question, "many [of the recommended] question-negotiation techniques lose their effectiveness" (1999: 54). This is because recommended interview skills function by tracking the question back to its origins in the life of the user, a process that is hampered when the user at the desk is not the person who generated the question. However, the agent will know *something* about the context. The whole trick in conducting an interview generated by an imposed query is to get the agent to talk about what he does know, not what he doesn't. A series of closed questions is even less efficient with an imposed query than it is with a self-generated question. Gross advises that the first step in conducting a successful reference interview is to identify the kind of question you are dealing with: Is it self-generated or is it an imposed query? This doesn't mean that it's a good idea to ask a closed question such as "Do you need this information on X for a school assignment?" It is better to ask something like "Can you tell me a bit about how this information will be used?"

Here are some common situations that give rise to imposed queries, together with some useful open questions that you can ask to get users to tell you what they know about the context of their question:

A student with a school assignment

A student with a high school assignment (see also section 5.4.3) might not know very much about the topic (the Globe Theatre in the time of Shakespeare) but there are many things that she does know that provide a useful context to the question: the subject or course for which she is writing the essay (e.g., English literature), the grade she is in, when the essay is due, how long the essay is supposed to be, what her teacher told her about the expectations for the assignment, and so on. In fact, the real context of this question—the situation, gaps, and uses—have to do with the student's needing to find materials to use in completing an assignment in order to pass a course. To get at this context, you can ask:

What did your teacher tell you about this assignment?
If you have the assignment sheet handy that your teacher
 gave you, it might help if I took a look at it.

A QUICK TIP

GHOST USERS

Users sometimes present their own information needs as those of a friend. Librarians are all familiar with "My friend thinks he may have herpes" and "My friend was in a hit-and-run accident." To ease awkwardness, you can work the conversation toward "people in general." Try "People who do X sometimes find this useful," or "Some people with X just want a list of symptoms, but others want to read about treatments" and then wait for the response. Besides, it could really be for a friend after all.

What requirements does your teacher have for this assignment?

Someone asking a question on behalf of a neighbor, friend, or family member

When a user says that material is needed "for a friend," this formulation is sometimes a defensive strategy to avoid self-disclosure about a sensitive topic. The person is saying in effect, "It's not really me who wants to know about pancreatic cancer or abortion or divorce proceedings or herpes; it's someone else who has this problem." In such cases, since the question is actually self-generated, the user is in a good position to describe what the "friend" is looking for. More frequent and more problematic are the cases in which the agent is in fact asking on behalf of someone else but doesn't indicate who the requested information is really for. Often certain individuals in a family or community act as information gatekeepers, bringing information into a social network for others to use. In immigrant families, for example, children may function as cultural mediators for parents and grandparents who are less proficient with English. In these situations, the following questions are useful:

Can you give me some idea of how your friend/husband/ daughter/father will be using this information?
Can you tell me a little bit about the situation your friend is in and how he will be using this information?

An employee asking a question for a boss or supervisor

This is often the trickiest situation of all. Often the only thing the user knows is that the boss has said, "Go to the library and get everything they have on illiteracy," possibly adding that she needs it for a report she is writing. All you can do in such cases is give the agent something to take back to the boss—your best guess as to what is really wanted—and then use a follow-up with a special twist. Essentially you are teaching the agent how to ask the right question of the supervisor in order to be a better go-between. You may also need to teach the intermediary how to ask an appropriate follow-up question. In this context, the follow-up question works the same way that it does in regular reference interviews to repair mistakes and offer a second chance to get it right. Say to the agent:

When you give this material to your supervisor, you could ask if it completely answers her question. If not, tell her that we can find other materials if she can tell you what specifically is missing in the materials provided.

ANALYZE THIS REFERENCE TRANSACTION

Case 18: I was just given this topic.

User: I need to find out something about this subject here. It's Generic Behavior Management Training for Parents.

Librarian: Where did you hear about this? (sense-making question)

User: I have this topic for a service proposal for school. It's an MRC course.

Librarian: What's MRC? (open question/acknowledgment)

User: Mental retardation.

Librarian: OK. And what is Generic Behavior Management Training . . .? (open question)

User: I don't really know . . .

Librarian: You don't know any . . . ?

User: No. I was just given this topic.

Librarian: You don't know if it's a certain kind of training that . . . ?

User: Supposedly. I guess so.

Librarian: I've never heard of it, but it sounds like some kind of a special program. We would have it listed in the catalog, if we have anything about it.

User: I checked the catalog under "Generic Behavior Management," but it's not there.

Librarian: Hmmm. Is that all you know—just the name of it? You don't know what it deals with, or anything? (closed question that functions like the open question What else do you know about it?)

User: I have to do a service proposal on it.

Librarian: What school is this for? (open question)

User: [Local community college]

Librarian: Is there anything else you can tell me about it? (closed question that functions as an open question)

User: No. Well, our service proposals are supposed to go to COMSOC, which is Community and Social Services or whatever.

Librarian: All I can suggest is that you give them a call and maybe they can give you some suggestions as to what to look for. Because if it's not in our catalog, I don't know where we could really start. If we had anything, it should be listed.

User: Oh, OK. Thank you.

Dewdney, Generic Behavior Management

Comment: In this interview, the question "Where did you hear about this?" worked well because it makes no assumptions while at the same time it encourages the user to talk about context. Examine the other questions that the librarian used. Which ones worked well? Which ones didn't?

For discussion:
1. How successful overall was this interview in finding out about the context of this imposed query?
2. Given the documented studies of users' failures in using the catalog, what do you think of the librarian's statement that since the user couldn't find "Generic Behavior Management" in the catalog that there would be nothing on the topic in the library?
3. How would you rate the helpfulness of the suggestion that the user give COMSOC a call?

DID YOU KNOW?

Carol Kuhlthau has done extensive research on students' information-seeking behavior. She points out that users working on a school assignment may have trouble explaining what they are looking for because the user and the librarian may have different models of the research project. According to Kuhlthau, "The bibliographic paradigm is based on certainty and order, whereas users' problems are characterized by uncertainty and confusion" (1991: 361). These differences may result in miscommunication and an unnecessarily lengthy search process.

ANALYZE THIS REFERENCE TRANSACTION

Case 19: Why can't a kid be more like a businessman?

In her doctoral thesis, Mary K. Chelton focused on the adult-adolescent service encounter and identified a number of barriers to providing good service to this user group. She quotes a reference librarian's posting on the listserv PUBYAC to illustrate how attitudes to specific user groups, specifically adolescents, can be a barrier to service:

> I'll be happy to tell you why I find this age group "problematic." So many come to the reference desk with no idea of why they are there. They shove a sheet of paper in my face and say, "This is my homework. Where can I find this?" When I ask them what the assignment is, they appear to be looking at it for the very first time. Or they simply mumble, "I don't know." It's a total lack of concern and the assumption that I'll figure it all out for them and go fetch the materials that irritates me.
>
> We have OPACS, and many of these patrons won't even go near them. When I ask them if they've checked the catalog, they reply they don't know how to use it. . . . They don't come to the library for any other purpose than to socialize and bother patrons who have legitimate business in the library . . . . Having homework assignments and reading lists shoved in my face by healthy, intelligent, able-bodied young people who have no interest in their own homework just plain bugs me. (Chelton, 1997: 193–94)

Comment: Sounds like another case of bad-guy users (see section 1.7). Chelton notes that this librarian has a tacit "theory of practice" that she uses to identify "legitimate" users and distinguish them from deadbeat users. Legitimate users are the ones who come prepared, are interested in their homework assignments, already know how to use the catalog, and expect to do most of the work themselves. Unfortunately, there is a mismatch between her perception of what is appropriate behavior and the actual behavior of most adolescents.

For discussion:
1. What difference might it make to the librarian's attitude if she reframed this situation by identifying it as a case of an imposed query? How prepared, interested, knowledgeable, and keen on work is a person likely to be when the question is generated by someone else?
2. How widespread in libraries do you think this attitude toward adolescents is? How problematic do you think such attitudes are when they do occur?

If this isn't the information that your supervisor wanted, it would help if you asked her what specifically she wants to know about X.

Another time when your supervisor asks you to get some information for him, we could be more helpful if you asked him how he plans to use the information and what kind of information about X would help him most.

5.4 THE REFERENCE INTERVIEW WITH CHILDREN AND YOUNG ADULTS

Section 5.4 was written by Lynne McKechnie, Associate Professor, Faculty of Information and Media Studies, the University of Western Ontario.

Conducting reference interviews with children and young adults presents special challenges for the reference librarian. Not only is this group of users developmentally different from adults, but they have less experience with libraries and information sources. Life contexts associated with their age have an important bearing on the reference interview, such as attendance at school, the need to develop information literacy skills, and their strong relationships with parents or other adult caretakers. In this section we focus on the skills needed to address the special needs of children and young adults in the context of the reference interview.

5.4.1 "GOT ANY BOOKS ON FLEAS?"

Here's a scenario that has been reconstructed from an actual reference question received at the reference desk of a public library. Jeremy, who was about six years old, approached the information desk with the following question.

Jeremy:	Got any books on fleas?
Librarian:	So you want some books on fleas.
Jeremy:	Yup. Fleas.
Librarian:	Well, I think we do. Come on over here with me where the insect books are.
Jeremy:	[As he and the librarian walk to the children's non-fiction section] Like with pictures.
Librarian:	Pictures?
Jeremy:	Yup. Pictures. And names. Like word names.

Librarian:	Pictures and word names? Do you want pictures of different kinds of fleas? Or maybe a picture book about fleas.
Jeremy:	Not a picture book! Them kinds of stories is for little kids. I need a book with real stuff, a book with facts.
Librarian:	Oh, a book with facts. A nonfiction book.
Jeremy:	Yup. A nonfiction book. With fleas. And words for names. Especially names of cats.
Librarian:	Cats!
Jeremy:	Especially cats.
Librarian:	Jeremy, I think it would really help if you could tell me what you want this nonfiction book for.
Jeremy:	We're going to get a cat. My Mom says I can pick the kind of cat. So, I need to know all, ALL the kinds of cats. To make sure we get the best kind.
Librarian:	I see. You need some information about cats. The different kinds of cats so that you can pick a breed, a type of cat, that you like.
Jeremy:	Yup. That's it. Breeds of cats. With pictures. And maybe yoyos.
Librarian:	Yoyos? . . .

Ten minutes later the librarian helps Jeremy check out two books about cats. The next summer Jeremy brings his Persian cat named Yoyo to the library's pet show.

This scenario demonstrates some of the special considerations that arise in interviews with children as a result of their state of cognitive development as well as their more limited experience with information sources and libraries. Jeremy's vocabulary is not yet large enough to include specific words like "breed." While it is clear that Jeremy understands what a picture book is, he did not understand the term "nonfiction" until the librarian explained the meaning of the concept. Although limited and inaccurate, Jeremy's request for a book on "fleas," a concept related to what he really wants, shows awareness of the library as an organized body of information. Jeremy's response to the offer of a picture book points to the need for age-appropriate materials, including items that are not only accessible in terms of reading level and other cognitive abilities, but also materials that are not considered by young library users themselves to be beneath or beyond their ability. Finally, this reference interview, like many with children and teens, took longer than it might have if Jeremy's mother or another adult had asked the question. As a result of asking this question himself and getting it satisfactorily answered, Jeremy's mental model (see section 1.4.2) of the public library has expanded; he now knows that the library is a good place to come to get books on "real stuff" and "facts" and that it's a good idea to ask the librarian for help.

Quick Tips for Meeting the Special Needs of Children and Young Adults

- Be respectful and nonjudgmental when interacting with children and young adults at the reference desk. Treat all of their questions as seriously as you would those from adults.
- Although children and young adults may have less experience with and knowledge of information sources and libraries, they are actively making sense of the world and are often eager to learn how things work. Involve them in the reference process. Ask what they know about the topic. Give them opportunities to browse shelves, search the library catalog, or find an article in an encyclopedia. Seek their feedback about the quality and suitability of resources found. This will increase their understanding, their self-confidence, and their sense of being a partner in the reference interaction.
- Many children and some young adults may have never asked for help at a library. They may feel shy, awkward, and reluctant to approach the reference desk. Be proactive. Approach children and teens in the library. Smile and make eye contact so that you appear open and welcoming. In the case of small children, try kneeling or bending over so that you are at their level, or at least closer to it.
- Remember that children and young adults are still developing language skills. They have more limited vocabularies than adults, may more frequently mispronounce words, and are still learning how to frame questions.
- Never assume that children and young adults understand library jargon. Unless they have been to library school, many adults do not know what a monograph or a periodical is. Children and young adults might never have encountered even more basic terms such as fiction, nonfiction, table of contents, index, or bibliography. Even adults often confuse biographies and bibliographies. Either avoid using this professional jargon or identify and explain it. For example, you could say, "To find the name of an organization to contact for your project on milk, we can look in this directory. A directory is like a specialized telephone book, with addresses and contact information."
- Accompany children and young adults to the shelves. They might not be able to retrieve items using call numbers.

DID YOU KNOW?

According to Behrmann and Vogliano, "[c]hildren are quick to discern a lack of respect for their needs or an unfairly small amount of time allocated to them" (1991:52). Patrick Jones (1998) states that many young people feel adults assume that all teenagers are troublemakers. Although equitable access to all services is a basic premise of providing library services for children and young adults, a study by Judith Dixon called "Are We Childproofing Our Public Libraries?" (1996) identified many barriers to library use by young people. It is neither correct nor fair to assume that children's and young adults' reference questions are simpler or less important than those asked by adults.

DID YOU KNOW?

According to Mary K. Chelton's 1997 Rutgers thesis, "Adult-Adolescent Service Encounters: The Library Context," school library media specialists are faced with special demands and challenges that are not acknowledged in such canonical statements as the RUSA "Guidelines for Behavioral Performance of Reference and Information Services Professionals" (1996). In her study, summarized in a 1999 RUSQ article, Chelton argues that information work is not the predominant activity in the school library media center. Reference work has to compete with routines of discipline and the enforcement of rules. The mental model of service held by both staff and students is that the school media center is a place where users can help themselves after the staff gets them started.

ANALYZE THIS REFERENCE TRANSACTION

Case 20: Self-help

Librarian: Do you need some help?
User: Yes. I need to find a picture of a baby.
Librarian: OK. (encourager) What kind of baby? (open question)
User: Just like a young baby.
Librarian: OK. Um, let's go up and look in the baby section.
User: OK.
Librarian: Let me take a quick look here for the call number. [Interruption by an interaction with another student.] OK, I got the number. You still here? 649. Here's some baby books.
User: I'd like a full-body picture.
Librarian: A full-body and a photograph picture. (acknowledgment)
User: Mm-hmmm.
Librarian: OK. Let's go down and look in Parents magazine. They have lots of pictures of babies. [Goes with the user. Some further discussion.]
User: Actually, I'm doing—I'm drawing a baby.
Librarian: Here's all the Parents magazines, and they often have pictures of babies in them.
User: OK.
Librarian: So you can [find] lots of babies. So you can just sit here and grab a stack of them and thumb through here and find the perfect baby.

(Reported in Chelton, 1999, and used with permission.)

Comment: In analyzing this reference transaction that she audio- and video-recorded in a school library media center, Mary K. Chelton (1999) points out that the librarian does not define her role as providing information, but rather as helping people find information on their own. The staff member points the user in the direction of some likely materials, but it's the user's job to evaluate and choose information on his own. "There is an embedded presumption of real or potential user competence here."

For discussion: Do you think that the model of information provision identified by Chelton is typical of school library media centers in general? How appropriate is this model for the school library media center? How appropriate would it be for a public library? for a special library? What other model could be used instead?

The time it takes to walk to and browse through the shelves can be used for further clarification of what the user really wants to know.

- Attempt to match information materials to the reading level and conceptual abilities of the child or young adult user. A quick way to assess reading level is to ask a child to read a few lines; if she makes many errors or struggles with the text, look for a document that is written at an easier level. You can also suggest materials at a variety of levels of difficulty, giving the child or young adult an opportunity to decide for himself what would be best.
- As recall memory does not fully develop until midway through childhood and emerges later than recognition memory (Gross, 2000), children tend not to remember book titles and author names. A study conducted in Denmark (Wanting, 1986) indicated that when children want specific titles, they often mention characters (both people and animals), the subject, and visual or auditory elements such as the cover illustration or a rhyme. Try to elicit clues like these during the reference interview.
- Children are multisensory learners. Give them opportunities to explore materials through their eyes (have them look at illustrations and other parts of documents like a table of contents or list of references), ears (have them read a portion of a source aloud or read selected bits to them), and hands (have them run their fingers along an index as they search for a specific entry).
- According to Patrick Jones (1998), young adults are proud of their growing independence and will therefore often not ask for help. Again, be proactive and approach teens in the library. But instead of asking if they "Need help?" try something like "Are you finding what you need?"
- Remember that reference interviews with children and young adults might take longer.

5.4.2 INFORMATION LITERACY

Most librarians believe that it is important for children and young adults to learn how to find information and use libraries, but a few carry this to the extreme of insisting that they do all this learning without any help. This tends to happen when a school assignment is involved because library staff may assume that the teacher has embedded an information search in the requirements. When it comes to child and teen users, there is often a debate about whether librarians should provide reference services or whether they should provide only instruction in information literacy.

This issue seldom arises in connection with other categories of library users. When an adult asks for the address of a particular company, the librarian provides the address and a citation for the source, possibly explaining how to use business directories in the course of finding the address. Child and adolescent library users deserve the same level of service. It is dangerous to assume that children and young adults have the skills needed to work independently. Some might, but it's important to check at the outset and use a follow-up question to invite the young user to return if she isn't finding what she needs. At the same time, librarians are also uniquely positioned to help young people acquire the information literacy skills essential for successful participation in the new knowledge society. A recommended compromise for the reference versus instruction dilemma is to incorporate instruction into the process of helping the user find the information needed. That is, you provide unobtrusive opportunities for young users to learn information literacy skills during the reference transaction.

5.4.3 THE SCHOOL ASSIGNMENT

Except for the very young, children and young adults spend a good deal of time at school or doing school-related work. Not surprisingly, many of the reference questions from this category of user also relate to schoolwork. For some children, especially those from social and cultural backgrounds without a strong tradition of library service, the first school project might be the stimulus for visiting a public library for the first time. Librarians should welcome this opportunity for helping the child develop a mental model of the library as a helpful and pleasurable place to visit.

Reference questions arising from school assignments differ from others in several ways. Almost all are secondhand queries that have been imposed by a teacher. The same assignment may have been given to every student in the class. As a result, a librarian may encounter, all in a short period of time, a number of questions from different students that are all generated by the same assignment. Patrick Jones (1998) talks about the "garbled assignment" problem, wherein it soon becomes clear that the student really doesn't understand what is required. As we have seen in section 5.3.1 on the imposed query, this kind of problem is very common when the question has not been self-generated.

Some students ask questions that are more concerned with how to do the project than with its information content—questions like "How do I do an outline/table of contents/bibliography?" or "How do I find a topic for a science project?" Some librarians find this kind of request frustrating and interpret it a request "to do their homework for them." However, it isn't doing their home-

---

ANALYZE THIS REFERENCE TRANSACTION

Case 21: My project is due tomorrow.

User: I have to write something for a seminar on the Mennonite family—or maybe Amish. I'm not sure if they are really the same thing or not.

Librarian: On Mennonites? (acknowledgment)

User: Yes, a seminar.

Librarian: What are you trying to write? The Mennonite family? Is that what you said? (acknowledgment to confirm that the topic was heard)

User: Yes. Like the children—how they grow up.

Librarian: OK, did you check some of our circulating books yet? Have you been over to our 282s? [They go to shelf.] You've already been to this section then? The Mennonites. Did you try this book?

User: Yes. It's too old. There wasn't anything about the family. [User has taken another copy of this book home.] There's nothing in there.

Librarian: You're sure. If this has education . . . ? You did see that there are some things in this book though? I just want to make sure before we give up on the book that you tried it, OK?

User: No . . . There's nothing about the family itself.

Librarian: OK. [She recommends that the user read particular pages.] Did you try the reference books? [Shows the user in turn entries on Mennonites in four different encyclopedias, but each time the user says the articles aren't what he wants. The librarian recommends a periodical search and suggests an index, but the user thinks it may take too long.]

User: You don't have videos that I could watch?

Librarian: [Librarian explains how to find videos in the catalog.] This project is due tomorrow? [And so on . . .]

Dewdney, Mennonites

Comment: This is a classic example of the frustrations that librarians often face in trying to answer questions generated by school assignments. The user's purpose here is to find materials—preferably ones that won't take too much time to access and process—so that he can achieve his real goal, which is to hand in a passing assignment by the next day. In this transcript (edited here for brevity because it goes on for five pages), the librarian, despite trying very hard, is never able to provide any information that the user is willing to accept. In the course of the interview, she asks one open question ("What are you trying to write?") and 23 closed questions. The problem seems to be that the user has a very specific understanding of what he means by Mennonite family life. Therefore the book that the librarian thought had lots of good material on the Mennonite family was rejected: "There wasn't anything about the family." That should have been a red warning flag to the librarian. At this point, instead of asking twelve more closed questions, she could have asked a sense-making question like, "If we could find the perfect book or article for you today, what specific information would it include?" or even, "What is missing from this book The Mennonites that you absolutely need to have?" Before she spends more time recommending sources and giving bibliographic instruction in their use, she needs a better idea of what she should be looking for (see section 3.2.3).

A QUICK TIP

ATTITUDE IS EVERYTHING

An experienced librarian from the Mental Models study said, "Many librarians say how resentful they are about doing school projects. But if you're interested or you can get yourself interested in their questions, then it's fun. I think it's great when kids come with their moms, because of two things. First, projects are fun a lot of times, especially if you find something; but also it's a social thing. They come for the kids' project, but the moms of the kids can also get a magazine or a video, so it's not all work for them. It's an opportunity for them both to combine business and pleasure. They come to get material for the project but at the same time they discover the library is a place to go for other stuff. And for the librarian there's that absolute pleasure you get when the kids clutch that little book to their breast and say, 'That's exactly what I wanted,' and it's just a book on sharks or monster trucks."

work for them to provide students with the help that they need to move through all the steps necessary to complete the assignment. This is why it's important, even if you think you have heard the question before, to conduct a reference interview with the student at the desk. Even when two students are working on the same assignment assigned by the same teacher, what each student needs to know may not be the same. One student could need help narrowing down the topic, another might need help with the proper format for doing a bibliography, and so on. Don't assume that the same information that suited the last student will help the next one. Some sense-making questions (section 3.2.3) that work well with children are:

> How did you get the idea for this?
> What are you going to do with this?
> What would you like to know about frogs/global warming/
> tree rings?

Quick Tips for the School Assignment

- Never assume that all reference questions are related to school assignments. The child who asks for information on diabetes might not be doing a science fair project on the topic. She could have a friend or family member who has just been diagnosed with the disease. To find out what is really needed, use open questions (section 3.2.1) like "It would be helpful if you could tell me what you plan to do with this information."
- Try to find out as much as you can about an assignment. Ask if the student has a copy of the teacher's written instructions that you can look at. Try to find out the due date, the length of the assignment, whether or not a specific number or types of resources are needed, if students are also required to report where and how they got the information, and if there are any other special requirements. This will help you determine exactly what type and amount of information is needed by the student to complete the assignment.
- If there is time, try to speak directly with the teacher who has given the assignment. As with all imposed queries, it is best to negotiate the question with the individual who originally asked it. Students may have misunderstood or completely missed the teacher's instructions.
- Don't expect all children and young adults to be interested in the questions they ask. Remember that many school-related topics have been assigned rather than freely chosen.

ANALYZE THIS REFERENCE TRANSACTION

Case 22: More is not always better.

User: I need some information—periodicals—on the war on terrorism. Something current. It's for an essay I have to write.

Librarian: All right. You need magazine articles? (acknowledgment)

User: Mm-hmm. Or books too.

Librarian: [Librarian explains how to use the Readers' Guide at some length.]

User: [After a while, the user returns to the desk, having apparently changed his topic to the Gulf War.] There was just too much on the terrorism subject. Pages and pages.

Librarian: There's a heck of a lot on the Gulf War. I hate to tell you. [laughs]

Dewdney, Adapted from Arms race

Comment: If you hold the view that information is a commodity (see section 1.5.1), then you may think that the more of this valuable commodity you can give the user the better. However, many users are overwhelmed by dozens of books, scores of periodical articles, or thousands of hits from a search engine. When students are working on an unfamiliar and diffuse topic, often they need help in eliminating material and finding a small number of sources that they can understand and use.

- While it is hard for library staff to stay enthusiastic about a reference question that they have already been asked 37 times from grade five children all doing the same project on ancient Egypt, remember that for the individual child in front of you, this is the first time the question has been asked.

5.4.4 PARENTS

Working with parents and other adult caretakers is part of doing reference work with children and young adults. Many children can't travel to the library on their own, and parents often want to continue to help their children once they arrive at the library. Some parents are an invaluable ally in the reference transaction. These parents are interested in their child's question, eager to find appropriate material to answer it, and usually want to help the child learn how to get help and find resources at the library. However, problems arise in the reference interview in two situations that involve parents. The first occurs when the parent arrives at the library alone to get materials for a child's project and the librarian can't talk directly to the child or teen. This is an imposed query (see section 5.3.1) made even trickier because now there are two filters standing between the librarian and the originator of the question: the child and the child's parent. The second problematic situation involves the overbearing parent. These parents arrive at the reference desk with a child or teenager in tow but completely dominate the interaction. Sometimes the young person utters not a single word, possibly even wandering off to another part of the library. Here is a list of strategies that you can use to make the adult-accompanied child a full participant in the reference interview while at the same time channeling parental involvement along productive lines.

- Smile at and establish eye contact with the child or young adult as well as with the parent so as to include them in the reference transaction right from the start.
- Make sure that you speak with the child or young adult throughout the entire reference interview. When a parent asks a question, redirect the reference interview to the child by using acknowledgment with him or by asking him the follow-up question. For example, in response to a mother who asks, "Do you have any books about trucks for my son?" you can turn and directly say to the four-year-old, "So, you're looking for some books about trucks."
- If possible separate an "overbearing" parent from the child. You can do this by offering to help the child find the information while the parent is looking for her or his own materials. For example, a librarian might say, "Sure. I would be happy to help Mary. We've got a great current magazine collection right here. Perhaps you would like to look through some of these while Mary and I look for information on pioneers." Alternately, you could leave the parent doing a task related to a query, such as checking encyclopedias for relevant articles while you and the child or teenager do another task, like searching the periodical index.

5.5 INTERVIEWING ADULTS WITH SPECIAL LANGUAGE-RELATED NEEDS

Because the basis of communication is a common language, communication accidents are more likely to happen when you and the user do not share the same first language or dialect, or when the user has a speech or hearing disability. Pay attention to cultural differences as well as to language differences. In your effort to understand what the user is saying, you might be sending other negative messages (such as asking too many questions or infringing on personal space) that hamper communication. It is important not to make assumptions about intelligence on the basis of language proficiency.

For people whose English language skills or ability to enunciate are not perfect, remember to listen patiently. Talk clearly and a bit more slowly than usual, but not louder. Above all, stay calm and be patient. Don't say to yourself, "I didn't understand a word of what he said—and I never will." Work through the strategies of acknowledgment, taking ownership, asking the user to write the question down, restating and paraphrasing the question. One of these will work in most situations.

1. Restate what you do understand (see section 2.4.3). If you catch the word "book" or "information," respond with some acknowledgment such as "You're looking for a book on . . . ?" or "You need some information . . . ?" This establishes your willingness to help, encourages the user to repeat or fill in the part you missed, and gives you a second chance to listen.
2. Take ownership of the problem. Say, "I'm sorry, I seem to be having trouble understanding people today. Could you tell me again?"
3. If you still do not understand what the user wants, ask him to write it down. Again, take ownership: "It would help me if you could just write the name (or topic) down on this paper." However, keep in mind that some people might not be able to write in English.
4. If all else fails, ask someone else to help. Sometimes another librarian will be able to hear immediately what the person is saying. Do this gracefully: "Maybe Mrs. Milne will be able to help. Let's just go over there and ask her." Often just moving with the user to a less public area will lessen tension or frustration for both of you and encourage the user to express the request in another way.

DID YOU KNOW?

Hendricks (1991) points out that a source of misunderstanding both in Japanese and in Spanish is that the negative response to a negatively phrased question is the reverse of the English practice. In reply to the question "You didn't bring any money either?" a response of "yes" would mean, "Yes, I did not," whereas "no" would mean, "No, I did."

DID YOU KNOW?

Especially with users who speak English as a second language, it is easy for similar-sounding words to be confused or misheard. In their article "Oranges and Peaches," Dewdney and Michell (1996) provide many examples such as bird control/birth control and laws/lace. They advise asking a question like "What would you like to know about lace?" If the user answers that he wants to know the laws regarding copyright, the librarian stands a good chance of repairing the miscommunication.

5.5.1 ENGLISH AS A SECOND LANGUAGE

In our increasingly multicultural societies, many library users do not speak English as their first language. Lack of fluency in English can create communication problems, but is not the only barrier to providing reference service. Many users come from countries where access to written materials is limited and where a library may simply be a large reading room with closed stacks. Questions, if asked at all, will focus on obtaining books from the stacks or on library holdings. Ziming Liu notes that it's not just working in a second language that deters university students from developing countries from asking reference questions but also "the lack of attention to reference services in their home countries" (1993: 28).

Libraries can help by training library staff in cross-cultural communication and by hiring staff members who can speak the dominant languages of the area served. In academic libraries, international students who are familiar with using North American libraries should be asked to participate in tours for new students. A large library system needs to determine which branches have different language concentrations and provide appropriate staffing, but it must also keep aware of changes in the population. Particular cultural groups may move to new areas, and collections and services (and sometimes staff) must move with them.

Here are some suggestions for improving reference communication with those who speak English as a second language (ESL).

- Make no assumptions (section 3.2.2). Assumptions are sometimes made about the level of service needed before users have gotten past the first few words of their question.
- Avoid using library jargon and acronyms (to be avoided with any user, but especially with ESL speakers).
- Don't raise your voice; the user's lack of fluency in English doesn't mean she can't hear you.
- Avoid using complex sentence structure and vocabulary. But don't just assume that the user will necessarily understand all the everyday words that you choose instead. Hendricks (1991) points out that many ESL speakers have learned English from textbooks and have never learned the everyday words.
- Don't ask negative questions such as "Don't you want this book?" or double-barreled questions like "Do you want to search yourself or do you want me to show you how?"
- Check often for comprehension, but don't just ask, "Did you understand?" Nonnative English speakers who want

A QUICK TIP

GET HELP FROM EXPERTS

As a staff training activity for reference staff, the library could invite a trainer or counselor from a local cross-cultural center or immigrant settlement service to come to talk to staff about common misconceptions that affect cross-cultural communication.

DID YOU KNOW?

Errol Lam (1988) points out that in reference transactions, African Americans rarely look at a speaking authority figure; white users, in contrast, tend to use eye contact more. African Americans use more eye contact when they are speaking and less when they are listening.

EXERCISE

CONSIDER THIS SCENARIO:

"An international student approaches the reference desk. In a quiet and retiring manner, the student asks for help. The librarian on the other side of the desk tenses while straining to understand the questions through the heavily accented, soft-spoken voice of the student. The librarian becomes agitated, thinking why doesn't this student speak up? Why can't he speak English? The foreign student senses the librarian's distress, apologizes and leaves without getting the needed information" (Hoffman and Popa, 1986: 356–60).

FOR DISCUSSION:

What cultural factors should the librarian have considered? How might the librarian have dealt with her own discomfort? What specific steps could she have taken to understand the question?

to be polite and respectful may say yes, even when they have not understood.

- Use visual aids such as handouts, and provide users with written library guides or pathfinders appropriate to their questions.
(Adapted from Greenfield, Johnston, and Williams, 1986; Janes and Meltzer, 1990; and Ormondroyd, 1990.)

5.5.2 CROSS-CULTURAL COMMUNICATION

Culture affects all types of communication. In this section, we point out a few of the communication accidents that can occur in the reference context directly as a result of cultural differences. If the number of "intercultural accidents" seems to be increasing, one reason is that we are all encountering cultural differences more often now than before. Contributing factors are increased ease of travel, changing immigration patterns, a greater mix of populations in large urban centers (especially immigrants taking courses), and new technology. Think, for example, of the multicultural nature of discussion groups and Web sites on the Internet. Daily we "meet" more people who are different from ourselves than we ever have before. We must therefore make a special effort to be aware of differing perspectives in order to avoid misunderstandings. First we need to educate ourselves about intercultural communication so that we are able to identify intercultural differences. Then we need a way of thinking about these differences that will enable us to develop intentional strategies for communicating effectively.

A good first step is to read as much as you can about the factors that affect intercultural communication and discuss them with knowledgeable people. The main differences between cultures are the different values and attitudes toward human relationships. These manifest themselves in differences in body language, in sense of time and personal space, and in general rules for etiquette or "being polite" or showing respect. Some differences seem quite arbitrary; for example, the "thumbs up" gesture means "all right" in North America, but to some people from Greece and Southern Italy, it means the equivalent of the American "middle finger."

Most cultural differences are internally logical. Many are based on concepts of time, space, and one's social position in any given situation. For example, in some cultures, being late is a mark of your importance—it shows you are busy. Personal space is also often culture-specific: a distance of two feet between two people may be perceived as "too close" (read "pushy") by the British participant and "too distant" (read "unfriendly") by the Latino. Touching is fraught with subtle cultural, social, and gender differences. A "friendly" tap on the shoulder of a South Asian female student by a male Euro-American librarian will likely be

A QUICK TIP

USE INCLUSION

Especially with international students, explain why you are asking questions. Yvonne De Souza (1996) explains that international students might not be aware that it is part of the reference librarian's job to conduct a reference interview and could therefore interpret your questions as some sort of test. If you ask, "What have you done/found so far?" the international user may be embarrassed to say, "Nothing," and be concerned about losing face. Use inclusion (section 4.1.1) to explain why you are asking open or sense-making questions.

DID YOU KNOW?

New technologies can help the hearing impaired participate in the reference interview. Teletypewriters (TTY) and telecommunication devices for the deaf (TDD) provide a way for the deaf to communicate through the telephone. Using TDD, a hearing impaired person can type a message over telephone lines and receive a response from a TDD-equipped library staff member. These services are now being supplemented by electronic reference services using e-mail and/or chat (see Chapter 6).

considered quite inappropriate. In some cultures, space is perceived as communal, permitting people to jump queues. Conflict then occurs when a person with this view of space comes to a culture that rigidly observes the "first come, first served" rule. Directness or "getting to the point" is valued by North Americans as an indication of efficiency and honesty, but in some Asian and Middle Eastern cultures it is perceived as impolite, if not downright offensive. The tolerance for conflict varies between cultures: saying "no" directly may be seen as a sign of disrespect by people whose culture values harmony.

Having given some examples of situations that call for cultural sensitivity, we must also say that a little knowledge is a dangerous thing: as we learn more about different cultures we are tempted to overgeneralize behavior within a particular culture. Vast individual differences exist within any one culture—consider, for example, your own way of communicating with that of someone else from your culture. Communication accidents arising between two people of different cultures may not, in fact, have their roots in culture but may have resulted from other individual or situational factors. So there are no general "rules" for cross-cultural communication, except perhaps to assess the situation on its merits, and show respect for the individual. However, here are a few tips for using nonverbal and speaking skills with people of another culture:

- Use body language (section 2.4.2) that suggests approachability, respect, and willingness to help: smiling, standing up, giving the user your full attention.
- Restate or paraphrase (section 3.2.4) the user's words to allow the other person to correct you.
- Do not assume that the user's smile means agreement—check it out.
- Recognize that the user's silence or lack of eye contact may mean agreement or demonstration of respect rather than lack of understanding.
- Keep your questions simple and wait for an answer.
- Use inclusion (section 4.1.1) to explain why you are asking sense-making questions (3.2.3) about what the user has done so far or how the information will be used.

5.5.3 INTERVIEWING PEOPLE WITH DISABILITIES

Libraries have worked hard to eliminate physical barriers that in the past hampered access to libraries and library materials by people with disabilities. The Americans with Disabilities Act (ADA), passed into law in 1990, covers most U.S. libraries in both public and private settings and has prompted the reassessment of

DID YOU KNOW?

Katy Lenn says that individuals with learning disabilities may "experience difficulties receiving, storing, processing, remembering or transmitting information" in either written or spoken form and may have difficulty concentrating or paying attention to detail (1996: 16). Users who find it hard to focus or remember may benefit from repetition. It can be helpful to use two channels of communication—speaking and writing down your questions and the answers—so that the user can both hear and see the process of the interview.

A QUICK TIP

AVOID UNMONITORED REFERRALS

Unmonitored referrals are problematic for all users, but are especially so for people with disabilities. Before you send a person with a disability upstairs, downstairs, or off to another library, make sure that you have understood the question and know for sure that the desired information will actually be at the distant location.

A QUICK TIP

BEWARE OF SPREAD

According to Wright and Davie, "spread" happens when you assume that a person with one disability also has problems in other areas as well: "You can observe this happening when people raise their voices in conversation with a blind person" (1991: 5).

library facilities, collections, and services. Libraries elsewhere are also paying greater attention to removing physical barriers to library access. On January 16, 2001, ALA Council approved the "Library Services for People with Disabilities Policy." This policy states: "Libraries must not discriminate against individuals with disabilities and shall ensure that individuals with disabilities have equal access to library resources." While emphasizing facilities, collections, and adaptive devices, the policy does not explicitly address communication skills needed by staff members who respond to the information needs of persons with disabilities. Nevertheless, helping library staff acquire appropriate communication skills is a crucial element in providing equal access.

The key, as with ESL speakers, is to respect the user and take every question seriously—possibly even more seriously than usual, since it can take more determination for a person with a disability to come to the library and approach a stranger with a request for help. A number of physical and mental conditions can make communication difficult. There are speech disorders, including problems of articulation, voice production, and rhythm, that can be caused by a variety of factors, including a cleft palate, hearing impairment, stroke, or cerebral palsy. Users with a mental illness may speak in a manner that appears inappropriate: incoherently or too loud, for example. Although the library literature sometimes refers to these users as "problem patrons," the Americans with Disabilities Act recognizes that mental impairment is a disability. The ADA defines mental impairments as "any mental or psychological disorder, such as metal retardation, organic brain syndrome, emotional or mental illness, and specific learning disabilities."

People with hearing difficulties have different ways of communicating, depending on when the problem began. People who have been profoundly deaf from very early childhood have never heard spoken language and will communicate using a sign language such as ASL (American Sign Language). For libraries serving such users, equitable access can be provided by hiring a staff member who can use sign language or by recruiting signing volunteers. Some who have been hearing impaired from birth but have residual hearing might wish to communicate by speaking. Because their pronunciation may be nonstandard, you need to listen carefully, use acknowledgment (section 2.4.3), ask for repetition when necessary, and sometimes ask the user to write down the question. Those with hearing loss in later life can speak without difficulty but may have a problem understanding your response.

In *Library Service to the Deaf and Hearing Impaired*, Phyllis Dalton provides these tips for communicating with people who have hearing loss:

- Speak clearly but do not exaggerate pronunciation of words in a way that could distort lip movement. Make it possible for the hearing impaired to maintain a clear view of your mouth.
- Maintain eye contact, even when an interpreter is present.
- Use mime, body language, and facial expression to augment the voice.
- Write it down. (1985: 30)

5.6 INTERVIEWING USERS WITH CONSUMER HEALTH AND LEGAL QUESTIONS

A librarian once told us that her least favorite reference questions concerned legal and medical information needs. Both types of queries undoubtedly present special challenges, especially for public librarians, who are unlikely to be specialists but have to cope with unfamiliar terminology, complicated or inadequate resources, and tricky ethical issues (including the "information vs. advice" problem). In addition, users who need consumer health or legal information may be reluctant to disclose the problem to the librarian. Yet effective service requires the librarian to determine not only the subject and scope of the question, but also the user's expectations and requirements, including that of privacy. This section deals with the first problem the librarian encounters in legal and health information service: finding out what the user really wants to know. Of course, the actual search for legal and health information raises other problems, owing to inherent difficulties of their respective literatures, but that's beyond our scope here.

Both the legal and the health reference interview follow the sequence of a good reference interview in general: establishing a good communication climate, asking questions, verifying details of the reference query, and following up. But legal and health queries pose at least two special problems. First, most users have no idea of the huge scope of these subject areas and commonly ask "too large" questions, such as "Where is your law section?" thinking they can find what they need by themselves. Or they may request "too specific" materials, such as "a book on plantar warts," when the information they need is likely in a medical encyclopedia or periodical article. Often they want very recent in-

A QUICK TIP

FIND THAT POTTED PALM

If you suspect that the user might describe the query more fully in private, invite her to walk with you away from the desk or catalog: "That's probably in the 600s—let's go that way." (Notice that this is one occasion when you appear to be making a premature diagnosis, but it's really a ruse to ensure privacy.) You may eventually have to come back to the desk for a medical encyclopedia or a Web search, but by then you'll know more about what you're looking for.

DID YOU KNOW?

In an analysis of 27 public library reference transactions that began with a user asking for legal information (a subset of Dewdney's dissertation data), the most common problem was getting from the initial question (e.g., "Where's your law section?") to the real information need (how to resolve a boundary dispute with a neighbor). In all but six interviews, the librarian made dysfunctional assumptions about the nature of the query or the user's purpose, rather than asking pertinent but sensitive questions. For example, one librarian assumed that the user wanted instructions for completing a tax return, when she simply wanted to read about financial planning. Librarians also tended to ask questions that the user was unable to answer, such as "Is this a federal law?" or "Civil or criminal?"

formation, such as new drug trials, that they cannot find in a catalog, and so the initial question may be "Can you show me how this catalog works?" Both the medical and legal literature are constantly changing. People may also have difficulty articulating the need because of the specialized terminology in these fields—hence the genealogy/gynecology mixup (see section 1.4.1).

The second and even trickier aspect of legal and health queries is that they often arise from personal needs involving sensitive or emotional factors. In particular, privacy and anonymity may be of great concern to the user. Consequently, certain interview skills described previously in this book must be used with special care, or even avoided. For example, the skills of acknowledgment or restatement (section 2.4.3)—repeating or paraphrasing what the user has said—must be used very carefully in legal and health reference interviews. A person who whispers his question to the librarian does not want "Sex education?" or "You were arrested?" broadcast to the rest of the library or even to nearby staff. Study the following stages and skills carefully to see how they differ from other types of interviewing.

Establish a good communication climate

- Demonstrate positive body language, such as initial eye contact and smiling (or sympathetic nodding, depending on the user's state of mind) to reassure and encourage the user (section 2.4.2).
- Use encouragers (section 2.4.4) such as, "Mm-hmm," "I see," or "and then?" in a supportive tone.
- Listen (section 2.4.5) to show you are interested and attentive. Don't interrupt unless the conversation gets way off track.
- Assure the user that she is not alone: "A lot of people ask us about that type of thing."
- Use reflection of feeling, but very carefully. "So that's really worrying you" or "You sound pretty upset about this" may help establish rapport, but equally it may provoke an emotional outburst that is hard to handle.

Find out what help is needed

- Avoid premature diagnosis (section 3.2.2). Don't jump to conclusions about what the information will be used for, or whether the user is simply pretending that he needs it for a friend. People often ask questions on behalf of family members or disabled friends who cannot come to the library—listen for clues (see the imposed query, 5.3.1).
- Use inclusion (section 4.1.1) or explain why you need to know more about the query: "There are a lot of Web sites

A QUICK TIP

QUESTIONS TO ASK THE DOCTOR

Sometimes people come to the library to find answers to questions they forgot to ask the doctor, or questions they do not know how to phrase. King County Library System in Washington has a very helpful handout for library users, Please Ask Your Doctor: An Interview Guide to Use with Health Care Professionals (www.kcls.org/askdoc/askdr.html). This helps the user and takes pressure off the librarian to provide advice or interpretation.

A QUICK TIP

UP CLOSE AND PERSONAL

With medical and legal questions, inexperienced librarians commonly ask, "Is this personal or for a project?" If it's a project, you can go on with your questioning. But if the user says, "Personal," where do you go from there? It's usually a conversation stopper, especially if the request was for material considered sensitive, such as abortion. A much better approach is to reassure the user by saying, "We have quite a bit of material on abortion," and then, "If you can tell me a little bit about what you'd like to know, I can help you better." Mentioning "a little bit" is crucial in sensitive questions because the user realizes she doesn't have to tell the whole story.

dealing with cancer, so if you could tell me a little bit more about it, I may be able to find something more helpful."

- Ask open questions (section 3.2.1) that the user can answer in her own words (e.g., "What aspect of the law/medicine are you looking for?") rather than closed questions such as "Is that a bylaw?" or "Is that a bacterium or a virus?"—questions to which the user may not know the answer.
- Ask sense-making questions (section 3.2.3) that leave the user in control but still give her an opportunity to describe the important aspects of the information.
- To get at the situation, ask, "Can you tell me a bit about how this problem arose?" or "Where did you come across this term?" or "What have you done so far to find out about this?" Answers to these questions may also help you to determine where the user is in the search process, and whether she has already consulted a lawyer or doctor.
- To get at the knowledge gap, ask, "What would you like to know?" and then "What do you already know about X?"
- To find out the intended use of the information, say, "If you can tell me a little bit about how you hope to use this information, I can help you better." The phrase "a little bit" is crucial with sensitive questions. These questions encourage the user to describe in her own words what she wants to be able to do as a result of the search. Sometimes the answer is "to make a decision," "to find out I'm not alone," or "to know what the doctor's talking about." The kind of materials needed in each case will be different.
- Ask closed questions to gather more detail: "Did you make a copy of that Web page?" Sometimes the user has taken notes or is working from a document such as a letter or pamphlet.
- Ask verifying questions to confirm your understanding: "You said this was German measles, not red measles?" or "You mentioned a particular Supreme Court case in 1999?"

Establish boundaries

- Explain that you provide information, not advice or interpretation. Contrary to the beliefs of many librarians, users rarely use the library for a cheap source of professional advice. More often they want to prepare themselves for an appointment with a doctor or lawyer or may just

A QUICK TIP

RESOURCES FOR LIBRARIANS

On the Web, there are some excellent resources for librarians who answer consumer health problems. Healthnet, from the library at the University of Connecticut Health Center, provides ten guidelines (including interview tips) to help library staff address personal medical concerns (http://library. uchc.edu/departm/hnet/guidelines. html). HealthInfoQuest, from the National Network of Librarians of Medicine, provides sample reference interviews and pathfinders for consumer health information providers (http://nnlm.gov/health infoquest/help). Follow the links in these two sites for other resources.

DID YOU KNOW?

Understanding the problem is the hardest challenge. In two public library mail surveys— one directed to librarians who answer legal reference questions and one directed to librarians who answer health questions—researchers identified eight categories of problems. The most frequent problem for both groups, according to these librarians, was the user's inability or unwillingness to express the query clearly or completely. More than 40 percent of these librarians said they "often" or "very often" had difficulty understanding what the user really wanted to know (Dewdney, Marshall, and Tiamiyu, 1991).

want to read more about what they have been told. Nevertheless, make it clear that the user should not depend on library or Internet materials for advice, that these are always changing (and sometimes are inaccurate), and that the user should consult a professional for advice.

- Do not make referrals to specific practitioners. Instead, refer the user to a service (e.g., hospital, law society) that gives out names of doctors or lawyers accepting new clients.
- Do not use self-disclosure ("I had that kind of problem myself . . .") or talk about other individuals' personal problems. You can put the user at ease without comparing problems, which may in fact not be similar at all.

Close the interview part of the transaction

- Give information about other search strategies. Let the user know that there are other routes to pursue, perhaps by offering a referral to another service or showing the user the links to other sources on the Web.
- Use closure (section 3.2.5) to finish a conversation with an overly talkative user. People with personal problems sometimes just need to talk about it, but occasionally you'll have to say, "I've given you the best information we have, so perhaps you'd like to take that home and have a look at it" or "I wish I had more time to talk, but do call the community center. Here's the number."
- Always ask a follow-up question (section 4.1.3). If the user was unable to get the help he needed, he should know that he can ask again or ask for a referral to another service or site. After looking at some material, the user may be better able to articulate his query. An all-purpose follow-up you can use: "If this information doesn't help, please ask again and I can suggest some other places to try." Even if the user hasn't been willing to describe the information need completely (or at all), a follow-up statement helps to ensure the user doesn't give up looking for help.

INITIAL AND NEGOTIATED HEALTH AND LEGAL QUESTIONS

The following question pairs, reported to us by public librarians, show why it is important to avoid premature diagnosis and to conduct a reference interview that gets beyond the initial statement of the question and discovers the real need.

Initial question
1. I'd like a book on becoming a lady.
2. I'd like to see the National Building Code.
3. Where are your phone books?
4. Can you get me a book from the Central Library on cosmetic surgery?
5. Have you got New Jersey laws?
6. Books on schizophrenia and homosexuality.
7. I want to read about the law.

Negotiated question
1. Information on menstruation for a young girl.
2. I'd like to see a map of seismic zones in this region.
3. An address for a California medical clinic.
4. Information on the risks of breast reduction.
5. Was a song by Bruce Springsteen adopted as the official state song?
6. Help in understanding a member of a family.
7. How to get a "deadbeat dad" to pay child support.

5.7 THE READERS' ADVISORY INTERVIEW

Some authorities, such as Mary K. Chelton, argue that the readers' advisory interview differs so substantially from other kinds of reference interviews that it should be thought of as an entirely separate animal. The readers' advisory interview is focused on helping readers find books they want to read, usually fiction books to be read for pleasure. Although no national statistics are gathered on what proportion fiction comprises of total public library circulation, Kenneth Shearer (1996) has used North Carolina's public library circulation statistics as the basis for estimating that fiction accounts for about 60 percent of total book circulation. As Francine Fialkoff, editor of *Library Journal*, has noted, "All the surveys we've seen, conducted by librarians as well as non-librarians, indicate that there is virtually no service library users value more highly than the ability to match a book with a reader or to answer the question, 'What do I read next?'" (1998:58). In this section we consider what library staff can do to find out from users what books they would enjoy and then help them choose.

There are two elements in effective readers' advisory work: the behind-the-scenes work, sometimes called "passive strategies" (but passive only in the sense of not involving direct contact with the user), and the face-to-face interaction of the readers' advisory interview. So-called passive strategies include putting spine labels on books, shelving books in separate genre collections such as Mysteries or Science Fiction, creating bookmarks and annotated book lists, and setting up attractive displays that are constantly replenished. This behind-the-scenes work sets the stage for the readers' advisory interview, which requires the same skills as other reference interviews, but there are some important differences. In readers' advisory transactions, you need above all to create a climate that encourages readers to talk about books and authors. A good open question that works for readers' advisers is "Can you tell me about a book you've read and really enjoyed?" followed up by a further probe, "What particularly did you like about it?" The ability to listen and distill the essence of what users say is a crucial skill for all reference interviews, but is especially challenging in the readers' advisory context. The readers' adviser has to pay close attention to what the reader says about a complex set of book appeal characteristics such as plot, characters, setting, pacing, preferred type of ending, difficulty, and length ("quick reads" versus "fat books"), and so on.

In addition to the skills needed for reference work in general, the readers' adviser should know something about reading and

DID YOU KNOW?

Readers' advisory as it is currently practiced operates from very different assumptions from those that used to underpin the Readers' Advisory movement of the 1920s and 1930s in North American public libaries. The idea behind that service was "reading with a purpose": systematic reading on socially significant topics for purposes of self-improvement and adult education, what is now called Adult Independent Learning. (See, for example, Jennie Flexner, A Readers' Advisory Service. New York: American Association for Adult Education, 1934.) The current emphasis in readers' advisory work is to recognize that readers have a variety of purposes that they would like to serve through reading: of these, pleasure is one of the most important. Duncan Smith's Talking with Readers: A Workbook for Readers' Advisory Service declares firmly: "Readers' advisory service is about establishing the library as a place of delight for the members of its community" (2000).

about popular genres of fiction. In readers' advisory work, there is seldom a single right answer—there are usually many books that would suit the reader. But there are also many wrong answers, books that would *not* be appropriate for that particular reader. The role of the readers' adviser is to help narrow down choices to a manageable number of suggestions that match the reader's stated interests and tastes. Does this mean that the readers' adviser needs to have read every book that she recommends? No, not any more than reference librarians working in other domains are expected to have all the answers in their heads. That's what reference tools are for. Fortunately, there is a growing number of excellent reference tools, including electronic resources, that the reference librarian can use, preferably along with the reader so that the readers' advisory transaction becomes a shared exploration of books.

Despite the growing awareness of the importance of readers' advisory work, it remains an area that many reference librarians find unfamiliar, difficult, and anxiety-inducing. One reason many librarians feel unequipped to provide readers' advisory help is that, as Dana Watson (2000) reports, only 14 of the 56 master's degree programs accredited by the American Library Association offer courses in readers' advisory services. Nor has readers' advisory work been given as much research attention as other areas of reference, with the result that we don't know nearly as much as would be desirable about the way that the readers' advisory interview is actually conducted in libraries. Kenneth Shearer (1996), Pauletta Brown Bracy (1996), and Anne May *et al.* (2000) are three researchers who have begun to address this gap by using unobtrusive methods to study the readers' advisory library visit. All three researchers have observed the same problems: Staff members fail to conduct an interview; they tend to rely on personal reading as their only source; they almost never use reference tools apart from the catalog (helpful only for a known author or title); and they do not follow up. May *et al.* report that the findings of an unobtrusive study of readers' advisory service in the Nassau, New York, Library System "underscored that a nonmethodical, informal, and serendipitous response was the norm to a patron's request for a 'good read'" (2000: 40–43).

Especially troubling in all three of these unobtrusive studies was the prevalence of a strategy of negative closure (section 3.1.5) in which the librarians used their own lack of personal interest in a particular author or genre as a reason for not providing any help. When reference staff was asked for help in finding a book similar to one the user had previously enjoyed, a not uncommon response was to say something along the lines of "I'm sorry but I've never read author X" or "I'm not very familiar with African-

American authors [or science fiction or fiction suitable for young adults], but maybe if you browse over there you'll find something." Underlying these reported problems with the readers' advisory transaction is a common factor: Librarians, by and large, do *not* view a readers' advisory as an area in which they can appropriately use their professional skills and training. With regular reference questions, librarians have received professional training and know what to do: conduct a reference interview, consult the appropriate reference tools, and provide an answer that is supported by authoritative sources. They would not consider it appropriate to respond to a question about, say, the current population of Sydney, Australia, by saying, "I'm sorry but I'm not very interested in Australian topics [or geographic topics or topics involving numbers] and don't know much about them, but maybe if you browse over there you'll find something."

For every other kind of reference work, it is understood that the professionalism of the reference librarian does not depend on his or her personal interest in or knowledge about the topic. Professional commitment to helping users motivates reference librarians to find answers in reference sources, irrespective of the topic. Moreover, they do not rely on whatever information happens to reside in their own heads. As Duncan Smith (2000) has pointed out, if a user asks for information on starting a small business, it is not acceptable for a reference librarian to say, "You know, I started a small business once and this is how I did it." Why, he wonders, can it be supposed that an acceptable answer to a readers' advisory question could be "You know, I read a book that you might like to read." Although the user *might* like to read the book most recently enjoyed by the librarian, it is also quite possible that the user's tastes and interests are very different from the librarian's. The readers' adviser should not rely on a lucky coincidence of tastes, but should use professional skills first to find out about the advisee's reading interests and, second, to use reference tools to find suitable books that match those interests.

In this section we stress that success in readers' advisory work depends on learning and systematically using a cluster of skills that can be acquired. It does *not* depend on some inborn knack that lucky people are born with but others can never learn.

5.7.1 SETTING THE STAGE FOR READERS' ADVISORY SERVICE

Setting the stage is even more important for readers' advisory work than for other kinds of reference. As we saw in section 2.1, users with reference questions are often diffident about asking their question at the reference desk, but at least they usually know that

A QUICK TIP

RESPECT THE READER'S TASTE

Users, sometimes with good reason, may fear that librarians will look down on their reading taste. According to Joyce Saricks and Nancy Brown (1997) Downers Grove (Illinois) Public Library reassures readers by posting behind the service desk a sign saying: ROSENBERG'S FIRST LAW OF READING: NEVER APOLOGIZE FOR YOUR READING TASTES. Saricks says that this sign is often commented on by users and has been the starting point for many satisfying readers' advisory interviews.

A QUICK TIP

SIGNAGE

Let users know that the library is the right place to ask for advice about what to read next. Put up signs that say FICTION DESK, FICTION SERVICES, or LOOKING FOR A GOOD BOOK TO READ? ASK US FOR SUGGESTIONS.

reference help is available. In contrast, readers looking for good books to read think of libraries, especially public libraries, as a storehouse where they can get books to read. However, they rarely think of librarians as experts on pleasure reading who can help them choose books. When asked why they wouldn't ask a librarian for suggestions about reading, users are apt to say that librarians wouldn't know what they liked or that librarians might try to improve their reading tastes. Or users may say that the librarians looked unapproachable and too busy to be bothered with questions about fiction, an area that users can observe being given short shrift in comparison with nonfiction and factual questions. This means that a library wanting to get into the business of providing readers' advisory service needs to take active steps to promote the service and let users know it exists. No one asks for a service that is invisible. But when users are encouraged to ask for help in choosing books and are satisfied with the help they get, they become repeat customers. Saricks and Brown note, "Only when readers have been helped and are made comfortable coming to the desk do we find substantial numbers of readers asking us directly for assistance" (1997: 67).

The first step is to create a physical environment that says, in effect, "In this library, we care about your reading interests and want to help you find books that you would enjoy. This is the place to come, not just for factual information, but for the delights of story." Libraries need to change the public's mental model of the library so that they see it as a place to get advice about books to read. Public libraries have a lot to learn from bookstores when it comes to creating a welcoming environment for readers. A good start is to provide comfortable chairs for reading near the fiction stacks. Readers' advisers need to be situated near the fiction collection so that they can be prepared to offer help. Clear and readable signs should advertise the existence of RA service by saying something like "Wondering what to read next? Ask us for suggestions."

Readers need help in narrowing down the book choices to a manageable number because of the phenomenon that Sharon Baker calls "overload." Fiction readers come to the library knowing the names of five or six favorite authors, hoping that one of these favorites has written a new book and that the new book will be on the shelf. When disappointed, readers resort to "browsing," defined by Baker as looking for something without a clear idea of what it is that you are looking for. Experienced readers have developed effective strategies for browsing, based on their broad familiarity with books, their knowledge of authors and genres, their ability to read the cues on book covers, their memory

DID YOU KNOW?

In readers' advisory interviews, the question "What did you like about that book?" is not used as often as it should be. In a study by Kenneth Shearer, student-users went into a library and said they had enjoyed a particular book (e.g., To Kill a Mockingbird or The Color Purple) and wanted to read another one just like it. In only one-quarter of instances did the library staff member ask a question designed to find out anything about the reader's experience of the book. In other words, for the most part, they didn't ask, "What did you like about The Color Purple?" Shearer's conclusion is that "the readers' advisory transaction is not about how similar the text of Book A is to the text of Book B." A successful readers' advisory transaction is "about relating Reader A's experience with Book A to the likelihood that Reader A would value the experience of reading Book B" (1996: 19).

DID YOU KNOW?

Ross's study of avid readers who read for pleasure found that the single most important strategy for picking books was to choose a book by a known and trusted author. Said a Salman Rushdie fan, "It's like finding a gold mine and following the vein when you find a good author like that" (2001: 14). Second to choosing by author, the next most popular strategy was to use genre to identify the kind of experience promised by a book. Genre was often used in conjunction with author.

of reviews or recommendations by friends, etc. But less practiced readers are daunted by the alphabetical arrangement of fiction and quite often end up choosing books at random and then being dissatisfied with the reading experience. Here's what one beginning reader said about her problem with finding new books of interest: "I go to the library and stand there for hours. So I end up picking just at random. I pick some books up, bring them home, and end up taking them all back. You read the first couple pages, and the author goes on and on about some long description. It's just so boring and you don't really get any excitement out of it" (Ross, 2001: 9).

Research shows circulation increases when libraries adopt the strategies that Sharon Baker (1986) describes as helping browsers cope with overload: separating popular genre titles into separate sections; putting genre labels on the spines of books; providing annotated lists; creating book displays; systematic weeding. Like the layout of the bookstore, the physical arrangement of the fiction collection should help readers choose books. In addition, when these strategies are pursued, the library itself becomes a prop for the readers' advisory conversation, which we discuss next.

5.7.2 CONDUCTING THE INTERVIEW

The readers' advisory interview is indispensable in the process of matching book to reader because, as we have seen, the term *good book* is relative. Readers mean: a good book for me; a book that matches my mood right now; a book that suits my level of reading ability; a book that satisfies my particular needs and interests; a book written in a style that maximizes the effects that I enjoy, whether what I'm looking for is something that scares me, soothes and reassures me, makes me laugh, lifts my spirits, unsettles my preconceived ideas, or opens my eyes to dangerous new possibilities. Therefore, it doesn't work to have a list of canonical "Good Books" such as *Middlemarch* or *Breakfast of Champions* and recommend these same good books to everyone. Nor does it work for readers' advisers to recommend their own personal favorites to everyone (e.g., "I've just read Kate Grenville's *The Idea of Perfection* and absolutely loved it; you are certain to love it too."). A key point to bear in mind is that you can't tell in advance whether a reader will enjoy a particular book by looking only at the text. It's the reader's *experience* of the text that is crucial.

A QUICK TIP

READERS LIKE RA TOOLS TOO

Assemble a small collection of readers' advisory tools and put them on a shelf that is available for users too, not just for librarians. Put a sign on the shelf: GUIDES FOR FINDING THE NEXT BOOK TO READ. At minimum, you will need Diana Tixier Herald's Genreflecting, Wilson's Fiction Catalog, Joyce Saricks's Readers' Advisory Guide to Genre Fiction, and some guides to individual genres, such as those mentioned at the end of this chapter.

A QUICK TIP

THE FIVE BOOK CHALLENGE

Read five books in a new genre every year to get an understanding of the genre. This is the five book challenge first issued by Ann Bouricius in her Romance Readers' Advisory (Chicago: American Library Association, 2000) and expanded by Joyce Saricks in The Readers' Advisory Guide to Genre Fiction (2001). For fifteen different genres, Saricks suggests five authors and titles that are good starting points for exploring a genre. To really expand your background, start by reading in the genre that you have read the least and have always thought you didn't like. The experience may surprise you.

That's why it's important to have a conversation with the reader about his or her experience of books. Good readers' advisers stress that the readers' advisory interview differs from the reference interview in at least one important way. For many avid readers, talking about books is an enjoyable experience in itself and an extension of the pleasurable reading experience. Therefore, the soul of a readers' advisory interview is the talk about books. Hence the question recommended by Joyce Saricks and Nancy Brown: Tell me about a book you really enjoyed. Duncan Smith, in his research involving the videotaping of readers, has very successfully used a variant: Tell me about a book you've read and enjoyed. The key is to get readers talking about their own engagement with a book.

The features of the book that readers choose to talk about are important clues to reading tastes and preferences. Listen very closely: Does the reader talk about fast-paced action and excitement? Does the reader emphasize the relationships that develop between or among characters? Is setting important? Is the reader looking for something that is soothing and comforting or challenging and quirky? Saricks and Brown point out that most fiction readers "are usually not looking for a book on a certain subject. They want a book with a particular 'feel'" (1997: 35). When asked to talk about a book they've enjoyed, readers mention being drawn into the story, or they talk about factors such as strong, empathetic characters or intriguing settings or an upbeat tone—elements that Saricks and Brown call "appeal factors." For Saricks and Brown, the important appeal factors of a book are its pacing, characterization, storyline, and frame, or the particular atmosphere or tone that the author constructs. Their book, *Readers' Advisory Service in the Public Library*, provides a list of useful questions that can be used to identify each of these appeal factors. For example, to identify pacing, they recommend, "Is there more dialogue or description?" To identify characterization, they recommend, "Is the focus on a single character or on several whose lives are intertwined?"

Factors that Affect Readers' Book Choices

The following list, adapted from Pejtersen and Austin (1983; 1984), shows what factors readers take into account when they look for a fiction book to read.

Subject—what is the book about?

What kind of *action* occurs in this book? Does the plot involve a conflict between two matched opponents, the uncovering of a mystery, the coming of age of the central character, a quest or

---

ANALYZE THIS REFERENCE TRANSACTION

Case 23: In the mood for challenging and quirky?

User: I was wondering if you could suggest some good books for me to read.

Librarian: What do you usually like to read? (open question that gets the user to talk about past reading preferences)

User: I enjoy contemporary fiction. Two writers that are among my favorites are Nabokov and Kundera.

Librarian: Um-hmmm [nods, smiles, and pauses].

User: And also I like contemporary Canadian fiction. In fact, today I'd like to find an interesting book by a new Canadian author that I haven't read yet.

Librarian: OK, the best place to start is this book; it lists all the important Canadian authors. [Goes to a nearby stack, finds John Moss's A Reader's Guide to the Canadian Novel, opens it, and shows the user the table of contents.] Another good starting point is this bulletin board where we post reading lists, reviews, upcoming events, and lists of award-winning books. In your case, the Giller Prize Shortlist and the Nominees for the 2001 Governor General's Literary Awards list could be helpful in suggesting authors. (bibliographic instruction using inclusion) What particular elements in a work of fiction are important to you? (open question)

User: I like challenging, quirky books. One that I really liked was Robertson Davies's Fifth Business.

Librarian: OK, here are some books I could suggest. Although Jane Urquhart's The Stone Carvers is on both shortlists, you might not find it so interesting since it doesn't have the quirkiness that you seem to enjoy. But you might want to try Gail Anderson-Dargatz's A Recipe for Bees and Ann-Marie MacDonald's Fall on Your Knees, which is also on the Oprah list. And another thing that might help you when you are browsing for Canadian books: all the books in the fiction section by Canadian authors have a maple leaf sticker on the spine.

User: Thanks, I really appreciate all your help.

Library Visit study

Comment: In this interview, the questions "What do you usually like to read?" and "What particular elements in a work of fiction are important to you?" worked well because they got the reader to talk about her experience with books. A big plus in this transaction is the way that the readers' adviser was able to go beyond her own personal reading by using a reference tool and the lists posted on the bulletin board as props in the interview.

   The user gave this transaction the highest possible rating and commented that the librarian's "informal, relaxed attitude made the experience of searching for a book enjoyable, and, more important, non-threatening. . . . I find this kind of behavior helpful because it is analogous to the experience of pleasure-reading itself. . . . In contrast, recommending too many books, relying too heavily on personal opinions, and not listening to what the user is saying would have been very detrimental. Essentially, the readers' advisory service should primarily offer an informative, congenial invitation to reading."

EXERCISE

THE PERFECT BOOK

The seven statements quoted below are accounts provided by avid readers when they were asked to describe what they considered to be a "perfect book." For each of the statements:

1. identify the appeal factors that the reader looks for in a book. What do you think are the most important clues, in each case, to the reader's preferences?
2. use readers' advisory tools to come up with a list of five books that you would suggest to the reader that he or she might enjoy.
3. if you are doing this as a group exercise, compare your lists with others and discuss the reasons for your choices.

A. Most of the books I read are British and written by women, for example, Fay Weldon, Barbara Pym, Miss Read. I like books that present family life, probably because I'm looking for security. I'm honestly interested in how people react under different conditions—how they get through life and face their problems. In fiction, you understand that things are tough for people, but they seem to be solved so easily. Things seem to work out. It doesn't work that way in real life. Maybe that's why I like reading about families, written from a woman's point of view. (female reader, age 31)

B. For a book to somehow touch me, I have to feel that whoever wrote it is sincere. And to me, in a novel especially—but even in a work of biography or history—there has to be something in it that tells me that the author, if not loves, then at least appreciates and is somehow able to understand the people that he or she has chosen to write about. There has to be some kind of grounding in reality for me. Even if the book is a total fantasy, like the devil coming to Moscow [in The Master and Margarita], I have to feel that there is a strong element of reality and a strong feeling that the author understands what it means to be alive. That's what a book needs to have to hold my attention. You know, in The Invisible Man, Ralph Ellison talks about how he and his little brother—this is a black writer in the South—how he and his little brother learned how to fish by reading novels by Ernest Hemingway. I've always enjoyed that. They'd go page by page and figure it out step by step. (male reader, age 26)

C. I like books about the life of a family—good, clean fiction without all the four-letter words. And not filled with sex, which is not necessary. A book can be written so that you can imagine it without putting it in plain words. I'm reading a good book right now that is really "high society," and it's all about all the fancy clothes they have to wear to their big parties. I also like those stories set in hospitals—doctor and nurse stories. (female reader, age 75)

EXERCISE (continued)

D. It would be long. I like books that are long because they're good and meaty. You get your value for your money. It would be about 500 to 800 pages. It would have lots of adventure in it. It would be suspenseful. It would have some instructional material in it. It would be very descriptive of places and people. During the book, there would be descriptions of how the people used to do things or the way things are done now or the way things are made—that sort of thing. The Tom Clancy books are good because they combine science fiction and instructional material right in them. (male reader, age 51)

E. Why don't we look at a book that I really thought was great and maybe that will tell me what I like? Well for instance, The Far Pavilions. I like books that can tell me details of cultures and religions that I'm not familiar with. I like lots of sort of nonfictional detail immersed in fiction. I'm very fond of that. I like to immerse myself in a different time space. Perhaps that's why I like the India stories so much, because it is so different. So I guess the perfect book for me takes me to a different time and space. But then there's another element too, when I think of The Bridges of Madison County, for instance. I just loved that book because it was about a real person, my age, and it was a beautifully crafted book in the literary sense. But it was about a person my age who had some feelings and so on, that she had to deal with. It also involved her family. So I guess I like to read about women I can identify with, in a historically based novel or real life. (female reader, age 46)

F. I would like to have a novel based on fact, that actually happened in the world. But put it into a novel form, so that there are fictitious characters in the book. I want to be able to relate the book to an actual country, a world, a situation that took place, an earthquake, or a fire, or a bombing, or an incident in a war that you know of or have heard of. The Bridge on the River Kwai is probably the movie that has stuck in my mind more than anything else. But, if you actually read the book On the Kwai River in Burma, it's not the exact situation of the movie, although some things are the same. There was a railway built, it was built by slaves, it was built by prisoners of war that the Japanese had. That's the type of book that I like. (male reader, age 60)

G. It would have to have strong characters, both good and bad. There's no use having strong heroines and weak villains because it doesn't make for an interesting book. One of the neat things about the Sherlock Holmes mysteries is that Moriarity is such an opponent. He matches Holmes move for move and word for word. The characters would be the most important thing. And it would have to have a good plot, something that followed and made sense, with a bit of suspense, even if it wasn't necessarily a mystery book. Even in a romance, you don't want to know what's going to happen, where the relationship's going. Those would be the main things— and a few interesting subplots, because they usually spice the book up, but not so many that you get confused. (female reader, age 26)

A QUICK TIP

INTERNET RESOURCES

For interactive access to the real experts—readers themselves—try the Internet. For example, science fiction readers have fanzines and discussion lists where they chat about the latest, the best and the worst. You can also find listservs featuring mysteries, romances, and other types of fiction (see, for example, Romance Readers Anonymous, rra-l@kentvm.kent.edu, accessible through listserv@kentvm.kent.edu). Post your difficult readers' advisory questions to the experts. And tell library users about these sites.

A QUICK TIP

MAKE SUGGESTIONS

Joyce Saricks encourages readers' advisers to suggest, not to recommend. Making a recommendation puts the readers' adviser in the role of expert and seems to imply: Take this book; it will be good for you. But suggesting "makes us partners with readers in exploring the various directions they might want to pursue. Simply altering our vocabulary [took] some of the pressure off us—and readers—as we shared books" (2001: 3).

EXAMPLE

User: Can you recommend a good book?

Librarian: You're looking for a book to read for enjoyment? (acknowledgment to confirm the reader's purpose)

User: Yes, I'm going on vacation and want a few books for cottage reading.

Librarian: OK. To give me an idea of the kind of thing you like, can you tell me about a book that you've read recently and enjoyed? (closed question that functions as an open question)

User: I've just finished Barbara Kingsolver's The Poisonwood Bible and loved that.

Librarian: What was it that you loved about that book?

User: The way the family life was developed over time and the relationship between the parents and the three sisters. I also liked the fact that the book was set in Africa. I felt that I was learning something about African life and politics. I like to learn about different places.

Librarian: OK. And are there types of books that you definitely would not like?

User: I don't like predictable books, which is why I don't want to waste my time reading those authors that just churn out the same book over and over.

Librarian: What sort of books are you in the mood for now?

User: I'd like to read some new authors—writers who could really surprise me with something unexpected. Amaze me!

---

journey, the gradual development of a love relationship, etc.? Is the action interior and psychological or is it external, involving a lot of activity such as fights and chase scenes?

What kinds of *characters* are featured in this book—a mother and daughter, a fellowship of elves, a strong woman who overcomes setbacks, a runaway, a private eye, members of a religious community, terrorists, an extended family, etc.? What sorts of relationships take place between characters?

What is the *theme*—love, war, survival, revenge, coping with illness, the conflict of good and evil, discovery of identity, etc.?

Setting

When does the story happen—past, present, or future? Time periods often offer clues to genre preferences, with the past associ-

DID YOU KNOW?

Electronic resources and Internet-based sites are increasingly valuable resources for readers' advisers. For an excellent crash course on Internet resources available for readers' advisory work, check out the guide by Roberta Johnson, Des Plaines (Illinois) Public Library, at www.fictional.org. The Downers Grove (Illinois) Public Library has taken a leadership role in becoming a gateway for electronic readers' advisory resources (www.webrary.org). Here are a few other sites too good to miss:

BookBrowser, www.bookbrowser.com/index.html

Bookwire's Index to Publishers, www.bookwire.com/bookwire/

Fiction_L Archive, www.webrary.org/rs/flmenu.html

Fiction_L Booklists, www.webrary.org/rs/flbklistmenu.html

SOME QUESTIONS FOR READERS' ADVISERS

To initiate a readers' advisory interview:
Is there a special book you are looking for?
Are you finding what you're looking for?

To get a picture of previous reading patterns:
So that I can get a picture of your reading interests, can you tell me about a book/author you've read and enjoyed?
What did you enjoy about that book (author/type of book)?
What do you not like and wouldn't want to read?
What elements do you usually look for in a novel (nonfiction book/biography/travel book)?

To determine current reading preferences:
What are you in the mood for today?
What have you looked at so far? [to a person who has been looking unsuccessfully for reading material]
What did you not like about these books that you looked at?
If we could find the perfect book for you today, what would it be like? (What would it be about? What would you like best about it? What elements would it include?)

To understand the function of the book:
What kind of reading experience are you wanting to find?
What do you want to get from this book? What do you find satisfying?
What would you like this book to do for you?

To follow up on a recommendation:
If you find that these books weren't to your taste, get back to me and we can suggest something else.
What else can I help you with?

---

ated with historical fiction or fantasy and the future associated with science fiction.

Where does the story happen—on another planet, a high school, a village in Kashmir, an advertising agency in Manhattan, the American frontier, a nursing home? Geographic settings also provide clues to genre preferences, with bestselling melodrama associated with wealth and glamor and the frontier associated with the Western or the family saga.

DID YOU KNOW?

During readers' advisory interviews, it can help to have an aide-mémoire to help jog your memory about authors and titles. As you talk to the user about what kind of mystery story he enjoys, you can show him the section on mysteries in Diana T. Herald's Genreflecting and use the categories provided to help narrow down whether the reader wants police procedurals, hard-boiled mysteries, mysteries with an anthropological interest, etc. Or you can use electronic readers' advisory resources such as EBSCO Publishing's NoveList. For a free trial of Novelist, contact novelist@epnet.com. With this online readers' advisory resource, adults and children can find new titles by genre, setting, characters, or subject, as well as find titles with similarities to titles they have read and enjoyed.

DID YOU KNOW?

Once the reader starts to browse within a range of books, the cover and the clues provided on the book itself become important. One reader interviewed by Ross explained: "When you're as genre-specific as I guess I am, and read as voraciously as I do, you're looking for some quick identifiers on what's a good book. It'll take me ten minutes to go in [to the science fiction section], get five books, and leave because I'm just so familiar with the genre in general" (2001: 14). The "quick identifiers" most frequently mentioned by readers in Ross's study were the cover, the blurb on the back, and the sample page.

TO-DO and NOT-TO-DO LIST for READERS' ADVISERS

This list was developed by students in a course taught by Mary K. Chelton in the Graduate School of Library and Information Studies, Queens College, Flushing, New York. Students were required to go to a library of their choice and ask for suggestions on good books to read. This checklist is based on their experiences as users of RA services.

Remember that fiction subject headings in normal cataloging are not specific enough to be useful to readers. Therefore:
- DO NOT refer a user to an OPAC.
- DO NOT use an OPAC yourself as a first resort.

Remember that your best source of information is the user asking you for a suggestion. Therefore:
- DO NOT ignore the user's unsolicited comments.
- DO NOT assume that the reader has not read other titles by the author without asking first.
- DO ask readers what they liked about the book and what they're in the mood for this time.
- DO talk to the user while you are searching in case clarifying information is offered or needed.

Remember to appear "askable." Therefore:
- DO say hello.
- DO project a friendly, NOT nervous, demeanor.
- DO follow up if you have to send the person off while you help someone else.

Remember that amazon.com "readalikes" are generated by sales figures, not by an analysis of what someone really likes or wants at the particular time you encounter them. Therefore:
- DO use readalikes, but only as an aide-mémoire of possible titles to suggest. Be aware that part of your role will be to help the advisees eliminate unsuitable titles from the readalike lists, so that they end up with some titles that match their own requirements.

Remember that libraries have user restrictions, such as residency requirements. Therefore:
- DO make sure you can help the person before offering interlibrary loan, if there are residency requirements.

Remember that research on RA shows that the largest problem is that librarians do not use readers' advisory tools. Therefore:
- DO NOT assume that you cannot help someone because you have not read the title yourself.
- DO use readers' advisory tools yourself and demonstrate their use to advisees as part of the RA transaction.

(Thanks to Mary K. Chelton for permission to use this checklist.)

EXERCISE

PRACTICING THE READERS' ADVISORY INTERVIEW

Here are two role-play scenarios to help you practice the readers' advisory interview. In pairs, one person takes the role of the librarian, who must find out what sort of book the user would like, and the other person, who acts the part of the user, is given one of these scripts. Switch roles for the other script. After each role-play, the actors should discuss how they felt about the interview, then invite comments or suggestions from observers. To expand this exercise, create additional scenarios that profile different kinds of readers, e.g., a reader of literary fiction; an adolescent boy who has just gotten turned on to reading by the Harry Potter books and wants other fantasy books that are "just the same"; a reader of historical fiction, preferably featuring naval or land battles; etc.

You like popular fiction and generally try to read what is on the bestseller list. In the past you have particularly enjoyed Sidney Sheldon, Robert Ludlum, and Ken Follett. You enjoy books that have a quick pace and are suspenseful, but you don't like anything with a historical bent. You approach the readers' adviser with this statement: "I'm looking for something good to read. I've checked your bestseller list but I can't seem to find any of them on the shelves."

You are a grade 12 student and your English assignment requires that you read one novel by each of three different authors that deal with a similar theme. You have decided to choose books that deal with YA problems–like drugs, pregnancy, or street kids. You approach the readers' adviser with this question: "Where are your books about teenagers?"

(Thanks to Heather Johnson, London Public Library, London, Ontario, for this exercise.)

Kind of reading experience offered by the book

Does the reader *learn something* from this book? For example: I learned so much about Islamic family life in postwar Cairo (or bee taxonomists or the fashion industry in Paris or how to break a horse).

Does the reader *feel something* as a result of reading this book? (e.g., It made me feel happy/sad/hopeful about human goodness. I was alarmed about the proliferation of land mines that maim civilians and children. It scared me. It made me laugh. It reassured me and confirmed my values. It was like comfort food. It challenged me to reassess my beliefs.) Does the book have a happy ending? What is the mood engendered by reading this book?

Accessibility

What *reading skills* are demanded by this book? Does this book use literary conventions that may be unfamiliar—stream-of-consciousness narrative method, an unreliable first-person narrator, flashbacks, postmodern reflexiveness, literary parody?

How *predictable* is it? The more conventional and formulaic the book is, the more the reader already knows about the content of the book and the easier it is to read. Depending on mood, sometimes readers want easy, predictable, safe reads and sometimes they seek challenging, unpredictable, risky reads.

How *accessible* is the book physically in terms of size and heaviness? In terms of the size of the type?

Not all of these factors will be salient for all readers. A reader with strong arms and good eyesight could find the physical characteristics of the book irrelevant. A reader might not care where the book is set, as long as it depicts strong, independent-minded female characters. On the other hand, a reader may refuse to read anything with too much sex and violence in it, or anything with confusing Russian names in it, or anything set in historical times. To find out which factors matter to an individual reader, ask open questions. The list SOME QUESTIONS FOR READERS' ADVISERS suggests some questions to choose from the next time someone says, "Can you recommend a good book?"

SOME QUICK TIPS FOR THE RA INTERVIEW

- Remember that you are trying to understand what the *reader* thinks is a good book. Don't fall into the trap of recommending the last book that you enjoyed, unless you have reason to think that the reader shares your reading tastes.
- Be careful with the term "well-written." When readers say that they are looking for a well-written book, they might

not mean a book that has a high degree of literary value, such as a recent Booker Prize winner. Readers are more likely to mean well-written to achieve the particular experience they are looking for—e.g., a well-written horror story scares the reader; a well-written romance depicts the growing relationship of two characters that the reader cares about; a well-written thriller is a page-turner; a well-written western is evocative of the place and time of the Old West. Check out what they mean by asking, "Can you tell me about a well-written book that you've enjoyed recently?" They might say Michael Ondaatje's *Anil's Ghost*, but then again, they may mention a genre book.

- Do not be judgmental or try to get readers to change their reading tastes. A reader who enjoys a category romance will definitely not welcome a comment like, "Why waste your time on that when you can be reading a really good book like *Jane Eyre*?"
- If you are in a library small enough for you to get to know readers, talk to them about their reading. Ask them what they liked or didn't like about the books they are returning. Show an active interest.
- Put readers' advisory tools close to the fiction collection where users can find them and where you can use them, along with the user, in order to explore reading preferences and narrow down choices of authors or books.

5.8 ANNOTATED REFERENCES

5.8.1 TELEPHONE REFERENCE

Adler, Ronald B., and Jeanne Marquardt Elmhorst. 1996. *Communicating at Work: Principles and Practices for Business and the Professions.* 5th ed. New York: McGraw-Hill. Good tips for using voicemail and other electronic media. Includes a chapter on interviewing.

Anderson, Eric, Josh Boyer, and Karen Ciccone. 2000. "Remote Reference Services at the North Carolina State University Libraries." a conference, Wash. [Online]. Available: www.vrd.org/con ferences/VRD2000/proceedings/ boyer-anderson-ciccone12-14.shtml.

Bond, Elizabeth. 1953. "Some Problems of Telephone Reference Service." *Wilson Library Bulletin* 27: 641–44.

Brown, Diane M. 1985. "Telephone Reference Questions: A Characterization by Subject, Answer Format, and Level of Complexity." *RQ* 24, no. 3 (spring): 290–303.

Gannett, Emily. 1936. "Reference Service by Telephone." *Library Journal* 61, 909–11.

Quinn, Brian. 1995. "Improving the Quality of Telephone Reference Service." *Reference Services Review* 23, no. 4 (winter): 39–50.

Rohlf, Robert, "Let's Consider a Telephone Department." *Library Journal* 83: 1–3.

Walters, Suzanne. 1994. *Customer Service: A How-To-Do-It Manual for Librarians.* New York: Neal-Schuman. See pages 45-47 for helpful hints on training staff to answer the telephone properly.

Yates, Rochelle. 1986. *Librarian's Guide to Telephone Reference Service.* Hamden, Conn.: Library Professional Publications.

5.8.2 THE IMPOSED QUERY

Chelton, Mary K. 1997. "Adult-Adolescent Service Encounters: The Library Context." Ph.D. diss., Rutgers University. Examines the place of the adolescent as "social construct and individual agent within the context of library theory and practice."

Gross, Melissa. 1995. "The Imposed Query." *RQ* 35, no. 2 (winter): 236–43. Deals with the theoretical and practical aspects of "secondhand" reference questions, whereby the inquirer is asking on behalf of someone else.

———. 1999. "Imposed versus Self-Generated Questions." *Reference and User Services Quarterly* 39, no. 1 (fall): 53-61. Argues that librarians need to identify questions as either imposed or self-generated and provide special treatment for imposed queries.

Kuhlthau, Carol. 1995. "Inside the Search Process: Information Seeking from the User's Perspective," *Journal of the American Society for Information Science* 42, no. 6 (June): 361–71.

5.8.3 INTERVIEWING CHILDREN AND YOUNG ADULTS

Behrmann, Christine and Dolores Vogliano, 1991. "On Training the Children's Reference Librarian." *Illinois Libraries* 73, no. 2 (February): 152-57. Describes the qualities of a good children's reference librarian and presents a model training workshop, including sample assignments.

Benne, Mae. 1991. "Staff Competencies." In *Principles of Children's Services in Public Libraries.* Chicago: American Library Association.

Bunge, Charles A. 1994. "Responsive Reference Service: Breaking Down Age Barriers." *School Library Journal* 44 (March): 142–45.

Burton, Melvin K. 1998. "Reference Interview: Strategies for Children." *North Carolina Libraries* 56, no 3. (fall): 110–13. Lists some special features of the reference interview with children, including the increased likelihood of ill-formed queries resulting from homophones and reconstructions (e.g., carnivorous/coniferous forest; *Rock Stew/Stone Soup*), the intermediating role of the parent; library staff's ambivalence over questions involving homework assignments; and the child's unfamiliarity with the library system and classification scheme.

Callaghan, Linda W. 1983. "Children's Questions: Reference Interviews with the Young." In *Reference Services for Children and Young Adults*, edited by Bill Katz and Ruth A. Fraley. New York: Haworth Press. First published in *The Reference Librarian* 7/8 (spring/summer 1983): 55–65.

Chelton, Mary K. 1999. "Structural and Theoretical Constraints on Reference Service in a High School Library Media Center." *Reference and User*

Services Quarterly 38, no. 3 (spring): 275–82. Finds that idealized standards for reference practice as articulated in the RUSA Behavioral Guidelines for Reference Service are not helpful to practitioners in school library media centers.

Dixon, Judith. 1996. "Are We Childproofing Our Public Libraries? Identifying the Barriers That Limit Use by Children." *Public Libraries* 35 (February): 50–56.

Gross, Melissa. 2000. "The Imposed Query and Information Services for Children." *Journal of Youth Services in Libraries* 13 (winter): 10-17.

Horning, Kathleen T. 1994 "Fishing for Questions." *Wilson Library Bulletin* 68 (May): 57–59.

———. 1994. "How Can I Help You? The Joys and Challenges of Reference Work with Children." *Show-Me Libraries* 45: 9–19.

Jones, Patrick. 1998. "Reference Services." In *Connecting Young Adults and Libraries*. 2d ed. New York: Neal-Schuman.

Kuhlthau, Carol C. 1991. "Inside the Search Process: Information Seeking from the User's Perspective." *Journal of the American Society for Information Science* 42, no. 6 (June): 361–71.

———. 1994. "Students and the Information Search Process: Zones of Intervention for Librarians." In *Advances in Librarianship*. Vol. 18. San Diego, Calif.: Academic Press.

———. 1998. "Meeting the Information Needs of Children and Young Adults: Basing Library Media Programs on Developmental States." *Journal of Youth Services in Libraries* 2 (fall): 51–57.

Loorie, Nancy. 1993. "Whose Homework Is It, Anyway? Helping Parents at the Reference Desk." *New Jersey Libraries* (February): 15–17.

Overmyer, Elizabeth. 1995. "Serving the Reference Needs of Children." *Wilson Library Bulletin* 69, no. 10 (June): 38-40. Uses examples from the San Francisco Bay Area regional reference center to focus on aspects of reference service to children, including resource sharing, online searching, telephone questions, and using the Internet.

Vaillancourt, Renee J. 2000. "The Reference Interview." In *Bare Bones Young Adult Services: Tips for Public Library Generalists*. Chicago: American Library Association.

Wanting, Birgit. 1986. "Some Results from an Investigation in Danish Libraries: How Do Children Ask Questions about Books in Children's Libraries?" *Scandinavian Public Library Quarterly* 19: 96-101.

Wronka, Gretchen. 1983. "From the Firing Line: Practical Advice for Reference Service with Children in the Public Library." In *Reference Services for Children and Young Adults*, edited by Bill Katz and Ruth A. Fraley. New York: Haworth Press. First published in *The Reference Librarian* 7/8 (spring/summer 1983): 143–50.

5.8.4 CROSS-CULTURAL COMMUNICATION

Abdullahi, Ismail. 1993. "Multicultural Issues for Readers' Advisory Services." *Collection Building* 12, no. 3/4: 85-88. Addresses the role of multicultural readers' advisers and how they should be trained.

Adler, Ronald B., and Jeanne Marquardt Elmhorst. 1996. *Communicating at Work: Principles and Practices for Business and the Professions*. 5th ed. New York: McGraw-Hill.

Alire, Camila, and Orlando Archibeque. 1998. *Serving Latino Communities: A How-to-Do-It Manual for Librarians.* New York: Neal-Schuman. Covers communication skills briefly. Concentrates on determining demographics, community needs, programming, collections, and resource directories.

American Library Association. 1995. *Differences Make Us Stronger: Diversity in the Library.* Produced by Library Video Network. 37 min. Videocassette. Interviews with librarians who deal regularly with diversity issues in customer service.

Behrens, S. J. 1990. "Cross-cultural Communication in the Reference Encounter: A South African Perspective." *South African Journal of Library and Information Science* 58, no. 1 (March): 87–97.

Dame, Melvina Azar. 1993. *Serving Linguistically and Culturally Diverse Students.* New York: Neal-Schuman.

De Souza, Yvonne. 1996. "Reference Work with International Students: Making the Most Use of the Neutral Question." *Reference Services Review* 24 no. 4 (winter): 41–48. Provides suggestions on how to use sense-making questions with international students without intimidating them.

Dewdney, Patricia, and Gillian Michell. 1996. "Oranges and Peaches: Understanding Communication Accidents in the Reference Interview." *RQ* 35 (4), summer: 520–36.

Fontana, David. 1990. *Social Skills at Work.* Leicester: British Psychological Society. Has a good chapter on communication with various populations, e.g., multicultural.

Frieband, Susan Jane. 1993. "Developing Readers' Advisory Service for Library Users Whose Primary Language Is Not English." *Collection Building* 12, no. 3/4: 79–84.

Greenfield, Louise, Susan Johnston, and Karen Williams. 1986. "Educating the World: Training Library Staff to Communicate Effectively with International Students." *The Journal of Academic Librarianship* 12, no. 4 (September): 227–31.

Hall, Edward T. 1959. *The Silent Language.* Garden City, N.Y.: Doubleday. The classic work on cross-cultural differences in communication.

Hendricks, Yoshi. 1991. "The Japanese as Library Patrons." *College and Research Library News* 52, no. 4 (July): 221–25.

Hoffman, Irene, and Opritsa Popa. 1986. "Library Orientation and Instruction for International Students: The University of California–Davis Experience." *RQ* 25: 356–60.

Janes, Phoebe, and Ellen Meltzer. 1990. "Origins and Attitudes: Training Reference Librarians for a Pluralistic World." *The Reference Librarian* 30: 145–55.

Lam, R. Errol. 1988. "The Reference Interview: Some Intercultural Considerations." *RQ* 27, no. 3 (spring): 390–93. Argues that librarians need to pay greater attention to understanding differences in verbal and nonverbal communication styles in order for white librarians to provide a positive environment for African American students.

Ormondroyd, Joan. 1990. "The International Student and Course-Integrated Instruction: The Librarian's Perspective." *Research Strategies* 7 (fall): 148–58.

Samovar, Larry A., and Richard E. Porter. 2000. *Intercultural Communication: A Reader.* 9th ed. Belmont, Calif.: Wadsworth. An excellent, research-based anthology of 42 articles that help the reader attain intercultural communication competence. The introduction and some of the shorter articles are useful for staff discussion.

Sarkodie-Mensah, Kwasi. 1992. "Dealing with International Students in a Multicultural Era." *The Journal of Academic Librarianship* 18, no. 2 (September): 214–16. Lots of practical tips on pronunciation problems, speech patterns, and taboo topics.

Wayman, Sally G. 1984. "The International Student in the Academic Library." *The Journal of Academic Librarianship* 9, no. 6 (January): 136–41. Covers many intercultural differences that can have an impact on communication.

5.8.5 COPING WITH LANGUAGE AND SPEECH BARRIERS

Many social-service agencies, health organizations, and self-help groups publish pamphlets that increase understanding of specific disabilities and include tips for communicating. Ask your local organizations to provide you with multiple copies for your staff and your public. They may also provide speakers for staff training.

American Library Association. 2001. Library Services for People with Disabilities Policy. [online]. Available: www.ala.org/ascla/access_policy.html. [17 February 2002]

————. 1993. *And Access for All: ADA and Your Library.* Produced by Library Video Network. 47 min. Videocassette with 165-page guide. A videotape and resource guide about the Americans with Disabilities Act. Although this video is mostly about physical access and employment services, it includes communication.

————. 1990. *People First: Serving and Employing People with Disabilities.* Produced by Library Video Network. 40 min. Videocassette with discussion guide. Focuses on both physical and communication barriers.

Dalton, Phyllis I. 1985. "Two-Way Communication." In *Library Service to the Deaf and Hearing Impaired.* Phoenix, Ariz.: Oryx Press. Chapter 4 discusses skills for working with groups and individuals, including American Sign Language and other systems.

DeCandido, GraceAnne A. 1999. "Issues and Innovations in Service to Users with Disabilities." SPEC Kit 243. Washington: Association of Research Libraries.

Deines-Jones, Courtney. 1995. *Preparing Staff to Serve Patrons with Disabilities: A How-To-Do-It Manual for Librarians.* New York: Neal-Schuman. Tips, resources and front-line procedures for library staff to use with special classes of users with special needs. Also includes sections on readers advisory and the special needs of children and young adults.

Hecker, Thomas E. 1996. "Patrons with Disabilities or Problem Patrons: Which Model Should Librarians Apply to People with Mental Illness?" *The Reference Librarian* 53: 5–12.

Katz, Bill, ed. 1990. *The Reference Library User: Problems and Solutions.* New York: Haworth Press. An issue dedicated to reference services for specialized user groups, including seniors, the learning disabled, the angry patron, and the deinstitutionalized.

Lenn, Katy. 1996. "Library Services to Disabled Students: Outreach and Education." *The Reference Librarian* 53: 13–25.

Liu, Ziming. 1993. "Difficulties and Characteristics of Students From Developing Countries in Using American Libraries." *College and Research Libraries* 54:25–31.

Reed, Sally G. 1992. "Breaking Through: Effective Reference Mediation for Nontraditional Public Library Users." *The Reference Librarian* 37: 109–16.

Velleman, Ruth A. 1990. *Meeting the Needs of People with Disabilities: A Guide for Librarians, Educators, and Other Service Professionals*. Phoenix, Ariz.: Oryx Press.

Whitlatch, Jo Bell, ed. 1995. *Library Users and Reference Services*. New York: Haworth Press. (Also published as *The Reference Librarian* 49/50, 1995.)

Wright, Keith C., and Judith F. Davie. 1991. *Serving the Disabled: A How-To-Do-It Manual for Librarians*. New York: Neal-Schuman. Focuses on attitudes rather than technologies, but includes a chapter on what "going electronic" means for the disabled. Provides exercises, tests and staff development simulations.

Zipkowitz, Fay, ed. 1996. *Reference Services for the Unserved*. New York: Haworth Press. (Also published as *The Reference Librarian* 53, 1996.)

5.8.6 ANSWERING LEGAL OR HEALTH QUESTIONS

Dewdney, Patricia, Joanne Marshall, and Muta Tiamiyu. 1991. "A Comparison of Legal and Health Information Services in Public Libraries." *RQ* 32, no. 2 (winter): 185–96.

Dewdney, Patricia, Sam Coghlan, Christine Sue-Chan, and Catherine S. Ross. 1988. "Legal Information Services in Ontario Public Libraries." *Canadian Library Journal* 45, no. 6 (December): 365–71.

Healthnet: Connecticut Consumer Health Information Network. 2001. "Guidelines for Providing Medical Information to Consumers" [online]. Available: http://library.uchc.edu/departm/hnet/guidelines.html [24 December 2001].

Internet Public Library [online]. Available: www.ipl.org/ref [28 December 2001].

King County Library System. 2001. "Please Ask Your Doctor: An Interview Guide to Use with Health Care Professionals" [online]. Available: www.kcls.org/askdoc/askdr.html [28 December 2001]. A handout for users.

Morris County Library, Highlands Regional Library Cooperative. "Legal Reference: Sources, Tips and Techniques." In *The Legal Reference Interview* [online]. Available: www.gti.net/mocolib1/demos/legalref.html [28 December 2001]

National Network of Librarians of Medicine, Pacific Northwest Region. 2002. *HealthInfoQuest* [online]. Available: http://nnlm.gov/healthinfoquest/help. [16 February 2002]. Provides interview tips and sample interviews.

5.8.7 READERS' ADVISORY
Evaluation of the Readers' Advisory Transaction

Bracy, Pauletta Brown. 1996. "The Nature of the Readers' Advisory Transaction in Children's and Young Adult Reading." In *Guiding the Reader to the Next Book*, edited by Kenneth D. Shearer. New York: Neal-Schuman. Adapting the method used by Shearer (1996), Bracy discovers that advisers frequently made unwarranted assumptions instead of conducting an interview.

May, Anne K., Elizabeth Olesh, Anne Weinlich Mitlenberg, and Catherine Patricia Lackner. 2000. "A Look at Readers' Advisory Services." *Library Journal* 125 (September 15): 40–43. Reports the results of an unobtrusive study of readers' advisory service provided at the 54 public libraries of the Nassau, New York, Library System.

Shearer, Kenneth D. 1996. "The Nature of the Readers' Advisory Transaction in Adult Reading." In *Guiding the Reader to the Next Book*, edited by Kenneth D. Shearer. New York: Neal-Schuman. Reports what happened in 54 public library transactions when students in Shearer's graduate course in an MLIS program at North Carolina Central University asked for help with finding a good book to read that was similar to one they had enjoyed earlier.

Indirect RA Services

Armstrong, Nora M. 2001. "No Thanks—I'd Rather Do It Myself: Indirect Advisory Services." In *The Readers' Advisor's Companion*, edited by Kenneth D. Shearer and Robert Burgin. Littleton, Colo.: Libraries Unlimited.

Baker, Sharon L. 1986. "Overload, Browsers, and Selections." *Library and Information Science Research* 8 (October-December): 315–29. Advocates ways to help browsers narrow selections using such techniques as book lists and book displays.

———. 1993. "Booklists: What We Know, What We Need to Know." *RQ* 33, no. 2 (winter): 177–80. Demonstrates how to write book list annotations that are interesting as well as informative.

———. 1996. "A Decade's Worth of Research on Browsing Fiction Collections." In *Guiding the Reader to the Next Book*, edited by Kenneth D. Shearer. New York: Neal-Schuman. Provides practical tips for helping browsers.

Saricks, Joyce G., and Nancy Brown. 1997. *Readers' Advisory Service in the Public Library*. 2d ed. Chicago: American Library Association. Chapter Six on Promotion provides an excellent discussion of book displays (e.g., stocking a Good Books You May Have Missed cart), creating bookmarks on sturdy stock card with a list of authors and titles, creating annotated reading lists with a targeted appeal (e.g., Gentle Reads or Novels with a Touch of Science), and booktalking.

Readers' Advisory and Reading

Chelton, Mary K. 1999. "What We Know and Don't Know about Reading, Readers, and Readers' Advisory Services." *Public Libraries* 38, no. 1 (January/February): 42–47. Summarizes research on reading and readers, along with suggestions about the implications of this research for public libraries.

De la Peña McCook, Kathleen, and Gary O. Rolstad, eds. 1993. *Developing Readers' Advisory Services: Concepts and Commitments*. New York: Neal-Schuman.

Jones, Patrick. 1992. *Connecting Young Adults and Libraries*. New York: Neal-Schuman. Has a useful section on talking with young adults.

Radway, Janice. 1994. "Beyond Mary Bailey and Old Maid Librarians: Reimagining Readers and Rethinking Reading." *Journal of Education for Library and Information Science* 35, no. 4 (fall): 275–96. Written originally as a talk for librarians, this article summarizes research on reading as a context for arguing for a new way of thinking about pleasure reading.

Ross, Catherine Sheldrick. 1991. "Readers' Advisory Services: New Directions." *RQ* 30, no. 4 (summer): 503–18.

———. 1995. "'If They Read Nancy Drew, So What?': Series Book Readers Talk Back." *Library and Information Science Research* 17, no. 3 (summer): 201–36. Research results based on interviews with readers suggest that series books can be allies in the making of readers.

———. 2001. "Making Choices: What Readers Say about Choosing Books to Read for Pleasure." *The Acquisitions Librarian* 25: 5–21. Analyzes 194 open-ended interviews with avid readers in order to understand how readers choose as well as reject books.

Ross, Catherine Sheldrick, and Mary Kay Chelton. 2001. "Reader's Advisory: Matching Mood and Material." *Library Journal* 126, no. 2 (February 1): 52–55. Draws out the implications for readers' advisers of Ross's research on the factors that influence readers' decisions when choosing a book to read for pleasure.

Saricks, Joyce G. 2001. *The Readers' Advisory Guide to Genre Fiction.* Chicago: American Library Association. Written by one of the world's best readers' advisers, this overview of 15 genres and their appeal to readers is a tremendous resource for readers' advisers. Each chapter contains a section on the readers' advisory interview for the particular genre under discussion.

Shearer, Kenneth D., and Robert Burgin, eds. 2001. *The Readers' Advisor's Companion.* Littleton, Colo.: Libraries Unlimited. Sixteen articles by researchers and noted practitioners, including Wayne Wiegand, Duncan Smith, Joyce Saricks, Robert Burgin, Roberta Johnson, and Glen Holt.

Smith, Duncan. 1993. "Reconstructing the Reader: Educating Readers' Advisors." *Collection Building* 12, no. 3/4: 21-30. Smith's article is one of a number of very useful articles in this special theme issue of *Collection Building* on readers' advisory.

Smith, Duncan. 2000. "Talking with Readers: A Competency Based Approach to Readers Advisory Service." *Reference & User Services Quarterly* 40, no. 2 (winter): 135–42. Describes a training manual, *Talking with Readers*, that Smith and others associated with NoveList developed for the Minnesota Division of Library Development and Services. The key competencies identified are a background in fiction and nonfiction; an understanding of readers; the appeal factors of books; the readers' advisory transaction.

———. 1996. "Librarians' Abilities to Recognize Reading Tastes." In *Guiding the Reader to the Next Book*, edited by Kenneth D. Shearer. New York: Neal-Schuman. An interesting and informed demonstration by three experienced readers' advisers of how to analyze a reader's response to "tell me about a book you've read and enjoyed" and make book suggestions.

Watson, Dana, and RUSA CODES Readers' Advisory Committee. 2000. "Time to Turn the Page: Library Education for Readers' Advisory Services." *Reference & User Services Quarterly* 40, no. 2 (winter): 143–46. Summarizes what is being taught in readers' advisory–related courses at 14 of the 56 ALA-accredited master's programs and recommends that other programs do more to provide RA training.

Readers' Advisory Interview

Chelton, Mary K. 1993. "Read Any Good Books Lately? Helping Patrons Find What They Want." *Library Journal* 118, no. 8 (May 1): 33–37. An excellent short introduction to RA skills.

Fialkoff, Francine. 1998. "New Twists on an Old Service." *Library Journal* 123 (October 15): 58.

Pejtersen, Annelise, and Jutta Austin. 1983-84. "Fiction Retrieval: Experimental Design and Evaluation of a Search System Based on Users' Value Criteria." Parts 1 and 2. *Journal of Documentation* 39, no. 4 (December): 230–46; 40, no. 1 (March): 25–35. As a preliminary to designing their classification system for fiction retrieval, the authors analyzed 300 user/librarian conversations as the basis for identifying the dimensions of fiction books that are important to readers.

Saricks, Joyce G. 2001. *The Readers' Advisory Guide to Genre Fiction.* Chicago and London: American Library Association. Contains sections on the readers' advisory interview tailored for each genre.

Saricks, Joyce G., and Nancy Brown. 1997. *Readers' Advisory Service in the Public Library.* 2d ed. Chicago: American Library Association. An indispensable guide that covers reference sources, appeal factors of books, promotion, passive strategies, and training. Contains a chapter on the readers' advisory interview which is defined as a conversation about books.

Guides for Readers' Advisers

After you have read Joyce G. Saricks's article, "The Best Tools for Advisors and How to Integrate Them into Successful Transactions" in *The Readers' Advisor's Companion* (Littleton Colo.: Libraries Unlimited), you will find these sources helpful.

American Library Association's Readers' Advisory Committee, Collection Development Section, RUSA. 1996. "Readers' Advisory Reference Tools: A Suggested List of Fiction Sources for All Libraries." *RQ* 36, no. 2 (winter): 206–29. This bibliography of recommended tools for readers' advisers is a good starting point.

Barron, Neil, Wayne Barton, Kristen Ramsdell, and Steven A. Stilwell. 1990. *What Do I Read Next? A Reader's Guide to Current Genre Fiction.* Detroit: Gale Research. An annual publication.

Berman, Matt. 1995-96. *What Else Should I Read? Guiding Kids to Good Books.* 2 vols. Littleton, Colo.: Libraries Unlimited. Helps students in grades 3 through 8 find books by subject, author, and genre.

Bouricius, Ann. 2000. *The Romance Readers' Advisory: The Librarian's Guide to Love in the Stacks.* Chicago: American Library Association.

Herald, Diana Tixier. 2000. *Genreflecting: A Guide to Reading Interests in Genre Fiction.* 5th ed. Littleton, Colo.: Libraries Unlimited. Invaluable for readers' advisory work. Lists authors and books, grouped by genres, themes, and types. See the *Genreflecting* Web site at http://genreflecting.com, sponsored by Libraries Unlimited, for information on genres, a list of LIS faculty who teach readers' advisory courses, and an "Ask the Experts" service.

———. 1999. Fluent in Fantasy: A Guide to Reading Interests. Littleton, Colo.: Libraries Unlimited.

Johnson, Roberta S. 2001. "The Global Conversation about Books, Readers, and Reading on the Internet." In *The Readers' Advisor's Companion*, edited by Kenneth D. Shearer and Robert Burgin. Littleton, Colo.: Libraries Unlimited. A compact and informative introduction to the art of getting the most from Internet resources.

NoveList [online]. EBSCO Publishing. Created by Duncan Smith, NoveList is a Web-based readers' advisory resource that provides access to nearly 100,000 titles of children's and adult fiction, many of them annotated, along with lists of award winners. Readers can find new titles by genre, setting, characters or subject. Available: http://novelist.epnet.com.

Ramsdell, Kristin. 1997. *What Romance Do I Read Next?* Detroit: Gale Research.

6 PERFORMING THE REFERENCE INTERVIEW IN AN ELECTRONIC ENVIRONMENT

In this chapter . . .

6.1 INTRODUCTION TO ELECTRONIC MEDIATION

Some libraries have noticed that users are making fewer trips to the library in person. People often don't need to visit a physical facility, because increasingly they can work at home and get access to electronic resources from remote workstations. Does this mean fewer reference interviews? Yes, some libraries have reported fewer face-to-face interviews, a trend that can be expected to continue. But we know, despite all the hype about the entire universe of information being "at people's fingertips at the touch of a button and at the speed of light," that many people simply won't find the information they need without professional assistance. So to help remote users navigate the information maze, libraries are experimenting with new ways of providing an old service: saving the time of users by connecting them with the information they need. With either asynchronous e-mail or real-time interviewing using chat or other instant messaging software, remote users can get their questions answered from their homes or workplaces.

DID YOU KNOW?

As a complement to their interactive electronic reference service, many libraries anticipate users' information needs by creating Web pages that locate and organize information to help users in commonly occurring situations. As a good example, Ann Viles (1999) highlights Penn State University's "Tell Me Where" service (www.lias.psu.edu:80/btellme.html). This service answers the question "Where is the best place to start searching for information on my topic?"

DID YOU KNOW?

A survey answered by 78 of the 122 Association of Research Libraries (ARL) members produced 51 respondents who provided data on the number of electronic reference questions received per month. The average numbers ranged from 2.3 to 3,200 questions per month, with a median of 35. The libraries getting the most questions were the Library of Congress (2,500) and the National Library of Medicine (3,200). And as for the library receiving 2.3 questions a month, we wonder what it is doing to publicize its service (Association of Research Libraries, 1999).

In "The Distributed Librarian," Karen Schneider, quoting Anne Lipow, says the goal is to "meet the users where they are, to seek them out, to market in language intelligible and attractive to our target communities, and to customize services based on the users' needs, preferences, and timetables" (2000: 64). In the context of digital, or electronic, reference service, the remote user is the person who is not physically in the library and therefore not available for a face-to-face transaction. Remote users are not necessarily located at great geographic distances from the library, and they are not necessarily working at off-hours—although they might be. The remote user of an academic library, for example, is often a student on campus during regular hours connecting from a wired university residence room or computer lab.

Of course, libraries have been serving remote users for a long time. Older technologies and delivery systems include telephone reference (see section 5.2) and mail reference, depending on an exchange of letters through the postal system. The advantage of electronic reference is the convergence of technologies, so that the same medium of communication can be used for the entire transaction. This convergence depends on parallel developments: Between 1995 and 2000, most libraries of any size established a Web presence and made their catalogs and electronic resources available online, including ready reference sources. Correspondingly, e-mail and Internet connectivity has moved beyond the offices and labs of scientists, engineers, and the military to become used by an increasing proportion of the general public. The next logical step has been to offer point-of-use reference help, available wherever the user is and taking advantage of the installed base of home and office computer technology.

With digital reference service, the library staff can transact the reference interview, refer the user to the online catalog and indexes, escort users through complex searches, provide bibliographic instruction and evaluation of sources, and deliver the required information in the form of Web sites or electronic journal articles or entries in electronic reference tools. The whole process can be conducted remotely, and at the end the user has electronic text or graphics that can be printed out or stored electronically. For the user, this service offers clear advantages over telephone reference, wherein answers must be read over the phone or faxed, and users are often advised to come to the library in person for anything that is not ready reference.

Sixty years after librarians first grappled with the best way to provide remote reference service using a relatively new technology—the telephone—we are now struggling with the problem of how to offer electronic reference service (see Ryan, 1996). The

A QUICK TIP

HIDING OUT

Publicize your service. In "My Patron Wrote Me a Letter," Karen Schneider says that most library e-ref services hide their "light under a bushel. Of over 30 librarians that responded [to her survey], almost all said that the primary publicity tool was a simple link from their library Web page. Yet many people won't think of a library Web site when they have a question."

DID YOU KNOW?

It's a mistake to carry policies developed for telephone reference into the digital environment because the two technologies are very different. There's a good reason to restrict telephone reference to ready reference questions that can be answered over the phone with a short answer. However, in the Web environment you have far more options for providing answers, including providing URLs and appending whole electronic documents. So why limit your service to ready reference? Particularly in libraries with the mandate of supporting distance learners, limiting service to ready reference is a disservice.

electronic reference interview requires the same skills that are needed in face-to-face interviews, but there are some additional considerations that relate to the electronic environment and the bias of the technology. This chapter focuses on the special features of the reference interview in the electronic context. Unlike the face-to-face interview or the telephone interview, the reference interview in the electronic context is a written medium, with all the constraints and advantages that writing entails. And in the spirit of "everything old is new again," we note that the online search form has been making a comeback in a new guise as a form for electronic reference. And the same system-centered versus user-centered choices (see section 1.5) are resurfacing with respect to structuring of the e-mail search request form.

A powerful reason to initiate electronic reference service is to put a human face on the digital library. Bernie Sloan (1997) has observed that most discussions and definitions of the digital library highlight its role as a "repository of information" or a networked "collection"—in short, a storehouse. More than 100 years ago, Melville Dewey issued a call for academic library staff to shift the emphasis from warehousing information to providing personal assistance that facilitates library use. The digital library needs to catch up.

The fundamental questions concerning the design of electronic reference services are often framed in terms of the technology, but in fact have far more to do with the library's orientation to users and with the library's policies about service. In this chapter we focus primarily on communication with users.

6.2 E-MAIL REFERENCE

Despite some experimental reference services offered in real-time, using chat or interactive video conferencing technology, the most popular form of electronic reference so far uses text-based e-mail as the means of communication. Most academic and special libraries and many public libraries have been offering at least some kind of e-mail reference since about 1995. In a useful article, "Virtual Reference Services," Suzanne M. Gray (2000) provides a summary of selected research on issues relating to virtual reference in libraries. She traces the growth of e-mail reference service from its beginnings in the mid-1980s, mainly in health sciences and engineering libraries. Initially a service that was used only by a small minority of early adopters, e-reference has established itself as a basic service that is increasingly popular with users.

Because the e-mail reference transaction is asynchronous and depends on the back-and-forth exchange of messages, users won't get an immediate answer. But they like its convenience anyway because they can ask a question when they think of it, at any time of the day or night. And they don't have to take time to make a special trip to the library. Moreover, they are more likely to get a specific answer and not an unmonitored referral. As we have seen in Chapter 3, some reference staff have discovered various ways of getting rid of users without actually helping them, such as advising them to search the catalog or to browse the shelves (e.g., "Our medical books/our encyclopedias are over there."). E-mail reference normally requires the staff to find a specific answer and send it to the user, not simply to say, "Have you done a Google search?"

Apart from these advantages, e-mail reference service offers specific benefits to particular groups of users. It offers advantages to users who:

- are shy and uneasy about asking questions in person or who are too proud to ask.
- do not speak English well enough to feel comfortable asking questions face-to-face or by telephone, but read and write English well enough to communicate. Transcription errors are avoided in the answer because it is written down by the librarian, not by the English-as-a-Second-Language user, who may have difficulty hearing and writing down a spoken answer.
- have constraints on mobility that prevent them from visiting a library in person. This group may well include an unexpected number of older users.
- live at a distance from urban centers and large libraries. This group includes an increasingly large number of distance learners.

E-mail reference offers advantages for staff as well:

- When questions arrive electronically, there is more time for thought and reflection than with in-person or telephone questions.
- Questions can be answered at quiet times or by librarians who are not working at the reference desk.
- It is easier to refer questions to the "resident expert," with the result that the expertise of the entire staff may be tapped as needed.
- The workload can be distributed among the staff, directed to appropriate individuals or subject specialists.

SOME QUICK TIPS
LOW BANDWIDTH

Make allowances for low bandwidth. Roseanne Allucquere Stone (1995) has called text-based environments "low bandwidth" in contrast to the "high bandwidth" richness of cues available in face-to-face communication. When people are in each other's physical presence, speakers use this extra bandwidth to communicate the emotional context of the message. Listeners use it to provide cues about how they are interpreting the message. In the low-bandwidth world of typed messages, small hints of emotion in the typed message can become magnified by the reader. Here are some tips for preventing the channel temperature from becoming too hot:

- Don't use uppercase or highlighting. It reads too much like shouting.
- Avoid emotive language.
- Don't respond in kind when you think that the other party has sent you a message that seems to you complaining, angry, hostile, sarcastic, or otherwise offensive.
- Recover from communication accidents that have happened because a user has misinterpreted one of your messages. Apologize and explain your previous message (e.g., you asked about intended uses because knowing context helps you do a better search).

- Because software can capture electronic questions and answers and put them into a database, it is easy to create a record that can be used for research and evaluation of reference services. The database can be used to develop FAQ files, which can answer questions that are commonly asked.

The drawbacks to e-mail reference all relate to its asynchronous, text-based technology and are the other side of the same coin:

- The text-based environment is impoverished and strips away both visual cues (in this respect resembling the telephone) and auditory cues. You can't use eye contact or establish a connection through a welcoming tone of voice. The problem of interpreting the tone of an e-mail exchange is well known for its role in creating flame wars in online discussion groups. To compensate for the loss of visual and auditory information, net-users have developed emoticons such as smileys— :-) —which say, in effect, "This is a joke. I'm just kidding. Please don't take this as an insult."
- Deprived of visual and auditory cues, you can't tell whether the user is a child or a senior citizen, male or female. You can't see how fashionably the user is dressed, whether the user has a disability or whether the user is a member of a visible minority. An advantage is that you will be less likely to jump to conclusions based on assumptions derived from physical appearance (see section 3.2.2). However, you still need to avoid making assumptions based on grammar, writing style, or spelling mistakes. For many topics, you will need to take extra steps to find out about the user's level of literacy and ability to make sense of specialized or technical information.
- Unless you use a well-designed form to encourage users to provide appropriate contextual details about the information need (see section 6.2.3), you are likely to need many back-and-forth e-mail messages. You cannot query the user while you are reading the question. Users who are infrequent e-mail users might take several days or a week to read your message asking for more information. The whole interview process could take considerable time before the question can finally be answered, by which time the answer may no longer be useful.
- The discourse of speed and immediacy leads some users

to have unrealistic expectations about an instantaneous answer. Input of the question can be 24/7, but for the most part, answering is done during normal hours. Except in the case of a few experimental services, an insomniac still has to wait till the library opens to get an answer. Moreover, the message might travel at the speed of light through fiber optic cables, but once it reaches the library, a human being deals with the question, finds and evaluates the sources, and types out an answer. You can address this problem of mismatch of service and expectations by having the software send an automatic message to the user saying that you have received the question and will answer within some specified period, such as 24 hours.

- Unlike a face-to-face interview, which has its own integrity, the e-mail reference transaction is often distributed across a number of separate messages. Software is therefore needed that manages the volume of e-mail traffic and links all the messages related to the same question, so that they can be read as a single thread or saved in a single folder.

- Providing a typed answer rather than a spoken answer takes more time and depends on an additional set of skills, including writing skills and the use of correct spelling and grammar. It may take longer to type the response than to find the answer in the first place. Sometimes the response involves retyping information from print sources into the reply message. Cutting and pasting from electronic resources can be done, but often requires some editing. Careful and complete identification of the sources used must be included with the reply.

- Because everything has to be typed out, bibliographic instruction is harder to do and may therefore get short-changed: it may seem like simply too much effort to explain how the information was found and evaluated.

- The service is susceptible to interruptions of the sort called "system vulnerability" in the literature—as one user put it, "If something is wrong with your e-mail system, then you're in trouble."

DID YOU KNOW?

Limiting service to ready reference doesn't work. In a survey of 22 U.S. public libraries offering e-mail reference service, Beth Garnsey and Ronald Powell (2000) discovered that 55 percent of the libraries said that their service was intended to answer ready reference questions that "can be answered quickly by consulting only one or two reference tools." An analysis by category of the questions asked showed that ready reference questions were a minority of the questions that users actually asked. The top three categories were: ready reference, 30 percent; complex research questions, 25 percent; and genealogy, 18 percent.

WHAT KINDS OF E-QUESTIONS DO USERS ASK?

Libraries that have reported on their electronic reference service say that the following types of questions are common:

- **Requests for technology instruction,** troubleshooting questions, and questions about the system itself. These questions often relate to getting access to library resources from outside the library. These questions can be answered in a FAQ file on the library Web page.
- **Questions on how to cite sources** using approved styles such as the Chicago Manual of Style or those of the American Psychological Association (APA) or the Modern Languages Association (MLA). These questions can be answered in a FAQ file on the library Web page.
- **Quick, short-answer questions.** Many libraries have guidelines that try to limit service to these kinds of questions, but see below for another view.
- **Research questions.** Academic libraries receive this kind of question often, even if the service is limited to ready reference questions. If these questions become too complex, the user is sometimes asked to come in and talk with the librarian. However, given the enormous expansion of courses offered to remote learners, academic libraries have a responsibility to provide reference service for research questions to users who cannot come to the library in person.
- **Genealogy questions.** Public libraries receive many genealogy questions from remote users who are tracking down every lead in order to construct a family tree.

If you provide several SAMPLE QUESTIONS for each of the categories, your users might better understand what kinds of questions are OK to ask from the perspective of the library system. These sample questions can be made accessible through a link from your service description. As many libraries have found, the strategy of saying, "We answer only ready reference questions" or "We answer only quick, short-answer questions" doesn't work. Who but a librarian knows what a "ready reference question" is anyway? Moreover, as we have seen, even librarians often don't know in advance if a question is easy or difficult (see section 1.6). Library users are even less likely to know what is quick and ready and what's slow and unready. And of course, as we have been saying throughout this book, the librarian doesn't really know what kind of question it is until after a good reference interview has happened.

In "Ready for Reference," Bernie Sloan lists 116 questions posted during the two busiest weeks of an experiment in real-time digital reference. He notes that there were relatively few quick "ready reference" questions asked and notes, "Handling only questions of a 'ready reference' nature might be a disservice to a sizable portion of the potential population of digital reference users" (2001: Online).

SAMPLE QUESTION

"EARL: Ask A Librarian" is a service provided in the UK by a consortium of British public libraries. It provides examples of sample questions and answers, to give users an idea of the type of question the service is best suited to answer. Here is a sample question and answer provided on the EARL: Ask A Librarian site *(www.ask-a-librarian.org.uk/)*:

Q: What did Florence Nightingale die from?
A: The consensus of opinion of her biographers seems to be that she died in her sleep of old age (age 90). The *Encyclopaedia Britannica* says, "It has never been shown that FN had any organic illness; her invalidism may have been partly neurotic and partly intentional."

6.2.1 SETTING THE STAGE

Before the user can ask an electronic question, you must do a lot of work behind the scenes. This work is the digital equivalent of setting the stage for an in-person question by paying close attention to making the physical environment a welcoming space. In the bricks-and-mortar library, this means using appropriate signage, positioning reference desks where they are easy to find, identifying the professional staff as the right people to receive the question, and so on (see section 2.2). The electronic counterpart to creating a welcoming physical environment is creating visible, easy-to-use Web links and well-designed, easy-to-navigate Web pages. Just as the reference service in the physical library should not be hidden away in an out-of-the way area but clearly marked and placed where users can find it, so the e-mail reference service should not be buried four levels deep in the Web site; it should be available through a link on the library's main page.

However elaborate your e-mail reference service is, the basic thing you need to provide is a means whereby users can e-mail their questions to the library. The simplest method—and the one that some libraries started with at the beginning of e-mail reference service—is to use a generic mail-to address that the user clicks on in order to send a regular e-mail (e.g., digref@lib.universityname.edu). In such a case, one central individual initially examines all questions received and routes them to appropriate people. Hence the technical questions are forwarded to technical staff, circulation questions are forwarded to circulation staff, and reference questions are routed to the reference department. This primitive system may be manageable when volume is low, but it has built-in inefficiencies that cause it to break down when volume increases. The main

---

ANALYZE THIS REFERENCE CASE

Case 24: Typical e-reference questions

Bernie Sloan (2001) has provided a list of questions that users have asked in the "Ready for Reference" service, which is a live, 24/7 Web-based reference service piloted by eight academic libraries in the Alliance Library System in Illinois. Here are some of the questions:

Do you know where I can find Chicago City Directories?
I would like to find information on Trinidad and Tobago, don't want to use encyclopedias—
    any suggestions as to where to begin my search?
Where can I find info about legislation concerning juvenile justice?
I need sources (that are not magazines) dealing with environmental racism.
I am giving a talk for a Mother-Daughter Banquet. My theme is "Sharing the Love of Story
    Across the Generations." I would like to open with reading a children's picture book that
    depicts the joy and value of grandmothers sharing their stories of life with their daughters
    and granddaughters. Or I would be interested in knowing some poetry on that topic.
I need info on early television reporters.
Where can I find data about the national deer populations over the past few years?
Information on phentermine.
I need help finding information on sexual activities among teenagers and young adults.
Looking for information on Native American families.

(Thanks to Bernie Sloan for permission to use these questions reported in "Ready for Reference:
        Academic Libraries Offer Live Web-Based Reference: Evaluating System Use.")

Comment: Bernie Sloan notes, "People working with digital reference projects often discuss the concept of creating logs of questions to use to automate part of the digital reference process. The general idea is that, after a user asks a question, the question is automatically matched against a list of previously asked questions to see if the question has already been asked and answered. If a match is found, that makes one less question a librarian will need to answer" (2001: Online).

For discussion:
Analyze the user questions listed above.

1. Do you think there are enough commonalties among these questions to make it feasible to automate the reference process?
2. Compare this list of questions with questions that are asked in person at the reference desk. What differences, if any, do you find?
3. Sloan notes that this list of questions asked contains few quick "ready reference" questions. His conclusion is that policy-makers need to rethink their inclination to restrict electronic reference to quick ready reference questions. Do you agree?

A QUICK TIP

MORE THAN A SEARCH ENGINE

To provide helpful service to information seekers at their point of need, go beyond what a search engine can do. On their own, Internet-using information seekers can type a keyword into a search engine. But search engines can't do reference interviews. What reference librarians can do (and search engines can't) is help users figure out what it is they really want to know.

problem is that users, unprompted, often don't provide enough information about the real question to allow the library staff either to answer the question or to make the appropriate referral. Making a referral without ascertaining the real question is the electronic counterpart of the unmonitored referral: it gets rid of the user, but all too frequently does not provide the user with the helpful answer. In the absence of a well-designed form, several back-and-forth messages may be needed to negotiate the question.

If you want to provide good electronic reference service, you need to do more than just the basics. Provide access to the service from the top-level library Web page as well as from every other page on the Web site and from the online catalog. Because you want people to use the service, give it a memorable name that clearly identifies it. Actively promote the service. When you advertise your electronic reference service, make sure that people understand your policy on the kinds of help they can (and can't) expect. You should provide a question form for users to submit their questions via e-mail, along with a description of the service offered and guidelines. Guidelines should specify who can use the service, the types of questions that can be answered, and how quickly a response can be expected. Instructions should be included both in the description and on the search form itself.

As you work behind the scenes to develop the service, you will notice that there are two categories of information you need to think about. There is information needed by users to access the service, and then there is information needed by staff to do their jobs. The first category of information goes onto your Web page. The second goes into your policy and procedures manual. When designing your Web page for the public, keep in mind your audience. Ask yourself: What does a *user* need to know about our library's service? What questions will be in the minds of our users? Here are some things that a *user* wants to know:

> What is the "Ask a Librarian" service and who provides it?
> Am I eligible to receive this service?
> What kinds of questions does this service answer?
> How long will it take to get an answer?
> What do I have to do to get this service?
> What kind of answer can I expect to get?
> How do I submit my question? (e.g., "Click here for question form")
> How can I contact the library directly? (Provide phone and fax numbers and physical location.)
> What kind of privacy can I expect?

DID YOU KNOW?

WebBots are automated programs that crawl the Web and find Web sites. "Bot" is short for "robot," which comes from the Greek word for work. See the BotSpot at http://botspot.com for a Web site that's all about Bots, including data-mining bots, knowledge bots, and search bots.

A QUICK TIP

WHO'S SENDING THOSE MESSAGES?

Use an autoresponder to acknowledge the user's question right away and explain that a librarian will reply within a specified time period. The text of the autoresponse message must be crafted to help the user understand the process. Joanna Richardson and colleagues (2000) found that an e-mail system that generates an autoresponse makes users think that the system will also send an automated answer. Meanwhile, staff were often totally unaware that their Ask a Librarian service generated an automatic response and had no idea what the response said.

Here are some things that *staff members* need to know:

> Who is eligible to receive this service and what do users have to do to demonstrate eligibility?
> What is the procedure for answering user's questions? If questions are received centrally and routed to subject experts, who is responsible for doing the routing?
> What are the policies on how frequently e-mail is checked?
> What are the policies on how to negotiate questions?
> What are the policies on how much time to devote to questions, what kinds of answers are appropriate, and privacy?

Obviously there is some overlap between these two sets of questions. But even when the question is the same (e.g., Who is eligible to receive service?), the text that provides the answer must be written differently to suit the intended audience. Staff members need a lot more detail. Users need to be told just enough to let them navigate the system. For example, users don't need to know about the procedures for handling questions within the library and routing, but they should be told how soon to expect an answer. Staff members, on the other hand, need clear and detailed guidelines for internal use on such matters as how often e-mail is checked, who opens the e-mail (does this responsibility rotate among staff or does one person do it?), and who is responsible for answering the question (is it done by one person or are the questions referred to appropriate individuals or departments?).

In your explanation of the service for users, special pains should be taken to write in a friendly, positive style that encourages users to use the service. Describing your service in this welcoming way must go hand-in-hand with the library's genuine commitment to the service. The description should come immediately after the user has clicked on the prominent "Ask a Librarian" link on the top-level page of the library Web site.

Once the e-mail reference service is established, monitor it closely, keeping track of questions and answers. You might want to provide a Frequently Asked Questions (FAQ) file that users can access on their own. For example, if you often get the question "How do I connect from home to the library's catalog/electronic journals?" provide the answer to this question. If the user bypasses the FAQ page and asks you anyway, you can answer by providing a link to your FAQ answer in your response to the user.

EXERCISE

LOOK-AND-FEEL

The look-and-feel of a library site is important—just like the first 15 seconds of an in-person contact. Bernie Sloan (1999) has identified a list of links to more than 90 libraries that provide electronic reference services. Use this list to heighten your awareness of best practices as well as horrible examples to avoid. Using any principle of selection you like (e.g., by type of library, size of library, geographic region, or random choice), pick three sites and evaluate them using the principles of good service and good design discussed in this chapter. You can find his complete list in "E-Mail Reference Sites," available at http://alexia.lis.uiuc.edu/~b-sloan/e-mail.html.

A QUICK TIP

A CLICK OR TWO AWAY

Don't let your service be a well-kept secret. Give the service a name that clearly identifies it. Provide access directly from the library's top-level home-page. Do not bury your e-mail reference form or make the user drill down many levels through your Web site to find it. Your e-mail form should be no more than two clicks away from the library home page.

• Click 1 should lead directly to a description of the service.
• Click 2 should lead directly to the form.

WHO CAN USE YOUR E-REFERENCE SERVICE?

You need to establish use guidelines for your e-mail reference question service at the outset, because the decision that you make here will have an impact on a lot of other decisions, including what kinds of questions to put on the forms. You might decide to have no limits and that you are prepared to welcome the world. Less ambitiously, you might decide that you have to concentrate your resources on certain classes of users who will have priority and that questions from others will be answered as time allows. Or you might limit your service to a defined user group. In any case, you need to make your eligibility policy clear in all descriptions of the service.

• In a public library, your service might be limited to card-holders, to local residents, or to residents of your state or province.
• In an academic library, you might limit your service to faculty, staff, students, and alumni of your own institution. In state-funded institutions you might serve all residents of the state or province.
• In a special library, your service might be limited to staff members, or it might include clients or members.

6.2.2 THE E-MAIL REFERENCE INTERVIEW

Setting the stage for e-reference by giving your service a name and putting links to the service on the library's main page is like having a centrally located, well-marked reference desk: it's a necessary first step in encouraging people to ask reference questions, but you still have to figure out what they really want. The reference interviewing skills discussed in Chapters 2 and 3 apply just as much in the electronic environment as they do face-to-face. The goal does not change just because you are working through e-mail. You still need to establish a welcoming environment, make contact with the user, find out what the user wants to know, link the user to the system, and confirm that the answer provided is actually what was wanted. The challenge is to find a way to provide these standard functions in the written, asynchronous environment of e-mail.

The key to conducting a successful e-mail interview is to take into account the bias of the medium. In face-to-face or telephone interviews, even very short ones, there is a lot of turn-taking, but frequent turn-taking does not increase the total length of the transaction. Turns are often short—remember those minimal encouragers such as "mm-hmm" or "That's interesting" discussed in

EXERCISE

ASK-A

Unlike search engines that retrieve static Web pages, "Ask-a" services connect users with real people who tailor their answer to the user's specific question. Ask-a services are often very specialized: Ask a High-Energy Astronomer, Ask the Archaeologist, Ask a Linguist, Ask Dr. Math, Ask a Volcanologist. Check out the competition by examining some of the Ask-a services that are becoming common in cyberspace. You can find them listed at the Virtual Reference Desk AskA + Locator project (http://vrd.org/locator/subject.html).

Before you go any further, think of a question that you would like to have answered. Ask your question in at least two Ask-a sites and compare your experience. On the basis of this experience, what conclusions can you draw about Ask-a services in relation to electronic reference?

See also Joann M. Wasik, "Information for Sale: Commercial Digital Reference and AskA Services" (vrd.org/AskA/commAskA.shtml), and L. Bry, "Setting up an Ask-an-Expert Service" (www.madsci.org/ask_expert/index.html).

FOR DISCUSSION:

1. How satisfied were you with the answers you got?
2. Compare your experience with Ask-a services against the experience you would expect to get from e-mail reference service offered by a library.
3. For users, what are the advantages/disadvantages of electronic reference service offered by libraries?

section 2.4.4—and the user's responses are immediate. But with the e-mail interview, turn-taking introduces delays, sometimes up to a week, depending on how frequently the user monitors her e-mail. The literature on e-reference refers to this phenomenon as "high dialog penalties." Quite simply, the fewer e-mail exchanges needed to clarify the real question, the faster the answer can be provided and the transaction completed. Moreover, when the negotiation of the question is stretched out over a prolonged series of e-mails, reference staff have the added work of linking the chain of messages and rereading earlier messages.

Many libraries have discovered that the secret to reducing turn-taking and its accompanying high dialog penalties is to develop a form that structures the information provided by the user along the lines needed by the staff member to answer the question. The purpose of a good digital reference form is to provide a framework in which the user is prompted to take many turns at once. *This means that the standard skills of welcoming the user, asking open and sense-making questions, using encouragers, and avoiding premature diagnosis all need to be incorporated into the form itself.* The equivalent of turn-taking in the reference interview is achieved through the series of well-designed questions on the form. Whereas the face-to-face interview takes place as a series of exchanges extended in time, the questions on the form are extended in space.

Here are some quick tips for the electronic reference interview:

- Provide a reference question form that users can access from the library Web page. If they do e-mail you directly, use a standard response explaining why they will get a more helpful answer if they fill out the form. Your reply should include a description of the service and the form, which they can fill out and return to you.
- For questions that arrive when the library is closed, program the system to send an automatic response saying, in effect, "Thank you for your electronic reference question. We will get back to you within 24 hours."
- Because you are using e-mail, you can't see those uncertain looks or signs of discouragement or impatience. All the messages that the user receives—from the initial form to the automatic response on receipt of the question to your individualized answer—must be friendly and welcome further communication.
- On the electronic form, ask the user to double-check the e-mail address. Explain why. The UK-based EARL: Ask A Librarian service explains, "We can't reply to your question if you haven't given us a workable email address." (See www.ask-a-librarian.org.uk/)

DID YOU KNOW?

Advertising makes a difference. Ilene Frank (1998) reports how the University of South Florida-Tampa changed its service from a "well-kept secret" by a systematic effort at marketing. To reach a wide audience, they decided to advertise the service in the campus newspaper, on the library's homepage, on the local university system, and on the local freenet; distribute bookmarks and business cards highlighting the service; mention the service in faculty-staff orientation sessions and bibliographic instruction lectures; and include a listing for the e-mail address in the campus phone directory.

A QUICK TIP

REFERRAL

If you're sure you can't help the user, suggest another way of getting help. When The Internet Public Library (www.ipl.org/ref) "Ask A Question" service is closed, such as for a holiday, this message appears: "We are temporarily closed . . . [but] it's certainly not our intention to leave anyone stranded. There are lots of places you can go for help." A list of such places is then provided.

- In your first individualized reply, acknowledge the question by restating what you understand the user has asked for (see acknowledgment, section 2.4.3). If your form has been well designed, you should be able to send some kind of answer in your first reply. But even with the best of forms, often some crucial piece of information will be missing. Suppose the user has said, "I am working on a sociology paper that needs references for the immigration patterns of Welsh immigrants 1870s-1890s. Any suggestions?" Your response might acknowledge the question by saying, "We understand that you want information on immigration patterns of Welsh immigrants 1870s-1890s. We have assumed that you are specifically interested in the pattern of immigration from Wales to the United States. Here are the URLs for two sites that provide information on this. If this information isn't helpful or you want Welsh immigration in general, please let us know what specifically is missing that you still need to know about."

- Suggest that users phrase their request in their own words. Encourage them to give some kind of context for the search (e.g., "It's often helpful if you tell us a little bit about how you plan to use this information so that we can find the most helpful materials"). You don't want to spend a long time looking for the exact, most up-to-date figures on literacy in Saudi Arabia when all they want to know is whether or not more than 50 percent of the population can read.

- Use inclusion (section 4.1.1) right on the form itself to explain to the users why you are asking for certain kind of information. The EARL: Ask A Librarian service has such a request on its form—"Please give us some background"—accompanied by the following explanation, which is an excellent example of inclusion: "Knowing the context of your enquiry can help us find the right answer for you. One of the difficulties of providing answers by email is that we can't interview you face-to-face to make sure we understand exactly what you want. You can help by explaining the context of your question, telling us in general terms why you are asking it and letting us know where you have already looked for the answer. Please add to your question any further information which you think may be useful to us. We are not being inquisitive. It really can help the librarians provide the information you need." (See www.ask-a-librarian.org.uk/)

EXERCISE

GETTING RID OF THE E-USER

For this exercise, pick the Web site of your own library or of a library in your area. Imagine that you are a user who is unfamiliar with the services offered and is exploring the site for the first time. Count how many features of the chosen site have the effect of discouraging the user from asking an e-question. Give a point for each of the following:

1. No link to the service is provided from the homepage.
2. The description of the electronic reference service gives priority to what the service does not do, not what it does do (e.g., we do not provide answers to X; we do not serve Y categories of users).
3. The page describing electronic reference service states that for good service you should come in person to the library.
4. High-end equipment or downloaded software is needed to make use of the service.
5. There is no digital form provided on which to submit your question.
6. The digital form looks very complicated and gives the impression that it would take 15 minutes or so to fill out.

If you give the site a score of 4 or more, the site needs improvement to make it more user-centered.

- Find out what the real question is before you try to answer it. A well-designed form should eliminate many of the too-general initial questions. But if the user's initial question is still unclear or too broad, there is no point in taking a scatter-gun approach to providing an answer, barraging the user with information in the hope that somehow some of it will be relevant. This approach doesn't work in face-to-face reference, and it won't work in the electronic environment. It is better to respond with a small amount of information plus a request for clarification. Make sure that you ask in the same e-mail *all* the questions that you need to get answered.
- Always include a follow-up (see section 3.3.3) with your answer or search output: "If this answer isn't helpful, please e-mail us again."
- Keep back-and-forth messaging to a minimum. If you find that routinely you need to send multiple messages before you understand the question, analyze the exchanges to pinpoint the problem. Do you need to introduce a form? Do you have a form that isn't working as well as it should?
- Prepare a list of frequently asked questions and make them available on the Web site.

6.2.3 USING FORMS

In the evolution of e-mail reference service, the first stage is often to provide a simple "mailto" e-mail address. Users mail a question to the reference department using the regular e-mail message space. The main advantage of this primitive system is that libraries can test the water and ease their way into e-mail reference service without having to spend much time on design. The drawback is that online users resemble face-to-face users: unless prompted, they do not provide enough information about themselves or about the question (see section 1.4). Although e-reference users probably won't say, "I need everything on transportation," they still tend to ask initial questions that are too broad. As we have been emphasizing throughout this book, most users do not understand what information librarians need to know in order to answer a question. The user's mental model of how bricks-and-mortar libraries work is apt to be sketchy; in the case of electronic reference, users may think that a computer is finding the answer for them. Hence the next stage is usually to design a form that structures the information that the users provide about their questions.

When designing the form, you need to be even more conscious of the difference between a systems-based approach and a user-based approach than you are in the face-to-face reference interview. Unfortunately, many forms consist almost entirely of questions that relate to system requirements—it's the same problem that used to beset the old online search forms. Often, the e-reference form requests a lot of demographic information; asks for limitations by geographic area, by language, by time period of published sources, by format of the preferred answer; and then says something like, "In the box below describe the topic of your search." Some forms provide even less direction to the user on what information to provide about the information need, being content to provide a box with a heading like "Your question?" or "Your message" or "Type your question." In describing the early years of the Internet Public Library (IPL) Reference Center, Nettie Lagace reported that many questions to the IPL consisted of "two or three keywords, with few clues specifying information" (1998: 6). This problem, she said, prompted a revision of the form. The revised form is one of the better forms being used anywhere.

Some Quick Tips for Creating Question Forms

A well-designed form will eliminate problems before they occur and provide the right framework for finding out what the user really wants to know.

- Use one standard form throughout the system. Some academic libraries have forms for each departmental library in the system, but students may be unaware of how the library system works and may therefore choose an inappropriate library for their question. Standard forms can be rerouted to any library.
- Name the form. You have already named the service, so the name of the question form can simply be an extension of the service name (e.g., "Ask-A-Librarian Question Form"). By giving the form a name, you make it easier to refer to it on the page that describes the service and easier for users to find it and recognize that they have found the right page.
- On the form, provide essential instructions and advice for completing it. Don't make the user click to another page to get necessary information. Be concise.
- Keep the form clean, functional, typographically simple, and easy to read. Don't use busy wallpaper designs in the background or animated graphics that compete for the reader's attention. These irritating bugaboos also make the Web page take longer to download.

A QUICK TIP

DESIGNING SPACE

Naturally, you want your Web pages to be attractive, uncluttered, easy to read, with clear instructions. But how to achieve this? Read Edward Tufte, the acknowledged authority on the visual display of information. He has written a dazzling series of books that set out principles for making information accessible to users in data-rich displays that are uncluttered. In his fourth book, Visual Explanations, he turns his attention to what's wrong with Web pages: interfaces based on a tedious series of binary choices; interfaces featuring clunky icons that require labels ("Why won't just the words do?" he asks); pages that are too cluttered, with too many pixels devoted to big buttons with no informational value or to distracting animations. Tufte recommends an evaluation of an interface by calculating the proportion of space on the screen devoted to information content in comparison with the space devoted to computer administration and system debris or to distracting analogies.

ANALYZE THIS REFERENCE CASE

Case 25: The Internet Public Library (IPL) and the Ask A Librarian service

The Internet Public Library (www.ipl.org/ref) is a pathbreaking experiment in providing virtual public library service on the Internet. The IPL electronic reference service was started in 1995 as an experiment in a graduate seminar at the University of Michigan School of Information and Library Studies. After two years, the volunteer librarians involved with the project had answered more than 6,000 questions from all parts of the world.

The Ask a Librarian (www.ask-a-librarian.org.uk/) service is an online reference service offered by a consortium of public libraries in the UK to "bring the resources of UK public reference libraries to people's desktops."

Examine these two sites and compare the information services they offer. What are the differences/similarities? Which do you prefer? Which features do you think could be adapted for an electronic service offered by an individual public library? How about academic libraries?

- Use boxes for each part of your form, which the user fills in. Indicate clearly which boxes are *not* optional—for example, the address to which they want the answer sent. Some software provides the capacity to prevent the user from submitting the form until the required boxes are filled in.
- Keep the form as short as possible so that it doesn't take so long to fill out that it becomes a formidable barrier to users. Look at every question on the form and ask yourself, "Why do I need to know that?" If the answer is, "Well, I'm not sure but Library X's form asks for this and so maybe we should ask for it too," then delete it. Be equally ruthless with all that demographic information that routinely gets added to forms. You will need some way of screening users, if your service policy puts restrictions on the types of users eligible to receive the service (e.g., restrictions to local residents for a public library service; members of the university community for academic libraries; staff for a special library). But if you don't plan to use the information for anything, don't ask it. Demographic information doesn't help you understand what the user wants to know.

COMPARING THE IN-PERSON AND THE E-MAIL REFERENCE INTERVIEW		
	In-Person	**E-mail**
Being approachable	Locate the reference desk in a prominent place. At the desk, look up at users, use welcoming body language, and smile. Do not bury your head in your work.	Create an easy-to-access and well-designed form that is not over-crowded. Question can be submitted at any-time, 24/7.
Using acknowledgment	Restate what you have understood of the user's original question. If necess-ary for a shared understanding, para-phrase.	If library is closed: send an auto-matic receipt notice explaining when a response from a librarian can be expected. If library is open: send user a reply that restates the question and asks for clarification if necessary. (You may provide an-swers to brief factual questions, but be sure to ask for confirmation that this is sufficient.)
Avoiding premature diagnosis	Don't assume that the question presented is the real question. Don't prejudge the user's need based on status, appearance, speech.	Don't assume that the question presented is the real question. Don't prejudge the questioner based on writing skills, spelling errors, typos, or e-mail address. (Children may use a parent's e-mail address.)
Using open or sense-making questions	Get the user to provide more informa-tion. Try to assess the situation, gaps, and kind of help wanted.	Use sense-making questions on the form in order to find out situations, gaps, or uses. If further clarifica-tion is needed, use open or sense-making questions in your e-mail response just as you would in per-son.
Using inclusion	Explain why the user's answers will help you to provide a more useful answer.	On the form, explain why the user's answers will help.
Paraphrasing your understanding of the information need	Rephrase the question as you now understand it. Ask for confirmation be-fore searching for final answer.	Rephrase the question as you now understand it. Ask for confirmation before searching for final answer.
Following up	After providing answer, say, "If this isn't what you are looking for, ask again." If the user goes to another section of the library, ask the user to come back if the answer cannot be found.	After providing answer, say, "If this isn't what you are looking for, e-mail us again." (If you recommend electronic sources or other external resources, ask the user to get back to you if the source did not turn out to be helpful.)

DID YOU KNOW?

When e-reference was young, some people thought that they would be able to create a database of questions and answers and be able to reuse the answers. Except for system questions asking about getting connected to library resources and questions about citing sources, it has turned out that very few questions are the same. Of course, this uniqueness of each question is exactly what should be expected, because every question has its source in the life of the information seeker. Just as in face-to-face reference, initial questions that sound the same often turn out to be completely different and need completely different answers.

PREFORMATTED MESSAGES

No matter how fast you type, you will feel that it's not fast enough. This is where preformatted messages come in. They work like boilerplate in a lawyer's preformatted form covering a situation that frequently recurs in a law practice. You can format these messages in advance and send them to your users as needed, but you need to be careful. When using a preformatted response, be sure that it is a relevant response and not just another way of getting rid of the user.

For referring users to the library FAQ page or online reference form:
You can find the answer to your question on the library FAQ page. The URL is XXX. If you need additional information, please let us know specifically what is missing that you still need to know. That way we can help you better.

For acknowledging the question:
This is to let you know that we got your question on X and will be getting back to you within one working day. Thanks for contacting the Ask a Librarian service of the Y Library.

For negotiating the question:
I'm not familiar with X. What else can you tell me about this subject?
What specifically would you like to know about X?
It would help me locate exactly what you need if you could tell me how you plan to use this information.

For follow-up:
If this information is not what you need, please let us know what specifically is missing so that we can help you further.

For real-time chat:
I'll need to search in a few places to find that. This might take about five minutes. Please hold on.
(With thanks to Cichanowicz, 2001, and Eichler and Halperin, 2000)

A QUICK TIP

BRUSH UP ON YOUR WRITING

In text-based electronic reference service, a crucial skill is being able to write clearly in an appropriate style that is correct but not too formal. In your answer, you need to start with a friendly greeting, summarize your understanding of the user's question, provide a concise answer, include sources, and end with a follow-up inviting the user to get back to you if the answer was incomplete. Check out the writing guides written to help question-answering volunteers in Ask an Expert services. For example, S. Foster has written a "Guide to Writing Responses" for the math experts who write for Dr. Math (www.mathforum.org/dr.math/guide). The EARL: Ask a Librarian site (www.ask-a-librarian.org.uk/) provides guidelines for structuring the response, with suggested formats for providing the answer.

A QUICK TIP

VIRTUAL EQUIVALENCIES

Ann Viles (1999) suggests that you try to find "virtual equivalencies" for the in-person interview. Here are some virtual equivalencies for nonverbal behavior, adapted from Viles.

Eye contact. The "Ask a Librarian" icon blinks once when the Web page first appears on the screen. (But it shouldn't keep blinking; additional blinking is distracting and annoying.)

Sitting or standing at the reference desk. "Ask a Librarian" is always in sight in a prominent place on the screen. Placing the pointer on "Ask a Librarian" flashes a message such as "Have a question? Click here."

Nodding. When users ask a question, they get an automatic acknowledgment.

- Aim for a form that doesn't take more than one screen, if possible. The form should *not* look like a census form that will take a half hour to fill out. With a compact form, you and the user can see the whole thing in one eyespan and recognize immediately that necessary information has been left out.
- After you have designed the form, analyze it. What percentage of your questions are system-based questions in comparison with questions that ask users to describe the answer wanted in their own words? What proportion of the questions are unnecessary for providing relevant answers but have been included anyway so that you can easily create reports that break down users by category (male/female; undergraduate/graduate student/staff/faculty)? Try to rewrite the system-based questions or delete them.
- Devote your greatest attention to refining the part of your form that elicits the information needed. This is the electronic equivalent of the reference interview. A box that says, "Type your question here" is *not* good enough. You can help the user understand what kinds of details you need by providing a link to an example of a form that has been filled out in a way that makes the context of the question clear.
- Provide a link to sample questions that shows examples of the types of questions that can (and cannot) be answered.
- Test your form by recruiting a novice user to help you. Get the user to use the form to ask a question, while you observe difficulties, if any. Revise and test again.
- After the user has clicked the submit or send button, let him know immediately that the transaction has worked by sending an automatic message that says you have received the question and will respond within a specified time period.
- Eliminate the need for some routine questions by providing the answers to frequently asked questions on your FAQ pages.
- Address privacy concerns by letting the user know what happens to the data after the question has been answered. On the form itself and/or in the description of the service, you can include a button (e.g., "Concerned about privacy?" or " Policy on privacy") that opens to the explanation.

EXERCISE

ANTHROPOLOGICAL STRANGENESS

This exercise is for librarians who are engaged in providing electronic reference.
Imagine that you are an anthropologist from Mars who is studying the communication that takes place during an electronic reference exchange. Select at random three reference questions received at your information service. Examine all the messages sent to each of these three users.

1. From the point of view that you have adopted of outsider to the library system, what do you notice about the nature of the communication exchange?
2. What, if anything, does this exercise suggest about ways to improve communication with users?

A QUICK TIP

WE ARE NOT MACHINES

Put a human face on the description of your electronic reference service. Too often library Web sites emphasize resources, collections, and databases, but the staff members and their crucial work are invisible. Let your users know that a person, not a robot or knowbot, will be answering the questions.

DID YOU KNOW?

MOOs and MUDs are likely to appeal disproportionately to younger users who increasingly use this technology for gaming and socializing.

What Information Should You Ask for on Your Form?

In a Public Library:

You probably want a fairly simple form that users can fill out easily. At a minimum, you will want basic contact information (e-mail address) and adequate detail about the context of the user's question, what the user wants to know about the topic, and how the requested information will be used. Optionally, you can ask for name, address, and home and work phone numbers, and you might have separate forms for adults and children.

In an Academic or Special Library:

For an academic or special library, your form probably needs to be more elaborate. If your service is limited to faculty, staff, and students, you need some way of determining eligibility, such as the user's name, affiliation, identification number.

You need contact information, which, in addition to an e-mail address, may include a telephone number, an address to which hard copy may be sent, and possibly an account to which search costs may be charged. Because users are often working on deadlines, find out the date after which the information is no longer needed.

For complex searches, additional elements may be needed. Instead of providing a long series of closed questions on languages preferred, the time period to be covered, preferred databases to be searched, you could use an open question asking for any additional relevant information that will help you narrow the search: What else can you tell us that will help us select information suitable for your needs? If relevant, you could tell us about language(s) preferred; any restrictions on publication dates (such as nothing that is more than five years old); preferred databases to be searched; etc.

In All Libraries:

The form needs to ask questions that tap the situation, gaps, and uses that are the context for the question. The core of the form should ask about the context of the user's question, what the user wants to know about the topic, and how the requested information will be used. Ask what the user has done about this search so far (sources searched; useful materials, if any, located on the topic; key authors who have written on this topic, if known).

Compare the request form below and the one on the next page. Which is better?

DIGITAL HELP REQUEST FORM

This service is **NOT** intended to replace in-depth research in the library. For help with subject-oriented inquiries, please visit our reference desk in person. **DigHelp may not be the best place to ask your question**. If the library is open, we recommend that you call us or visit us.

Our Digital Help service is intended for ready reference questions only. We do **NOT** research topics or do your class assignments for you. This service is provided to help patrons become self-sufficient in their research endeavors. We **CANNOT** be expected to perform information searches or provide comprehensive bibliographies or checklists nor can we retrieve or hold library materials for requesters. We do **NOT** answer medical or legal questions or give advice.

If extensive time is required to answer any question, DigHelp may contact the requester to clarify the question. Please make your question clear and concise. If a question is not clear, DigHelp will respond by asking for more detailed information.

The information collected here is under the authority of the Freedom of Information and Protection of Privacy Act and will be used for statistical purposes. Please send us your brief factual or statistical question.

Click here to download plug-in before proceeding.

REQUESTER NAME _____

REQUESTER TITLE _____

INTERNET E-MAIL ADDRESS _____

BUSINESS TELEPHONE _____

HOME TELEPHONE _____

CHOOSE A STATUS _____

CHOOSE A LIBRARY _____

If you know the SUBJECT, enter it here. _____

ENTER YOUR REQUEST HERE (Please include all important keywords).

_____

LANGUAGES PREFERRED (Please click all that apply.) _____

TIME PERIOD COVERED_____

PREFERRED DATABASES TO BE SEARCHED _____

PREFERRED FORMAT (Please click all that apply.) _____

JUSTIFICATION OF THE REQUEST if outside scope of service._____

_____

ASK A RIVERBRIDGE LIBRARIAN REQUEST FORM

This form allows you to send your question to the professional library staff at the Riverbridge University Library. We try to answer all questions within one working day, but if your question is a frequent one, we might have the answer for you right away. Click on our Frequently Asked Questions page to get an immediate answer on any of the following: library cards, borrowing books, getting periodical articles, getting connected, citing electronic sources, interlibrary loans, special services for distance learners, troubleshooting computer problems.

If you have any problems sending this form, you can e-mail your question to us directly at libref@riverbridge.edu.

Concerned about privacy? Click here to see how your personal information is protected.

1. Contact information
Name:
E-mail address:
Phone number:

2. Your connection to the University of Riverbridge
(Some of our resources are limited to registered students, staff, and faculty. If we know your connection to the University of Riverbridge and how far away you are from the campus library, we will not waste your time by referring you to resources that you cannot access.)

O Current on-campus student   O Distance student   O Faculty or staff

O Alum   O Other

3. What do you want to find out? Click here for a sample form that illustrates the kinds of details about your question that it helps us to know.
What specifically would you like to find out?
   (If you want to know the cost of a student ticket for a return bus trip from Oxford to London, ask for this information specifically and not something general, such as "information on bus travel.")
Please give us some background that will provide a context for your question.
   (We can't interview you to make sure we understand exactly what you want. But you can help us search for the most useful materials if you say a bit about how this question arose and what aspect of the topic interests you most. If you have already looked for an answer, please tell us what you have done so far.)
How do you plan to use this information?
   (If you tell us a little bit about what you are trying to do and what you want to get out of the answer, we can do a better job of selecting helpful sources.)

4. What requirements do you have for a helpful answer?
Is there a deadline after which the information is no longer useful to you?
Is there anything else you can tell us about the features that you are looking for in the answer?

A QUICK TIP

WE'RE NOT NOSY; IT'S OUR JOB

When designing your form, adapt best practices. A good place to start is the Internet Public Library reference question form (www.ipl.org/ref/QUE/FefFormQRC.html). We think it is one of the best. One big strength of this form is that it asks the sense-making question "How will you use this information?" followed by an explanation: "It really helps librarians to know this part! Sometimes we can use our subject knowledge and imaginations to think of other places to look for answers and information, if we know how you will use it or what you want to get out of the answer."

A QUICK TIP

IF YOU KNOW . . .

Avoid asking users for information that they are ill-equipped to tell you. For example, we really hate seeing the request, "If you know the subject, enter it here." What is actually meant is, "If you know the LC subject heading verbatim, . . ." but few people do. Another problematic request is "Please select the most appropriate library for your question" with a list such as The Betty and Billy Blaisdell Library, The Woolley Business Library, The Stevenson Library, and so on.

EXERCISE

EVALUATING YOUR E-MAIL REFERENCE FORM

In the summer 2001 term, students in Carole Farber's MLIS course at The University of Western Ontario on "Issues in Distance Learning" evaluated e-reference forms being used in a range of public and academic libraries. Use their list of criteria below to evaluate the e-mail reference form in your library or a library nearby. The students concluded that a good form should ask questions designed to get answers to the following:

Eligibility. The Who and Where questions that allow the library to determine whether the user is eligible to use this service.

History of the question. What have you done so far? What is the most useful source you have found so far?

Gaps. What would you like to find out?

Uses. How do you plan to use this information?

Features of the perfect answer. For example, "The perfect answer would be an annotated bibliography of the best articles published in the past five years in top tier research journals on Topic X" or "an email address and/or telephone number for an expert on Topic X that I could contact" or "an introduction to Topic X written for nonspecialists."

Time constraints. What is the time after which the answer is no longer useful?

(Thanks to Carole Farber, Associate Professor, Faculty of Information and Media Studies, The University of Western Ontario.)

6.3 REAL-TIME CHAT AND INSTANT MESSAGING

Electronic reference started with e-mail, but some libraries are augmenting, not replacing, their e-mail reference service with a real-time electronic reference service. The increasing popularity, especially among young people, of chat and instant messaging, of MOOs and MUDs, has prompted some libraries to launch pilot services. Experiments that use video have been limited by the fact that most people do not have the necessary hardware and software at home to allow them to send and receive video images from their desktops. Because real-time reference service is still experimental, much of the discussion about it is framed in the context of the library of the future. Enthusiastic exponents envisage a collaborative network of linked libraries that would allow an insomniac user in California to ask a question in the middle of the night and have it negotiated in real time by a librarian who is at a desk in Australia or England or India. Everyone acknowledges that there are still problems to be worked out, but technophiles think that just around the corner will come the improvements in computer technology that will make this service feasible on more than an experimental basis: faster and better connections and interactive audio or video capacity built in to the standard home computer.

In the meantime, most real-time reference trials have used communication software mounted on the library system that allows users who are at a distance to interact with live librarians through typed messages. Despite low use of such experimental services to date, advocates, such as Edana Cichanowicz, see real-time electronic reference evolving into a standard service: "We believe that live reference chat (and its descendants) will evolve into a service as ubiquitous as telephone reference. It will become merely another channel of communication for users and librarians to exploit. It increases the market penetration of libraries by bringing service to the personal desktop" (2001: 53).

Here are some advantages of providing real-time reference using messaging software:

- As with e-mail reference, you are providing access to users at a distance. The difference is that a librarian can respond immediately. With this synchronous service, you can conduct your reference interview at a faster pace than is possible with e-mail. The time lag between turns is a matter of seconds and minutes, not days. You can ask the

DID YOU KNOW?

When Temple University was beginning to design its experiment in real-time remote reference service, staff members formulated a number of requirements for the system: it had to be easy to use, directly accessible from the library Web page, and not involve staff in doing any programming or users in downloading any software; the program should allow staff to limit interactions to one-on-one discussions rather than group chat in order to provide privacy; and the service should be low-cost and not require the library to show advertising (Meola and Stormont, 1999). Temple University's "Talkback" service promises to connect students within two minutes to a librarian who conducts a typed interview.

EXERCISE

THE FUTURE IS HERE

The Library of Congress has started a project to provide collaborate remote reference service on a 24/7 basis, "using a variety of Internet communications technologies (e.g., e-mail, chat, etc.) toward a potential goal of reference service for users any time any where." Check out the service at http://lcweb.loc.gov/rr/digiref/phil99.html. Put yourself in the role of a user. Is the user interface welcoming? How easy would it be for a user to submit a question? How well designed is the question form? Are there model elements in this service that your library could adopt?

user to provide clarification or supplementary information and expect an immediate response.

- Some of the electronic messaging technology allows you to send URLs or push Web pages to the user. You can demonstrate to the user how to find something on the Web. This allows you to walk your user through the source to find the answers. Newer technologies such as the Voice over Internet Protocol (VoIP) allow you to talk to and hear users while connected and while showing the sources.
- When the library is not open, the service can be provided by a librarian working at home or in some other time zone.
- You can establish a chat room and work with several users at once (such as students working on team projects) or you can work on a one-to-one basis.
- Transaction logs of each chat session can be archived (with the consent of the user) so that a full transcript of the reference transaction is available, complete with URLs and instructions provided.

Conversely, there are some drawbacks to e-reference that uses chat or messaging software:

- As with e-mail reference, chat software does not allow you to get visual or aural cues: you can neither see nor hear the user. All you have to go on are the written words. You may infer, say, impatience or frustration from the user's text, but the environment is impoverished in comparison with the opportunities for nonverbal cues offered in face-to-face interactions. Newer Voice over Internet Protocol (VoIP) technology solves part of the problem by providing the cues of tone of voice.
- Real-time reference is labor-intensive. If the service is part of your regular reference desk duties, you will find that it competes for attention with face-to-face users—in this respect, it's similar to telephone reference. Demand is unpredictable, and if the questions come in while the desk is busy with walk-in users, you need to find some way to juggle the requests.
- Some librarians find that providing real-time reference service is stressful because the remote user is waiting for your reply but cannot see what you are doing. You need to tell the user what you are doing.
- As in the e-mail reference interview, communication in the chat mode requires you to type each of your queries to your user, and the answer and source must be put into

EXERCISE

EXPERIMENTS

We are at the stage with real-time reference that no single model has established itself. Check out some of the experiments to evaluate the features that you like/don't like:

- A pioneer in chat reference, Temple University uses "TalkBack" and promises to connect users within two minutes to a paging service at the reference desk for a real-time typed conversation with a librarian (www.library.temple.edu/ref/tbabout.htm).
- North Carolina State University (NCSU) launched a new service in January 2001 using Virtual Reference Desk after an earlier experiment failed because users found it too complicated to figure out how to meet a librarian in the chat room (Boyer, 2001).
- Unlike the many decentralized services, the University of California, Irvine (UCI) established a centralized format for answering questions, in which one member of the electronic reference service team has responsibility for answering all questions received during a particular day (Horn, 2001).

written form. Unlike e-mail, as you type, the user can be watching the words appear on the screen. You can only type so fast, and your haste can cause typos and spelling errors that you would clean up if you were using e-mail. Chat is more demanding than e-mail.

6.3.1 CONDUCTING THE REAL-TIME ELECTRONIC REFERENCE INTERVIEW

The principles for the reference interview remain the same, no matter what the environment. Review the table in section 6.2.2 that compares face-to-face reference and e-mail reference. The adaptations needed for electronic real-time interviewing all relate to the medium. Like the e-mail reference interview, the chat interview can involve several back-and-forth messages. The key point to remember is that you should not get engaged in a frustrating game of twenty questions. If the question appears complex, you might ask the user to complete a question form, which structures the information provided by the user along the lines needed for you to understand what the user really wants to know.

ANALYZE THIS REFERENCE TRANSACTION

Case 26: Ask a Librarian Live

The Business and Economics Resource Center (BERC) of the University of Chicago began in September 2000 to use LiveAssistance.com for chat hosting. BERC has found that a librarian can handle four chat sessions at once. An audio cue—"Incoming chat request"—alerts the librarian to the fact that someone has logged on to the service. LiveAssistance allows the librarian to push Web pages to users. A transcript of the interaction is e-mailed to the user after each session. Here is the first part of a 54-minute chat interview posted on the BERC Web site, with original spelling and punctuation retained:

Librarian: Hi patron. I am working on the question you sent to bus-ref this morning! What can I do for you?

User: Same question. Didn't know when someone would get back to me. Still looking for infromation about the brewing industry in the 1950s. In particular, I am looking for # of breweries, sales by region, and marketing/advertising cost for Anheuser-Busch for any given year (choose 1955) during the period. Hope you can help.

Librarian: I've found a number of books on Anheuser-Busch in our stacks. I will send it to your e-mail right now.

User: Thanks. I'll check them out and let you know if they are what i am looing for.

Librarian: It also seems like some of the info you need can be found in annual repotrs. Have you checked there yet?

User: can't find a location that has annual reports that old. any advice?

Librarian: We don't seem to have Anheuser or Miller in the 50s. From 1969 forward, we do keep it in microfilm, located here on the A-level. You can also find annual reports in Lexis-Nexis back to 1970 for some companies.

Librarian: Can I ask where you are connecting to? Are you in class?

Librarian: You can interlibrary loan annual reports from the 50s. I will send you a record from WorldCat (if I can find one) for the 2 companies. You will have to tell Interlibrary loan what years you need.

User: I am in the Walker computer lab. I think I have Lexis Nexus access here (with appropriate password) but I really need data from the 1950s. What is this WorldCat thing?

Librarian: WorldCat is basically a huge catalog of hundreds of libraries. We use it to request items from other libraries.

Comment: Because this transaction was one of only two sample transcripts that Ask a Librarian Live chose for posting, it is hard to know how typical this transaction is. Nevertheless, it does provide an illustration of an unedited interview transcript that can be examined and analyzed.

For discussion:
Compare this transaction with interviews conducted face-to-face or on the telephone. What are the strengths/weaknesses of live chat in comparison with other formats for:

1. finding out what the user really wants to know?
2. providing answers?

6.4 ANNOTATED REFERENCES

6.4.1 BIBLIOGRAPHIES AND DISCUSSION GROUPS

See the Dig_Ref Listserv Archives at http://groups.yahoo.com/group/dig_ref/ for a discussion of digital reference services hosted by the Virtual Reference Desk. Whereas the Dig_Ref listserv entertains discussion of the range of electronic reference, LiveReference is restricted only to real-time reference.

Bernie Sloan has a very useful Web site, which he updates with materials, bibliographies, and articles related to digital reference service. His bibliography, "The Reference Interview in the Digital Library: A Bibliography" is available at http://alexia.lis.uiuc.edu/~b-sloan/interview.htm [18 February 2002].

The Information Institute of Syracuse has begun a project, "Assessing Quality in Digital Reference." The Web site (http://quartz.syr.edu/quality) includes reports, bibliographies, and conference information on digital reference.

6.4.2 ELECTRONIC REFERENCE

Abels, Eileen G. 1996. "The E-Mail Reference Interview." *RQ* 35, no. 3 (spring): 345–58. Suggests a systematic approach to "interviewing" remote clients and provides a model for the e-mail interview, including a search request form to initiate the process.

Abels, Eileen G., Colleen Shannon, Eileen Deegan, and Ann R. Sweeney. 2000. "Conducting the Reference Interview by E-mail and the Intranet." Panel presentation at the Special Libraries Association Annual Conference, Philadelphia [online]. Available: www.library.northwestern.edu/transportation/slatran/philpresents/ReferenceLinks.htm [18 February 2002].

Association of Research Libraries. 1999. *Electronic Reference Service: A SPEC Kit.* Washington, D.C.: Association of Research Libraries. SPEC Kit 251 was compiled by Lori Goetsch et al. with the goal of reporting the results of a survey of ARL libraries' electronic reference services and of offering "a snapshot of the types of users reached, questions received, policies established, data-gathering techniques utilized, and innovations implemented." For a summary, see www.arl.org/spec/251sum.html.

Booth, Andrew, Alan J. O'Rourke, and Nigel Ford. 2000. "Structuring the Pre-search Reference Interview: A Useful Technique for Handling Clinical Questions." *Bulletin of the Medical Library Association* 88, no. 3 (July): 239–46. Compares the results of using minimally structured forms with the results of using forms structured according to an evidence-based medicine anatomy (EBM) and ends saying "considerable work remains on making these forms acceptable to both librarians and users." Apart from one question, the EBM form provided in the Appendix focuses almost entirely on demographic data and system-derived categories.

Boyer, Joshua. 2001. "Virtual Reference at the NCSU Libraries: The First One Hundred Days." In *Information Technologies and Libraries* 20, no. 3 [online]. Available: www.lita.org/ital/2003_boyer.html [18 February 2002].

Broughton, Kelly. 2001. "Our Experiment in Online, Real-Time Reference." *Computers in Libraries* 21, no. 4 (April): 26-31.

Bushallow, Wilbur L., Gemma DeVinney, and Fritz Whitcomb. 1996. "Electronic Mail Reference Service: A Study." *RQ* 35, no. 3 (spring): 359–71.

Business and Economics Resource Center, University of Chicago. 2000. Ask a Librarian Live [online], Available: www.lib.uchicago.edu/e/busecon/transoct2000.html [18 February 2002].

Cichanowicz, Edana M. 2001. "Sunday Night Live!—An Experiment in Real Time Reference Chat—on a Shoestring Budget." *The Charleston Advisor* 2, no. 4 (April 15): 49–51. Available online: www.charlestonco.com/features.cfm?id-59&type-fr.

Coffman, Steve. 2001. "Distance Education and Virtual Reference: Where Are We Headed?" *Computers in Libraries* 21, no. 4 (April): 20–25.

Diamond, Wendy, and Barbara Pease. 2002. "Digital Reference: A Case Study of Question Types in an Academic Library. *Reference Services Review* 29, no. 3 (fall): 210–18. Analyzes categories of questions received between August 1997 and May 1999 in a medium-size academic library. Suggests that an "Answer Checklist" can stand in for a reference interview in the digital environment and remind librarians to reply in a systematic way.

EARL: the Consortium for Public Library Networking. No date. *Ask A Librarian Service: Manual for Participating Libraries* [online]. Available: www.ask-a-librarian.org.uk/ [18 February 2002]. This is the manual used by a consortium of UK public libraries that provide an electronic reference service called Ask A Librarian.

Eichler, Linda, and Michael Halperin. 2000. "LivePerson: Keeping Reference Alive and Clicking." In *Econtent* (June) [online]. Available: www.ecmag.net/awards/award13.html [18 February 2002]. Describes how Lippincott Library added online chat to its reference service in September 1999, using a commercial service provided by LivePerson. Explains useful features of LivePerson and provides a sample transaction.

Francoeur, Stephen. 2001. "An Analytical Survey of Chat Reference Services." *Reference Services Review* 29, no. 3 (fall): 188–203.

Frank, Ilene. 1998. "E-mail Reference Service at the University of South Florida: A Well-Kept Secret." *Art Documentation* 17, no. 1: 8–9, 44.

Garnsey, Beth A., and Ronald R. Powell. 2000, "Electronic Mail Reference Services in the Public Library." *Reference & User Services Quarterly* 39, no. 3 (spring): 245–54.

Gray, Suzanne M. 2000. "Virtual Reference Services: Directions and Agendas." *Reference & User Services Quarterly* 39, no. 4 (summer): 365–75. Analyzes Web sites of ten large research libraries belonging to the Association for Research Libraries (ARL) in 1998 and 1999 in terms of centralization of service, use of search forms, and guidelines for types of questions handled.

Hahn, Karla. 1997. *An Investigation of an E-mail-Based Help Service* [online]. Available: www.clis.umd.edu/research/reports/tr97/03/9703.html [18 February 2002].

Haines, Annette, and Alison Grodzinski. 1999. "Web Forms: Improving, Expanding, and Promoting Remote Reference Services." *College and Research Libraries* 60, no. 4 (July): 271–72.

Horn, Judy. 2001. "The Future is Now." Paper presented at the ACRL Tenth National Conference, Denver, Colorado [online]. Available: *www.ala.org/acrl/papers01/horn.pdf* [18 February 2002].

Hulshof, Robert. 1999. "Providing Services to Virtual Patrons." *Information Outlook* 3, no. 1 (January): 20–23.

Janes, Joseph, David Carter, and Patricia Memmott. 1999. "Digital Reference Services in Academic Libraries." *Reference & User Services Quarterly* 39, no. 2 (winter): 145–50. Reports the results of examining 150 academic library Web sites. Includes a helpful review of the related literature.

Janes, Joseph, ed. 1999. *The Internet Public Library Handbook.* New York: Neal-Schuman. Edited by the founder of the Internet Public Library, this collection is a good starting point for any library wanting to start a new e-reference service or review an established one.

Kasowitz, Abby W. 1998. "AskA Service Question Submission Forms." In *Virtual Reference Desk* [online]. Available: www.vrd.org/AskA/askaforms. shtml [18 February 2002]. Compares the request form for seven popular Ask-A services, with links to the forms and homepages.

Lagace, Nettie. 1998. "The Internet Public Library's 'Ask A Question' Worldwide Reference Service." *Art Documentation* 17, no. 1: 5–7.

———. 1999. "Establishing Online Reference Services." In *The Internet Public Library Handbook*, edited by Joseph Janes, et al. New York: Neal-Schuman.

Lankes, David, John W. Collins, and Abby S. Kasowitz, eds. 2000. *Digital Reference Service in the New Millennium: Planning, Management, and Evaluation.* New York: Neal-Schuman, Contains a list of citations to works on digital reference, subdivided by type of service and type of library. The list "Digital Reference Resources," compiled by Joann Wasik, is updated regularly and available at www.vrd.org/pubinfo/proceedings99_bib.shtml.

Lankes, R. David. 1998. "AskA's: Lessons Learned from K-12 Digital Reference Services." *Reference & Users Services Quarterly* 38, no. 1 (fall): 63-71. Reports the criteria of good digital reference service that emerged from the electronic discussion of an expert panel: authoritative, accessible, has fast response time, protects privacy, is consistent with good reference practice, establishes clear expectations for users, is reviewed regularly, provides access to related information, is noncommercial, well-publicized, instructive, and offers training to experts.

Lankes, R. David, and Abby S. Kasowitz. 1998. *AskA Starter Kit: How to Build and Maintain Digital Reference Services.* Syracuse, N.Y.: Syracuse University. Draws on experience and research in order to provide a set of guidelines for developing and operating a digital reference service.

Levesque, Suzanne. 2001. "Developing an Electronic Research Request Form." *Wired West* 4, no. 2 [online]. Available: www.sla.org/chapter/cwcn/wwest/v4n2/slform.htm [18 February 2002]. Levesque summarizes what she learned in the process of consulting colleagues and examining existing forms.

Lipow, Anne G. 1999. "Serving the Remote User: Reference Service in the Digital Environment." In *Proceedings of the Australasian Information Online & On Disc Conference* [online]. Available: http://csu.edu.au/special/online99/proceedings99/day2.htm [15 October 2001]. Lipow argues in this keynote address that the information seeker in the digital environment is a user "whose need for personalised human-delivered reference service is greater than ever" and that libraries need to develop organizational structures that put reference librarians center-stage.

Meola, Marc, and Sam Stormont. 1999. "Real-Time Reference Service for the Remote User: From the Telephone and Electronic Mail to Internet Chat, Instant Messaging, and Collaborative Software." *The Reference Librarian* 67/68: 29–40. Reviews various technologies and collaborative software for serving remote users and reports the results of a trial project at Temple University in 1998 using an interactive pager program, TalkBack.

Nardi, Bonnie A., and Vicki L. O'Day. 1998. "Application and Implications of Agent Technology for Libraries." *The Electronic Library* 16, no. 5 (September): 325–37.

Regan, Caroline. 2001. "Virtual Reference: 24 x 7 in Your Library/Information Centre." In *Online Currents* 16, no. 2 (March) [online]. Available: www.sofcom.au/olc/Sample.html [18 February 2002].

Richardson, Joanna, Janet Fletcher, Alison Hunter, and Phillippa Westerman. 2000. "Ask A Librarian Electronic Reference Services." Paper presented at AusWeb2K, the Sixth Australian World Wide Web Conference, Cairns [online]. Available: www.bond.edu.au/library/jpr/ausweb2k/ [18 February 2002].

Ryan, Sara. 1996. "Reference Service for the Internet Community: A Case Study of the Internet Public Library Reference Division." *Library and Information Science Research* 18, no. 3 (summer): 241–59. To put into context the efforts of the Internet Public Library to integrate Internet technology into reference service, Ryan considers efforts to adapt three earlier technologies for reference service: postal service, teletype, and telephone. Concludes with recommendations for how previous strategies can be used in the Internet environment.

Schneider, Karen G. 2000. "The Distributed Librarian—Live, Online, Real-Time Reference." *American Libraries* 31, no. 10 (November): 64. Available online at: www.ala.org/alonline/netlib/ill00.html [18 February 2002]. Argues that libraries need to collaborate to offer 24/7 online real-time reference or lose their market share to commercial Web-based services.

———. 2000. "My Patron Wrote Me a Letter: The Joy of E-mail Reference." In *American Libraries* 31, no. 1 (January) [online]. Available: www.ala.org/alonline/netlib/ill00.html [18 February 2002].

Shaw, Elizabeth. 1996. *Real-Time Reference in a MOO: Promise and Problems* [online]. Available: www-personal.si-umich.edu/~ejshaw/research2.html [18 February 2002].

Sloan, Bernie. 1997. *Service Perspectives in the Digital Library: Remote Reference Services* [online]. Available: www.lis.uiuc.edu/~b-sloan/e-ref.html [11 October 2001]. Emphasizes the crucial role of the human intermediary in the digital library. The article profiles a number of experimental projects that use e-mail and/or video to provide guidance to users; ends with a proposal for a model service.

———. 1999. *E-Mail Reference Sites* [online]. Available: http://lis.uiuc.edu/~b-sloan/e-mail.html [18 February 2002]. A useful listing.

———. 2001. *Ready for Reference: Academic Libraries Offer Live Web-Based Reference: Evaluating System Use* [online]. Available: www.lis.uiuc.edu/~b-sloan/r4r.final.htm [18 February 2002]. Describes the Ready for Reference service, which is a collaborative 24/7 live reference service being piloted by eight academic libraries in the Alliance Library System in Illinois.

Stacy-Bates, Kristine K. 2000. "Ready-Reference Resources and E-mail Reference on Academic ARL Web Sites." *Reference & User Services Quarterly* 40, no. 1 (fall): 61–73. Reports the findings of an examination of the ready-reference and e-mail reference pages on the Web sites of 110 academic libraries in the Association of Research Libraries (ARL). Looks at the wording of Web page titles and links, number of steps from library's homepage to the service pages, response time, and the prevalence of forms, and makes recommendations for improvements.

Stone, Roseanne Allucquere. 1995. *War of Desire and Technology at the Close of the Mechanical Age.* Cambridge, Mass.: MIT Press.

Straw, Joseph E. 2000. "A Virtual Understanding: The Reference Interview and Question Negotiation in the Digital Age." *Reference & User Services Quarterly* 39, no. 4 (summer): 376–79

Taylor, Gil, and Martin Kalfatovic. 2000. "Emailing the Experts: Responding to Electronic Public Queries at the Smithsonian Libraries." Text and charts presented at the American Library Association Annual Conference, Chicago [online]. Available: www.sil.si.edu/staff/ALA-2000/libmail [18 February 2002].

Thomsen, Elizabeth. 1999. *Rethinking Reference: The Reference Librarian's Practical Guide for Surviving Constant Change.* New York: Neal-Schuman.

Tibbo, Helen R. 1995. "Interviewing Techniques for Remote Reference: Electronic Versus Traditional Environments." *American Archivist* 58, no. 3: 294–310.

Tufte, Edward. 1997. *Visual Explanations: Images and Quantities, Evidence and Narrative.* Chesure, Conn.: Graphics Press.

Viles, Ann. 1999. "The Virtual Reference Interview: Equivalencies." In *International Federation of Library Associations and Institutions* [online]. Available: www.ifla.org/VII/dg/dgrw/dp99-06.htm [18 February 2002]. Discussion Group on Reference Work report from the meeting held at the 65th IFLA General Conference, Bangkok, August 23, 1999.

Wasik, Joann. 1999. *Building and Maintaining Digital Reference Services.* Syracuse, N.Y.: Syracuse University. Provides an overview of digital reference, with emphasis on David Lankes's six-step process for setting up and operating digital reference services. Available online at http://ericit.org/digests/EDO-IR-1999-04.shtml [18 February 2002].

———. 1999. "Information for Sale: Commercial Digital Reference and AskA Services." In *Virtual Reference Desk* [online]. Available: www.vrd.org/AskA/commAskA.shtml [18 February 2002].

Weissman, Sara K. 2001. "Considering a Launch?" *Library Journal* 126, no. 2 (February 1): 49.

White, Marilyn Domas. 2000. "Questioning Behavior on a Consumer Health Electronic List." *Library Quarterly* 70, no. 3 (July): 302–34.

Zick, Laura. 2000. "The Work of Information Mediators: A Comparison of Librarians and Intelligent Software Agents." In *First Monday* 5, no. 5 (May 1) [online]. Available: firstmonday.org/issues/issue5_5/zick/index.html [18 February 2002]. Compares librarians and intelligent software agents as information mediators, illustrating the former with an example of a user's request in a medical library. Article concludes with some scenarios involving collaboration of librarians and software agents and a useful bibliography and list of further reading on intelligent agents.

7 ESTABLISHING POLICY AND TRAINING FOR THE REFERENCE INTERVIEW

In this chapter . . .

7.1 THE LIBRARY CONTEXT

Throughout this book, we have stressed that a reference question is an information need that arises in the context of the user's day-to-day life. A reference interview is a structured conversation that links the user's world to our information systems in a way that makes sense to the user. As we have said in our discussion of Brenda Dervin's sense-making theory (section 3.2.3), information-seeking occurs within this larger context of the user's situation, the specific information that the user wants to know in that situation (the gap), and the specific goal that the user wants to achieve in the situation (the uses to which the information will be put). Situations in which people need information are diverse and numerous: a person may want to write a speech; find a research topic; make an important personal decision; cope with a legal, health, or family emergency; prepare for a career; apply for a job; find comfort or consolation; or simply find relaxation in a hobby. In each situation, the gaps in the user's understanding—that is, what the person wants to know—differs from one individual to the next and can't be predicted from the situation alone. For this reason, a well-conducted reference interview is a crucial element in the process of linking the user's information need to the store of information.

In this final chapter, we raise for discussion some of the issues that affect information service providers within the library system and we place particular emphasis on institutional policy and training. It is not enough for an individual librarian to want to provide excellent service to users by conducting an effective reference interview and linking users to sources. The library as an institutional system must support the individual librarian through the articulation of policies that support service goals and through the provision of training.

A QUICK TIP

POLICY FOR E-REFERENCE

Policies for electronic service differ from policies for walk-in and telephone service, although the goal of effective information service remains the same. Different methods of communication have different advantages and different constraints. As discussed in Chapter 6, electronic service requires longer turn-taking in the "interview" and does not provide instant feedback. These differences in the means of communication demand different ways of establishing rapport and asking questions. Other aspects that may differ include level of service and user eligibility rules, especially for long-distance learners. The concept of intentionality (see Chapter 1) will help you adapt personal skills so that a reference interview can be conducted successfully in the electronic environment. For example, you can still always ask a follow-up question by including it on the search form.

7.2 INSTITUTIONAL POLICY AND THE REFERENCE INTERVIEW

7.2.1 TYPICAL POLICIES

The librarian at work operates within a system that provides guidelines and constraints in the form of written policy. This policy is usually drawn from a broader mission statement (e.g., to serve the information needs of residents of X county or to serve the students and faculty of educational institution Y or to serve the employees of company Z) and from a set of legal statements approved by the governing body. Parts of a library's policy, and the law that governs it, are usually based on even broader professional guidelines such as "freedom of information" and the right of the user to have access to information service. The content of library policies will differ depending on the type and size of the library. Because part of the mission of academic libraries, for example, is to educate students in the finding of information, bibliographic instruction will be a more important component than would be the case in public libraries. Public library policies themselves may take different approaches according to the type of user: students working on a project may be encouraged to learn how to find information themselves, while seniors wanting information on home care may be given the information and helped to make contact with appropriate local services. In special libraries, the level of service is generally higher, with the librarian providing not only directions but also printouts of the material, all within very tight time frames.

In addition to general library policies, some libraries have policies specifically covering the delivery of reference services—in person, by telephone, by mail, and by electronic means. A written reference policy is important because it helps to set service

DID YOU KNOW?

A SAMPLE POSTING

The George A. Smathers Library of the University of Florida has an excellent Library Staff Toolbox (http://web.uflib.ufl.edu/toolbox/). Under "Policies and Procedures Manuals—Public Services—Reference Policies," you can find "Guidelines for Performance Standards" based in part on the Reference and User Services Association (RUSA) "Guidelines for Behavioral Performance of Reference and Information Services Professionals." Although the major focus of the Florida guidelines is on knowledge of sources, searching, and system-based procedures, it includes specific reference behaviors that we have covered in this book, with sections that deal with approachability, interest, listening/inquiring, and follow-up.

priorities, establish standards and levels of service, ensure consistency in staff response to similar situations, provide a basis for staff training and evaluation, and clarify goals and objectives (see, for example, Easley, 1985; DeMiller, 1994).

All of these policies have two intended audiences: the library users and the library staff. Usually two different kinds of policy statements are produced, a shorter statement for library patrons and a longer policy manual for staff. Policy statements written for library users list a library's policies with respect to nature of the collections, services available to them, expected user behavior, and any necessary limits on service. These policy statements sometimes refer to library association guidelines, such as the American Library Association's Library Bill of Rights and its Freedom to Read Statement. Libraries also have written policies and procedures manuals exclusively for staff members, which cover, among other things, standards of service, levels and limits of service to users, priorities of service, and the operation of the library. Staff manuals might also include recommended procedures that ensure consistency in practical service delivery. These staff manuals also often refer to library association guidelines, such as the ALA Code of Ethics, and sometimes to specific state or provincial legislation as well. The staff policy and procedures manual, which is more detailed than the statements designed for users, not only serves current employees but is used to train new recruits and to evaluate staff. Both the public and the staff documents should be reviewed regularly to ensure that they remain current. Sometimes older policies become outdated, and new unwritten policies develop (especially with the rapid growth of electronic service) that should be incorporated into the written documents.

Reference department policy statements directed at users should be available to walk-in users and also published on library Web sites. There are many advantages to posting a reference policy on your library Web site, including: (1) you can refer to it from your library homepage or from other appropriate pages in your site and provide links to it, and (2) you can provide links from the posted reference policy to relevant sections of your own Web site as well as to the various library association statements that you wish to highlight for users. In this way, the policy document itself can be more concise.

In contrast to policy statements, reference department staff manuals are usually mounted on library Intranets requiring password access and are not considered public documents. This limitation to an internal audience is appropriate, as staff manuals provide a great deal of detail that is not of general interest to the public. The focus of many staff manuals is system based, with names and addresses of people, information about buildings,

YOUR POLICY MANUAL SHOULD INCLUDE THESE ELEMENTS

- a statement that the reference interview (at least a brief one) is mandatory
- a short explanation of the value of the reference interview and why it is required
- a listing of the model reference behaviors that will help elicit information from users
- a reference to guidelines such as the Maryland Model Reference Behaviors or RUSA's "Guidelines for Behavioral Performance of Reference and Information Services Professionals," the complete text of which should be available in print form either as an appendix or as a separate document
- a statement that the guidelines will be used for purposes of training and evaluation

EXERCISE

POLICIES FROM OTHER LIBRARIES

Look at some Web sites belonging to libraries that are similar to your own. Do they publish a reference department policy for users? If so, what are the most common elements? How readable are they for the typical user? What features do you like best? Least? What's missing from the policy?

forms, and other internal procedural information. Some have links to training modules or to performance standards.

7.2.2 WHAT SHOULD BE IN THE REFERENCE SERVICE POLICY?

Typically, a reference department policy consists of two main parts, one general and one more specific. The general statement usually shows how reference department activities fit into the library's overall mission statement. This section might include a separate mission statement for different kinds of reference service (walk-in, telephone, and electronic), explain the purpose of reference guidelines, and describe the general role of reference staff. A more specific section usually deals with guidelines for reference service to library users, such as general guidelines for desk service, specific desk service guidelines, specific question guidelines, online searching, and loan of reference materials (Grodinsky, 1991). A procedures manual, which is even more specific, should complement the policy manual.

The Dorchester County Public Library in Maryland has a Web site with a clearly stated reference policy and procedures manual that is available to the public. It includes a section on "Courtesy and Interest" and another on the "Reference Interview" (see the POLICY DISCUSSION exercise). The policy refers to, but does not include, a Model Reference Behaviors Checklist. In addition to the sections quoted in the exercise, the policy provides some guidelines on such topics as walk-in and telephone inquiries, leaving the information desk, and evaluation.

The problem with many reference staff manuals is that often the reference interview is taken for granted but invisible. Sometimes it is not mentioned at all or is mentioned only in passing in a subordinate clause such as, "After you have conducted a reference interview . . . ." Quite often there is no discussion of the interview process itself, no list of model behaviors, and usually no explicitly stated requirement regarding reference interviews. Even the RUSA "Guidelines for Information Services" (available at *www.ala.org/rusa/stnd_consumer.html*) do not explicitly mention the reference interview. Guideline 1.1 states that "The goal of information services is to provide the information sought by the user," but it does not indicate how the librarian determines that information need. The RUSA "Guidelines for Behavioral Performance of Reference and Information Services Professionals" *do* emphasize the behaviors necessary in a good reference interview. Nevertheless, the reference interview seems to be assumed in most library policies, rather like breathing. This is not good enough. We believe that the reference interview should not only be mentioned explicitly, but should also be *required*. One simple

EXERCISE

POLICY DISCUSSION

Discuss the following excerpt from The Dorchester County Public Library in Maryland. Does it give you any ideas for your own reference policy? Would you post something like this on your Web site and/or put it in your staff manual?

Reference Interview: The reference interview shall be conducted in accordance with the Model Reference Behaviors Checklist and in such a manner as to draw out as much information from the patron as is necessary to answer the request accurately and fully. If the patron's question is a broad, general one, the librarian should skillfully question him to learn exactly what the patron is seeking. Conversely, if the question is exceedingly specific, the library staff member may attempt to negotiate to a broader level in order to obtain the necessary information for the patron. During the course of the reference interview, the library staff member should paraphrase, summarize, and verify the question to make sure the patron and the library staff member have the same understanding of the question. Points to be covered in the reference interview include whether there is a deadline and the level of information required (basic or technical). If instructions are given to the patron, they should be simple, explicit and not relayed in library jargon. The library staff member should accompany the patron when searching for sources and not simply direct him to an area. The source of all answers must be cited by the staff member. When the staff member feels that the question has been answered, he should always ask, "Does this completely answer your question?" If the reply is negative, the library staff member should begin the reference interview again. (Dorchester County Public Library).

thing that all libraries could, and should, do right away is to add a paragraph to their reference policies along the lines of:

> A *reference interview must be conducted with every user who asks an information question.* This means that when a user asks, "Where are your books on transportation?" you should not just say, "Our books on transportation are over there," but also add, "We have a lot of materials on this topic. Is there a specific aspect of transportation you are interested in?"

Why require a reference interview? After all, it could be argued that most librarians have learned about interviewing in their professional education and are able to judge when an interview is needed. However, as we have emphasized throughout this book, in practice, staff members bypass the interview about half the time, and in these cases usually provide less than satisfactory service. A truly effective information service can be achieved only when reference interviews are routinely conducted by all staff members, even if the reference interview consists of the minimal "Are you finding what you are looking for?" or "If you don't find the information there, please ask again." If the policy statement explicitly requires a reference interview, staff members will grow more attuned to assessing whether people are really finding out what they want to know. The more reference interviews librarians conduct, after proper training, the better they will be able to serve library users. As staff members begin to use reference interviews consistently and skillfully, they will come to realize the value of the process. There is a final advantage to requiring staff to conduct reference interviews: When there is an explicit statement requiring its use rather than, as at present, a tacit assumption that somehow interviews just happen, management is more likely to pay attention to the reference interview. This means a greater likelihood that training will be provided and that interviewing skills will be evaluated.

Sample Guidelines for Reference Behavior

Guidelines for reference behavior are readily available on the Internet. One of the best is The Maryland Model Reference Behaviors, which can be found on the *Ohio Reference Excellence on the Web* site at www.olc.org/ore/3model.htm. Another excellent set of guidelines is the American Library Association's Reference and User Services Association (RUSA) "Guidelines for Behavioral Performance of Reference and Information Services Professionals" (www.ala.org/rusa/stnd_behavior.html).

BEFORE TRAINING, ASK THESE QUESTIONS

- To whom are the events of the training program geared? professionals only? support staff? new staff? a mix?
- Is in-service training designed for a particular library more appropriate than mixing staff from different types of libraries?
- What are the goals of the overall training program (i.e., all events)? What are the objectives of a specific training event? How will you know whether these objectives are achieved?
- Is the content of each session manageable? Is there sufficient time for trainees to learn without being overwhelmed? If skills are taught in a series of events, is there enough time between events for trainees to practice on the job? Are sessions scheduled closely enough together so that trainees will not forget too much between sessions?
- What provision is there for participants to evaluate the training event itself? What are you trying to evaluate—participants' general satisfaction with the trainer's approach? new knowledge learned by participants? the trainer's success in teaching new skills? the learner's ability to use the skills? effect of training on performance? These are all different outcomes and require different means of evaluation.
- What specific recommendations are there for follow-up training and reinforcement of the new skills?
- What evaluation instruments are recommended? Are these designed primarily to provide feedback and support? Are they tied to job performance ratings? (Two separate strategies might be designed for these two different purposes.)

7.3 TRAINING STAFF IN REFERENCE INTERVIEW SKILLS

A library that truly believes in its mission as an information service must hire managers who value and support the front-line staff members who deliver the service. One way of demonstrating support for staff is to provide staff training, so that reference workers develop the skills to do their jobs well and at the same time experience job satisfaction and professional growth. Contrary to what some managers and even some new librarians believe, reference librarians do not spring fully formed from library school. Nor does prolonged experience in itself ensure that librarians are providing good service: lengthy experience reinforcing certain behaviors such as the "without speaking she began to type" maneuver or strategies of negative closure can scarcely be considered an advantage.

In the Library Visit study, users sometimes attributed unsatisfactory service to the librarian's indifference, but is this the case? The decisive question here is: Could the reference librarian have provided a satisfactory answer if his or her life depended on it? If the answer is yes, then the problem to be addressed is the librarian's attitude toward the user. However, there is evidence in the Library Visit study that at least part of the problem may lie elsewhere. Users who had received less than satisfactory service often said things like "He looked puzzled," "She looked scared," or "The computer screen was being used as a shield." It seems that sometimes professional staff feel overwhelmed and defensive, in which case the answer may be in-service training that gives staff the tools to do the good job they would really like to do. In particular, libraries should examine the type of support they provide to new staff, including orientation according to accepted guidelines for public service behavior.

Training should be ongoing and available throughout the staff member's career. It must not be left to chance but be an explicit objective in the library's policies. In budget planning, administrators should earmark funds to regular training activities for both new and experienced employees. Even if employees leave a particular library system, their training is transferable to other settings and enriches the profession as a whole. In addition to library-funded training programs, individual librarians must take responsibility for their own continuing education through memberships in library associations and attendance at training sessions that these associations provide. The following sections give an overview of ways for using this book for independent and group training. For a more complete discussion of the theory and practice of training library staff, read Chapter 10 in *Communicating Professionally* (Ross and Dewdney, 1998).

7.3.1 INDEPENDENT LEARNING

Reference service policy ideally includes "off-desk" time for staff to upgrade their skills and continue their education through reading or using distance-education programs. However, in practice, other duties and demands often encroach on the time available, which is one reason that we have written this book in a modular format that can be read in short periods. It is possible for an independent learner to work his way through this book, focusing on learning one skill at a time, and practicing each new skill with library users and noting the results. For example, a list of general-purpose open questions can be taped to the desk as a reminder, or a name tag worn as an experiment for a shift or two. Some of the suggested exercises can be done alone. There are a few good self-study programs on the Web, notably the *Ohio Reference Excellence on the Web*, which consists of six modules and allows for supervisor input and feedback. However, because the reference interview is an act of communication, a better way of learning is to practice with others—perhaps with other staff at first—and with the support of a skilled trainer.

7.3.2 GROUP LEARNING

A more successful way of training staff in reference interview skills is to work in small groups using the microtraining method described in section 2.4.1. The essence of this approach is identifying and defining single skill or behaviors that facilitate any interview, observing the skill as modeled by others, reading about the skill and its underlying concepts, practicing the skill in a supportive environment, using the skill with real library users, and finally, teaching the skill to others. Allen Ivey, who developed microtraining, calls this the "Learn, Do and Teach" approach. The most difficult stage is fine-tuning the new skills and integrating them seamlessly into existing behavior. Check out section 4.2 for proven tips on integrating skills. It is natural for trainees to feel awkward at first. The key is practice—trying the skills out first in nonthreatening or simple situations and gradually increasing confidence with experience. In any group training, a leader with professional knowledge of group dynamics is essential. This book can be used by experienced leaders to introduce new skills and approaches. In-group sessions can be supplemented not only

DID YOU KNOW?

According to one Maryland study, the factors that make the most difference to the success of the reference transaction are communication skills that are within the control of the individual librarian. Factors outside the librarian's control, such as the size of the reference collection, the size of the staff, or how busy the library was, turned out not to be important factors. In particular, two behaviors made the most difference to the success of the transaction: verifying that you really understand the question before trying to answer it, and checking, or following up, with the user afterward to be sure that you really did provide the answer that was wanted (Gers and Seward, 1985).

DID YOU KNOW?

Microtraining works. Many studies by Allen Ivey have shown that people can learn microskills fairly easily. In a controlled experiment, Elaine Jennerich found that prospective librarians could learn basic microskills within a short time. Using a pretest, posttest research design in a public library setting, Patricia Dewdney found that, after three training sessions, librarians trained in microskills used acknowledgment and encouragers more often, and asked more sense-making and open questions. The habit that librarians seemed to find hardest to break was asking too many closed questions. (From Ivey, 1994; Jennerich, 1997; and Dewdney, 1986.)

with reading but also through peer coaching, so that trainees can continue to get feedback, evaluation, and support.

There are many ways to set up the necessary training for staff. Often, skilled leaders offer workshops at professional library conferences, and more communication training is becoming available through the Internet. Many of the basic skills, such as listening, paraphrasing, and asking open questions, apply to all kinds of interview situations, and courses are offered at local colleges. However, to be truly effective, training must be ongoing rather than a one-shot event, and must be explicitly relevant to information service. A regular series of workshops for new or for more senior employees can be arranged for individual libraries or groups of libraries. Library managers proposing to hire a trainer should always check out his or her qualifications and obtain references from other organizations who have used this trainer. Whether the library uses a professional consultant or relies on its own staff as trainers, objectives must be specific and must take into account that a broad training program will need to include many events at different times and for different types of staff.

It is often effective to use an approach to training that combines outside training with in-house support for practice, peer coaching, and follow-up. The first step may be to invite an outside expert to provide staff training in reference skills and reinforce the point that skills can be learned. One value in bringing in the outside person is that it signals the fact that the library system takes reference training seriously and is willing to invest in staff training. Another advantage is that trainees may be more open and less self-conscious with a trainer who is not also a supervisor. The next step should then be ongoing reinforcement of skills within the library system itself, using peer coaching. Peer coaching can be a very effective approach as long as the environment is supportive and not threatening. When practicing new skills, trainees need to feel that it's OK to make some mistakes at first, that success is measured when each attempt comes a bit closer to the desired behavior, and that asking for feedback is a helpful element when mastering a skill. As a tool for peer coaching, you may wish to use the MODEL REFERENCE BEHAVIORS CHECKLIST, adapted from the very successful checklist used in Maryland. Work in pairs and take turns, with one person conducting the interview and the partner observing the interview and recording what happened. The checklist becomes a useful tool for providing feedback.

Model Reference Behaviors Checklist

The user's initial question (record the user's words verbatim):

What the user really wanted (as clarified in the interview):

Model behaviors (put a check beside each behavior that the staff member displayed during the interview). For verbal skills, record as accurately as possible what the librarian says.

SKILL (check if present)	**OBSERVED** (record verbatim)	**LIBRARIAN'S WORDS**

Being approachable
The staff member:
   Smiles
   Looks up
   Makes eye contact
   Gives a friendly greeting
   Is at eye level with the user

Establishing a comfortable environment
The staff member:
   Speaks in a pleasant tone of voice
   Appears unhurried and willing to
     take time with the user's question
   Maintains a distance that seems
   comfortable to the user

Showing interest
The staff member:
   Puts aside competing activities
   Maintains appropriate eye contact
   Makes short comments such as
     "Um-hmm," "That's interesting,"
     or "Yes?" to encourage the
     user to say more
   Gives full attention to the user
   Doesn't just point to distant
     resources but goes with the user

Model Reference Behaviors Checklist (Continued)

Listening

The staff member:

Does not interrupt

Uses acknowledgment or
restatement

Clarifies

Asking questions

The staff member:

Asks open questions

Uses probes such as "What do
you mean by X?"

Checks that his/her understanding of what the user
wants is   correct

Informing

The staff member:

Speaks clearly

Lets the user know what s/he
is doing (*inclusion*)

Checks if answer is understood

Offers help in using/evaluating
a source

Cites source used

Following up

Asks "Does this completely
answer your question?"
or equivalent question

Encourages the user to come
back if the answer provided
is not adequate or complete

(Adapted from Dyson, 1992)

GUIDELINES FOR PROVIDING FEEDBACK

If you are called upon to provide feedback in a peer coaching situation, here are some guidelines:

- **Start first with one or two positive comments**, even when the overall performance was not very good. Find something good that you can praise. You could say to the interviewer, "You did a good job of creating a welcoming climate by looking up and smiling" or "You showed a real interest in the user's question." Feedback that is entirely negative discourages further effort. The person getting the entirely negative feedback is apt to think, "What's the point of trying? I'm never going to be able to do this."

- **Be specific**. Focus on concrete instances of behavior, not generalities. Don't say, "Your interviewing skills need brushing up." Better to say, "I noticed that you asked two closed questions: 'Is this for a school project?' and 'Do you need magazine articles?' but you didn't find out what specifically the user wanted to know. An open question might have worked here, such as, 'What particular aspect of environmentalism are you interested in?'"

- **Be descriptive** rather than simply providing a global evaluation. Saying something is excellent or terrible is not very helpful. Especially when you are making suggestions for improvements, it is important to stick to observable facts and behaviors. Not "That last reference interview had problems" or even "When you were negotiating that interview, you didn't use inclusion." It is better to say, "When the user asked his question, you walked away to get the information he needed, but you didn't tell him what you were doing. I thought the user seemed confused about whether he should follow you or not."

- **Be realistic**. Suggest improvements that are within the capability of the person. Improvements are usually made one step at a time. An interviewer who has relied for years on the "without speaking she began to type" maneuver could be encouraged, to start with, to look at the user, smile, and use acknowledgment.

- **Limit your suggestions** for improvements to the most important one or two areas. It's better for the trainee to focus on one skill at a time. Once one skill is mastered, other areas can be focused on.

- **Suggest rather than prescribe**. In most situations, it works best to suggest a change tentatively, as in "You might want to ask an open question here."

- **Consider the needs of the receiver of your feedback**. Provide the amount of information that the receiver can use, rather than everything that can be said. Before giving feedback, you could ask, "Which particular areas would you like feedback on?" The trainee may want to focus on a specific skill, such as asking open questions or using a follow-up.

- **Seek out opportunities to offer sincere praise** (people will recognize and resent insincerity). People work and learn better when their value is recognized and acknowledged.

- **Create a climate that is positive and encouraging**—that's the key to providing helpful coaching.

A QUICK TIP

TRAINING EVALUATION

Exit questionnaires are an easy—but not completely reliable—method of evaluating the training event. It's a good idea to ask, "In what ways did this workshop help you? not help you?" so trainees can be specific. Ideally, participants should be surveyed again six weeks after an individual training event to assess the durability of the training.

A QUICK TIP

INTEGRATION OF SKILLS, 1938 STYLE

"Learn each bit of the routine so thoroughly that to do it right is an established habit, and is done as unconsciously as the act of walking. Walking is not such a simple matter, as any baby can tell you, but when you mastered it, you did it completely and no longer need to think how to keep your balance or to turn corners. At first you walked in order to walk, but now your attention is given to getting somewhere" (Carnegie Library of Pittsburgh, 1938).

7.3.3 RESISTANCE TO TRAINING—AND SOME ANSWERS

Some staff have questions about the usefulness of training for the reference interview. Here are some common objections that trainees raise, together with our responses.

1. **Good communication skills are inborn and cannot be learned.**
   It's true that some people seem to have a "talent" for communication, but they probably learned it from modeling others. Most of us have to learn systematically how to do effective interviews. A large body of research now shows that people *can* change their communication behavior through training. We are beginning to get some solid evidence that a good reference interview is positively correlated with good search outcomes.

2. **Reference interviews are rarely necessary, so training is a waste of time.**
   We hope by now to have convinced you otherwise. If not, please take another look at Chapter 1 and the myth of the face value rule. Of course it's silly to interview the user with books to check out who asks for directions to the circulation desk. But many questions requiring an interview do begin as directional questions. At the very least, training teaches you to offer the user an opportunity to describe her information need more clearly and more completely so that you can provide better service. If you are using the appropriate skills and she doesn't accept your invitation, that is her choice. If all that is learned from training is to use a follow-up such as "If that doesn't help you, please ask again," using this additional skill alone would bring about a big improvement in typical reference service.

3. **It takes too long to use these skills. We're too busy to repeat what users are saying or ask open questions.**
   In that case, you are probably also too busy to be going off into the stacks (or mining the Web), looking for something that isn't required, wasn't asked for, and won't help the user. Have you ever seen users surreptitiously leave materials behind when you were sure your long search yielded the very best sources? We are not claiming that time spent doing an interview *always* shortens search time—sometimes you can guess and be lucky—but it often does.

4. **Using microskills is manipulative, not genuine; it's like requiring retail staff to say "Have a good day!"**
   We're assuming that librarians entered the profession because they have a genuine desire to help people find the

information they need. Using appropriate skills makes that desire explicit to the user, much as using correct grammar and spelling enhances your ability to communicate in writing.

5. **The trouble with conducting a good reference interview is that you then have to find the materials that will help the user.**

So true. But that's why we have librarians. At least you know, after the interview, what you're looking for, and you may well save your own time and the time of the user. We also advocate training programs that will help librarians find the best sources—we just think they should know what the question is first.

7.4 ANNOTATED REFERENCES

7.4.1 POLICIES FOR REFERENCE STAFF

Carnegie Library of Pittsburgh. 1938. *Staff Manual, Lawrenceville Branch* [online]. Available: www.clpgh.org/clp/LV/centennial/rules.html [17 February 2002].

DeMiller, Anna L., comp. 1994. *Reference Service Policies in ARL Libraries.* Washington, D.C.: Association of Research Libraries, Office of Management Services. *SPEC Kit and Flyer 203* provides examples of actual policies.

Dorchester County Public Library (Maryland). *Reference Policy.* Available: www.dorchesterlibrary.org/library/refpolicy.html [1 February 2002].

Easley, Janet. 1985. "Reference Services Policies." *Reference Services Review* 13 (summer): 79–82.

Grodinsky, Deborah. 1991. "Developing a Model Reference Policy." *Illinois Libraries* 73 (November): 513–14.

The George A. Smathers Library, University of Florida. 2002. "Policies and Procedures Manuals—Public Services—Reference Policies." In *Library Staff Toolbox* [online]. Available: http://web.uflib.ufl.edu/toolbox/ [3 January 2002]. Useful information on policies for reference staff.

7.4.2 TRAINING

American Library Association. RUSA "Guidelines for Behavioral Performance of Reference and Information Service Professionals" [online]. Available: www.ala.org/rusa/stnd_behavior.html [18 February 2002].

———. RUSA "Guidelines for Information Services" [online]. Available: www.ala.org/rusa/stnd_consumer.html [18 February 2002].

Angus, Helen Y. 1993. *Leading Seminars and Training Sessions: Great Ideas, Information and Inspiration.* North Vancouver, B.C.: Self Counsel Press.

Written for the seminar or workshop leader, this manual offers practical tips for preparing for presentations.

Arthur, Gwen. 1992. "Using Video for Reference Staff Training and Development: A Selective Bibliography." *Reference Services Review* 20, no. 4: 63–68. An annotated bibliography that reviews the videos useful for library staff training and development, including some focusing on reference service.

Dewdney, Patricia H. 1986. "The Effects of Training Reference Librarians in Interview Skills: a Field Experiment." Ph.D. diss., University of Western Ontario.

Dyson, Lillie Seward. 1992. "Improving Reference Services: A Maryland Training Program Brings Positive Results." *Public Libraries* 31 (September/October): 284–89.

Gers, Ralph, and Lillie J. Seward. 1985. "Improving Reference Performance: Results of a Statewide Study." *Library Journal* 110, no. 8 (November 1): 32–35.

Isenstein, Laura. 1992. "Get your Reference Staff on the STAR Track." *Library Journal* 117 (April 15): 34–37. Good example of a skills-based training program. Describes a program for training reference staff to use open questions, paraphrase, and follow up in which reference staff increased their success rate from 60 to almost 80 percent.

Isenstein, Laura J. 1991. "On the Road to STARdom: Improving Reference Accuracy." *Illinois Libraries* 73, no. 2 (February): 146-51. Describes a training program developed by Baltimore County Public Library to improve the success of the reference interview.

Kalvee, Debbie. 1996. "Successful Reference Training on a Shoestring." *Library Administration & Management* 10, no. 4 (fall): 210–13. Describes how a training firm trained ten librarians who then trained other staff in a program modeled on the Maryland program.

Layman, Mary, and Sharon Vandercook. "Statewide Reference Improvement: Developing Personnel and Collections." *Wilson Library Bulletin* (January): 26-31. Describes how the California State Library undertook a two-year project to help local public libraries improve reference service.

Ohio Library Council. 2000. *Ohio Reference Excellence on the Web* [online]. Available: www.olc.org/ore/. [2002 January 3]. Based on *Ohio Reference Excellence: A Self-study Reference Course*, 2d ed. An excellent Web-based training program, with support for supervisors doing their own one-on-one training.

Ohles, Judith K., and Julie McDaniel. 1993. *Training Paraprofessionals for Reference Service: A How-To-Do-It Manual for Librarians*. New York: Neal-Schuman. A guide for librarians who need to create, implement, and evaluate reference training programs for paraprofessionals.

Ross, Catherine S., and Patricia Dewdney. 1998. *Communicating Professionally*. 2d ed. N.Y.: Neal-Schuman. See Chapter 10 on training and development, with an extensive bibliography.

Zemke, Ron, and Susan Zemke. 1995. "Adult Learning: What Do We Know for Sure?" *Training Magazine* (June): 31-39. A brief discussion of adult learning theory, including what motivates adults to learn, and suggestions on how to design effective curricula for adult learners.

INDEX

ABOUT THE AUTHORS

The authors are all faculty members at the Faculty of Information and Media Studies, the University of Western Ontario, London, Ontario, Canada.

DR. CATHERINE SHELDRICK ROSS, Professor and Dean, teaches graduate courses in reference services and readers' advisory work in the MLIS program and has presented more than 50 workshops to library professionals in the United States and Canada. Together with Patricia Dewdney, she has written two editions of *Communicating Professionally* (Neal-Schuman, 2nd ed., 1998) and is a three-time winner of the Reference Services Press Award.

DR. KIRSTI NILSEN, Assistant Professor, has taught reference courses at the introductory and advanced level in the MLIS programs at both the University of Western Ontario and the University of Toronto. In addition, she has taught Government Information, Collection Development, Special Libraries and Information Policy. She is the editor of the latest (8th) edition of the *Guide to Reference Materials for Canadian Libraries* (University of Toronto Press, 1992).

DR. PATRICIA DEWDNEY, Associate Professor, worked for many years in public libraries and has taught MLIS reference courses as well as workshops for librarians. She has conducted extensive field research on the reference interview and has won several awards for publications on information services.

To contact the authors, send an e-mail to ross@uwo.ca.